# Evolutionary Computation

# Evolutionary Computation

## Toward a New Philosophy of Machine Intelligence

**David B. Fogel**

Natural Selection, Inc.

**IEEE PRESS**

IEEE Neural Networks Council, *Sponsor*

The Institute of Electrical and Electronics Engineers, Inc., New York

This book may be purchased at a discount from the publisher when ordered in bulk quantities. For more information contact:

IEEE PRESS Marketing
Attn: Special Sales
P.O. Box 1331
445 Hoes Lane
Piscataway, NJ 08855-1331
Fax: (908) 981-8062

© 1995 by the Institute of Electrical and Electronics Engineers, Inc.
345 East 47th Street, New York, NY 10017-2394

Printed in the United States of America

10 9 8 7 6 5 4 3 2 1

**ISBN 0-7803-1038-1**

**IEEE Order Number: PC3871**

**Library of Congress Cataloging-in-Publication Data**

Fogel, David B.
    Evolutionary computation : toward a new philosophy of machine
intelligence / David B. Fogel.
       p. cm.
    Includes bibliographical references and index.
    ISBN 0-7803-1038-1
    1. Computer simulation.   2. Artificial intelligence.   I. Title.
QA76.9.C65F64   1995
006.3—dc20                      94-26693
                              CIP

*to mom, dad, and gary*

# Contents

# Preface

Intelligence and evolution are intimately connected. Intelligence is a natural part of life. It is also, however, a mechanical process that can be simulated and emulated. Intelligence is not a property that can be limited philosophically solely to biological structures. It must be equally applicable to machines. Although such efforts for generating intelligence in machines are typically described by the term *artificial intelligence*, this is in fact a misnomer. If intelligence were to be properly represented as to its process there would be nothing artificial about it. If the process is understood, methods for its generation should converge functionally and become fundamentally identical, relying on the same physics whether the intelligence occurs in a living system or a machine.

The majority of research in artificial intelligence has simulated symptoms of intelligent behavior as observed in humans. In contrast, I propose a definition of intelligence that does not rely only in its comparisons to human behavior. Intelligence is defined as the capability of a system to adapt its behavior to meet its goals in a range of environments. The form of the intelligent system is irrelevant, for its functionality is the same whether intelligence occurs within an evolving species, an individual, or a social group. Rather than focus on ourselves and attempt to emulate our own behaviors and cognitive processes, it would appear more prudent to recognize that we are products of evolution and that by modeling evolutionary processes we can create entities capable of generating intelligent behavior. Evolutionary computation, the field of simulating evolution on a computer, provides the basis for moving toward a new philosophy of machine intelligence.

Evolution is categorized by several levels of hierarchy: the gene, the chromosome, the individual, the species, the ecosystem. Thus there is an inevitable choice that must be made when constructing a simulation of evolution. Inevitably, attention must be focused at a particular level in the hierarchy, and the remainder of the simulation is to some extent determined by that perspective. Ultimately, the question that must be answered is, "What exactly is being evolved?" All the symptoms of the simulation will reflect the answer to this question, whether by conscious design or not. If intelligence is viewed in terms of adaptation, then the answer to the question must be that what is evolved is functional behavior. To construct a useful model, evolution must be abstracted in terms of the behavioral relationships between units of evolution, rather than the mechanisms that give rise to these relationships.

The result of such modeling is a series of optimization algorithms that rely on very simple rules. These various procedures are implemented as population-based searches over a fitness response surface. The optimization process inherent in selection iteratively improves the quality of these solutions. The rate of improvement is primarily determined by the shape of the response surface, but the procedures generally converge to near-optimal solutions despite the existence of topological pathologies. In some cases, it is provable that the procedures will asymptotically converge to the best solutions; in others, it is provable that they will never converge at all. Nonetheless, these methods offer potential for addressing engineering problems that have resisted solution by classic techniques.

More importantly, however, these methods may be used to address a range of problems, rather than any one specific problem. They have proven themselves to be robust and may be applied toward general problem solving. This latter attribute represents the greatest potential for evolutionary computation, yet there have been few investigations in this regard. The real promise of evolutionary computation remains mostly unfulfilled.

This book is an attempt to integrate the inspiration, philosophy, history, mathematics, actualizations, and perspectives of evolutionary computation. It will have been successful if this integration adds to the reader's understanding of the field of research. My hope is that it will encourage further investigation into the potential of these techniques for generating machine intelligence.

There are many people to thank for their time and effort spent helping me prepare the manuscript and offering comments on this work. Dudley Kay, Lisa Mizrahi, Val Zaborski, and Karen Henley of IEEE Press and copyeditor Kathleen Lafferty were most supportive. Teresa Moniz and Mike MacVittie assisted with the artwork, and I would like to thank them and ORINCON Corporation, and especially Terry Rickard, for making their time and skills available. I also greatly appreciate the help received from Scott Haffner, Brian Moon, and Rob Redfield converting and debugging computer programs for execution on different machines. Chapters and sections, including those taken from recent publications, were reviewed by Lee Altenberg, Russell Anderson, Pete Angeline, Valerie Atmar, Wirt Atmar, Thomas Bäck, Rick Barton, Hans Bremermann, Tom Brotherton, Cliff Brunk, George Burgin, Michael Conrad, Lawrence (Dave) Davis, Hugo de Garis, Ken De Jong, Marco Dorigo, Tom English, Gary Fogel, Larry Fogel, Steve Frank, John Grefenstette, Paul Harrald, David Honig, Gerry Joyce, Mark Kent, Avi Krieger, Charles Marshall, Ernst Mayr, Zbyszek Michalewicz, Mike O'Hagan, Bill Porto, Bob Powell, Tom Ray, Ingo Rechenberg, Bob Reynolds, Matt Rizki, Stuart Rubin, Günter Rudolph, N. (Saravan) Saravanan, Bill Schopf, Hans-Paul Schwefel, Brad Scurlock, Tony Sebald, Pat Simpson, Chris Wills, Xin Yao, and several anonymous referees. Their criticisms have been invaluable. I would be remiss if I did not acknowledge the encouragement of John McDonnell, Ward Page, and Jennifer Schlenzig, and I am deeply grateful to Wirt Atmar and Tony Sebald for years of guidance and friendship. Finally, I thank my family for their constant support.

David B. Fogel
La Jolla, CA

# 1

# Defining Artificial Intelligence

## 1.1 BACKGROUND

Although most scientific disciplines, such as mathematics, physics, chemistry, and biology, are well defined, the field of artificial intelligence (AI) remains enigmatic. Indeed, Hofstadter (1985, p. 633) remarks, "The central problem of AI is the question: *What is the letter 'a'?* Donald Knuth, on hearing me make this claim once, appended, 'And what is the letter "i"?'— an amendment that I gladly accept." Despite nearly 40 years of research in the field, no widely accepted definition of artificial intelligence exists.

Artificial intelligence is sometimes defined as the manipulation of symbols for problem solving (e.g., Buchanan and Shortliffe, 1985, p. 3) or by tautological statements such as artificial intelligence is "the part of computer science concerned with developing intelligent computer programs" (Waterman, 1986, p. 10). Rich (1983, p. 1) offered, "Artificial intelligence (AI) is the study of how to make computers do things at which, at the moment, people are better." But this definition, if regarded statically, precludes the very existence of artificial intelligence. Once a computer program exceeds the capabilities of a human, the program is no longer in the domain of AI.

The majority of proffered definitions of artificial intelligence rely on comparisons to human behavior. Staugaard (1987, p. 23) attributes a definition to Marvin Minsky—"the science of making machines do things that would require intelligence if done by men"—and suggests that some define AI as the "mechanization, or duplication, of the human thought process." Charniak and McDermott (1985, p. 6) offer, "Artificial intelligence is the study of mental faculties through the use of computational models," while Schildt (1987, p. 11) claims, "An intelligent program is one that exhibits behavior similar to that of a human when confronted with a similar problem. It is not necessary that the program actually solve, or attempt to solve, the problem in the same way that a human would."

The question, "What is AI?" would become mere semantics if only the answers did not suggest or imply radically different avenues of research: "Some researchers simply want machines to do the various sorts of things that people call intelligent. Others hope to understand what enables people to do such things. Still other researchers want to simplify programming" (Minsky, 1991). Yet Minsky also laments, "Why can't we build, once and for all, machines that grow and improve themselves by learning from experience? Why can't we simply explain what we want, and then let our machines do experiments or read some books or go to school, the sorts of things that people do. Our machines today do no such things."

## 1.2 THE TURING TEST

Turing (1950) considered the question, "Can machines think?" Rather than define the terms *machines* or *think*, he proposed a test which begins with three people, a man (A), a woman (B), and an interrogator (C). The interrogator is to be separated from both A and B, say, in a closed room (Figure 1-1) but may ask questions of both A and B. The interrogator's objective is to determine which of A and B is the man and which is the woman. It is A's objective to cause C to make an incorrect identification. Turing (1950) provided the following example of a question posed to the man:

"C: Will X [C's name for A] please tell me the length of his or her hair?"

"A: My hair is shingled, and the longest strands are about nine inches long."

**Figure 1-1**    The Turing test. An interrogator (C) questions both a man (A) and a woman (B) and attempts to determine which is the woman.

Player A may be deceitful, if he so desires. In contrast, the object for B is to help the interrogator. Turing suggested that the probable best strategy for her is to give truthful answers. In order that the pitch of the voice or other external clues may not aid in C's decision, a teleprinter was to be used for communication between the rooms.

Turing then replaced the original question, "Can machines think?" with the following: "We now ask the question, 'What will happen when a machine takes the part of A in this game?' Will the interrogator decide wrongly as often when the game is played like this as he does when the game is played between a man and a woman?" (Turing, 1950). This question separates the physical and intellectual capacities of humans. The form of interrogation prevents C from using sensory information regarding A's or B's physical characteristics. Presumably, if the interrogator were able to show no increased ability to decide between A and B when the machine was playing as opposed to when the man was playing, then the machine would be declared to have passed the test. Whether or not the machine should then be judged capable of thinking was left unanswered. Turing (1950) in fact dismissed the original question as being "too meaningless to deserve discussion."

Turing (1950) limited the possible machines to be the set of all digital computers. He indicated through considerable analysis that these machines are *universal*, that is, all computable processes can be executed by such machines. With respect to the suitability of the test itself, Turing (1950) thought the game might be weighted "too heavily against the machine. If the man were to try and pretend to be the machine he would clearly make a very poor showing." (Hofstadter, 1985, pp. 514–520, relates an amusing counterexample in which he was temporarily fooled in such a manner.)

Turing (1950) considered and rejected a number of objections to the plausibility of a "thinking machine," although somewhat remarkably he felt an argument supporting the existence of extrasensory perception in humans was the most compelling of all objections. The *Lady Lovelace* objection (Countess of Lovelace, 1842), referring to a memoir by the Countess of Lovelace on Babbage's Analytical Engine, is the most common of present refutations of a thinking machine. The argument asserts that a computer can only do what it is programmed to do and therefore will never be capable of generating anything new. Turing (1950) countered this argument by equating it with a statement that a machine can never take us by surprise. But he noted that machines often act in unexpected ways because the entire determining set of initial conditions of the machine is generally unknown; therefore, an accurate prediction of all possible behavior of the mechanism is impossible.

Moreover, he suggested that a thinking machine should be a learning machine, capable of altering its own configuration through a series of rewards and punishments. Thus it could modify its own programming and generate unexpected behavior. He speculated that "in about fifty years' time it will be possible to programme computers, with a storage capacity of about $10^9$ [bits], to make them play the imitation game so well that an average interrogator will not have more than a 70 per cent chance of making the right identification after five minutes of questioning" (Turing, 1950).

## 1.3  SIMULATION OF HUMAN EXPERTISE

The acceptance of the "Turing Test" focused attention on mimicking human behavior. At the time (1950), it was beyond any reasonable consideration that a computer could pass the Turing Test. Rather than focus on imitating human behavior in conversation, attention was turned to more limited domains of interest. Simple two-person games of strategy were selected. These games received attention for at least three reasons: (1) Their rules are static, known to both players, and easy to express in a computer program, (2) they are examples from a class of problems concerned with reasoning about actions, and (3) the ability of a game-playing computer can be measured against human experts.

The majority of research in game playing has been aimed at the development of heuristics that can be applied to two-person, zero-sum, nonrandom games of perfect information (Jackson, 1985). The term *zero-sum* indicates that any potential gain to one player will be reflected as a corresponding loss to the other player. The term *nonrandom* means that the allocation and positioning of resources in the game (e.g., pieces on a chess board) is purely deterministic. *Perfect information* indicates that both players have complete knowledge regarding the disposition of both players' resources (e.g., tic-tac-toe, not poker).

The general protocol was to examine an expert's decisions during a game so as to discover a consistent set of parameters or questions that are evaluated during his or her decision-making process. These conditions could then be formulated in an algorithm capable of generating behavior similar to that of the expert when faced with identical situations. It was believed that if a sufficient quantity or "coverage" of heuristics could be programmed into the computer, the sheer speed and infallible computational ability of the computer would enable it to match or even exceed the ability of the human expert.

### 1.3.1  Samuel's Checker Program

One of the earliest efforts along these lines was offered by Samuel (1959), who wrote a computer program that learned to play checkers. Checkers was chosen for several reasons: (1) There is no known algorithm that provides for a guaranteed win or draw, (2) the game is well defined with an obvious goal, (3) the rules are fixed and well known, (4) there are human experts who can be consulted and against which progress of the program can be tested, and (5) the activity is familiar to many people. The general procedure of the program was to look ahead a few moves at a time and evaluate the resulting board positions.

This evaluation was made with respect to several selected parameters. These parameters were then included in a linear polynomial with variable coefficients. The result of the polynomial indicated the worth of the prospective board under evaluation. The most critical and obvious parameter was the inability for one side or the other to move. This can occur only once in a game and was tested separately. Another clearly important consideration was the relative piece advantage. Kings were given 50 percent more weight than regular pieces. Samuel (1959) tried two alternative methods for including additional parameters. Initially, Samuel himself chose these terms, but he later allowed the program to make a subset selection from a large list of possible parameters.

To determine a move, the game tree of possible new boards was searched. A minimax procedure was used to discover the best move. The *ply*, or number of levels to be searched in the tree, was initially set at three unless the next move was a jump, the last move was a jump, or an exchange offer was possible. The analysis proceeded backward from the evaluated board position through the tree of possible moves, with the assumption that at each move the opponent would always attempt to minimize the machine's score while the machine would act to maximize its score. Under these conditions the search was continued until these circumstances were no longer encountered or until a maximum of 20 levels had been searched.

After initial experiments in which the selected polynomial had four terms (piece advantage, denial of occupancy, mobility, and a hybrid term that combined control of the center and piece advancement), the program was allowed to select a subset of 16 parameters from a list of 38 chosen parameters. Samuel allowed the computer to compete against itself; one version, Alpha, constantly modified the coefficients and parameters of its polynomial, and the other version, Beta, remained fixed (i.e., it was replaced by Alpha after a loss). A record of the correlation existing between the signs of the individual term contributions in the initial scoring polynomial and the sign of the change between the scores was maintained, along with the number of times that each particular term with a nonzero value was used. The coefficient for the polynomial term of Alpha with the then-largest correlation coefficient was set at a prescribed maximum value with proportionate values determined for all the remaining coefficients. Samuel noted some possible instabilities with this modification technique and developed heuristic solutions to overcome these problems. Term replacement was made when a particular parameter had the lowest correlation eight times. Upon reaching this arbitrary limit, it was placed at the bottom of the reserve list and the first parameter in the reserve list was inserted into the scoring polynomial.

After a series of 28 games, Samuel described the program as being a better-than-average player. "A detailed analysis of these results indicated that the learning procedure did work and that the rate of learning was surprisingly high, but that the learning was quite erratic and none too stable" (Samuel, 1959). Refinements were made to the method of altering the scoring polynomial to help prevent this problem.

In 1962, at the request of Edward Feigenbaum and Julian Feldman, Samuel arranged for a match between his program and Robert W. Nealy, a former Connecticut checkers champion. Samuel's program defeated Nealy, who commented (cited in Samuel, 1963):

> Our game . . . did have its points. Up to the 31st move, all of our play had been previously published, except where I evaded "the book" several times in a vain effort to throw the computer's timing off. At the 32–27 [a specific move] loser and onwards, all the play is original with us, so far as I have been able to find. It is very interesting to me to note that computer had to make several star moves in order to get the win, and that I had several opportunities to draw otherwise. That is why I kept the game going. The machine, therefore, played a perfect ending without one misstep. In the matter of the end game, I have not had such competition from any human being since 1954, when I lost my last game.

The moves of the game appear in Samuel (1963).

## 1.3.2  Chess Programs

Researchers in artificial intelligence have also been concerned with developing chess programs. Initial considerations of making machines play chess date to Charles Babbage (1792–1871). Babbage had described the Analytical Engine, a theoretic mechanical device that was a digital computer, although not electronic. This machine was never built (but an earlier design, the Difference Engine, was in fact successfully constructed only as recently as 1991; Swade, 1993). Babbage recognized that, in principle, his Analytical Engine was capable of playing games such as checkers and chess by looking forward to possible alternative outcomes based on current potential moves.

Shannon (1950) was one of the first researchers to propose a computer program to play chess. He, like Samuel later, chose to have an evaluation function such that a program could assess the relative worth of different configurations of pieces on the board. The notion of an evaluation function has been an integral component of every chess program ever since. The suggested parameters included material advantage, pawn formation, positions of pieces, mobility, commitments, attacks, and options (cited in Levy and Newborn, 1991, pp. 27–28). Shannon noted that the best move can be found in at least two ways, although the methods may be combined: (1) Search to a given number of moves ahead and then use a minimax algorithm or (2) selectively search different branches of the game tree to different levels (i.e., moves ahead). The second method offers the advantage of preventing the machine from wasting time searching down branches in which one or more bad moves must be made. This method, later termed the *alpha-beta algorithm*, has been incorporated in many current chess playing programs.

Turing (1953) is credited with writing the first algorithm for automatic chess play. He never completed programming the procedure on a computer but was able to play at least one game by hand simulation. Turing's evaluation function included parameters of mobility, piece safety, castling, pawn position, and checks and mate threats. The one recorded game (cited in Levy and Newborn, 1991, pp. 35–38) used a search depth of two ply and then continued the search down prospective branches until "dead" positions (e.g., mate or the capture of an undefended piece) were reached. In this game, the algorithm was played against "a weak human opponent" (Levy and Newborn, 1991, p. 35) and subsequently lost. Turing attributed the weakness of the program to its "caricature of his own play" (cited in Levy and Newborn, 1991, p. 38).

The first documented working chess program was created in 1956 at Los Alamos. An unconfirmed account of a running program in the Soviet Union was reported earlier by *Pravda* (Levy and Newborn, 1991, p. 39). Bernstein et al. (1958) described their computer program, which played a fair opening game but weak middle game because the program only searched to a depth of four ply. Newell et al. (1958) were the first to use the alpha-beta algorithm (Shannon, 1950). Greenblatt et al. (1967) are credited with creating the first program, called MACHACK VI, to beat a human in tournament play. The program was made an honorary member of the United

States Chess Federation (USCF), receiving their rating of 1640. MACHACK VI used a search of at least nine ply.

In 1978, CHESS 4.7, a revised version of a program originally written by Atkin, Gorlen, and Slate of Northwestern University, defeated David Levy, Scottish chess champion, in a tournament game. Levy was "attempting to beat the program at its own game" and returned in the next match to a "no-nonsense approach," presumably to win (Levy and Newborn, 1991, pp. 98, 100). BELLE, written by Thompson and Condon, was the first program that qualified, in 1983, for the title of U.S. Master.

In the 1980s, efforts were directed at making application-specific hardware capable of searching large numbers of possible boards and quickly calculating appropriate evaluations. Berliner created HITECH, a 64-processor system. Hsu produced an even more powerful chip and its resident program, now known as DEEP THOUGHT, quickly outperformed HITECH. DEEP THOUGHT was able to search to a level of 10 ply and became the first program to defeat a world-class grand master, Bent Larsen. In 1989, DEEP THOUGHT, then rated at 2745, played a four-game match against David Levy. Levy admits, "It was the first time that [I] had ever played a program rated higher than [I] was at [my] best" (Levy and Newborn, 1991, p. 127), and correctly predicted that the machine would win 4–0. In 1990, Anatoly Karpov, the former world champion, lost a game to a MEPHISTO chess computer while giving a simultaneous exhibition against 24 opponents.

Judging by the nearly linear improvement in the USCF rating of chess programs since the 1960s (Levy and Newborn, 1991, p. 6), the efforts of researchers to program computers to play chess must be regarded as highly successful. But there is a legitimate question as to whether or not these programs are rightly described as intelligent. Schank (1984, p. 30) commented, "The moment people succeeded in writing good chess programs, they began to wonder whether or not they had really created a piece of Artificial Intelligence. The programs played chess well because they could make complex calculations with extraordinary speed, not because they knew the kinds of things that human chess masters know about chess." Simply making machines do things that people would describe as requiring intelligence is insufficient (cf. Staugaard, 1987, p. 23). "Such programs did not embody intelligence and did not contribute to the quest for intelligent machines. A person isn't intelligent because he or she is a chess master; rather, that person is able to master the game of chess because he or she is intelligent" (Schank, 1984, p. 30).

### 1.3.3 Expert Systems

The focus of artificial intelligence narrowed considerably from the early 1960s through the mid-1980s (Waterman, 1986, p. 4). Initially, the desire was to create general problem-solving programs (Newell and Simon, 1963), but when preliminary attempts were unsuccessful, attention was turned to the discovery of efficient search mechanisms that could process complex data structures. The focus grew even more myopic in that research was aimed at applying these specific search algorithms (formerly termed *heuristic programming*) to very narrowly defined problems. Human experts were interrogated about their knowledge in their particular field of expertise, and this knowledge was then represented in a form that supported reasoning activities on a computer. Such an *expert system* could offer potential advantages over human expertise: It is "permanent, consistent, easy to transfer and document, and cheaper" (Waterman, 1986, p. xvii). Nor does it suffer from human frailties such as aging, sickness, or fatigue.

The programming languages often used in these applications are LISP (McCarthy et al., 1962) and Prolog (invented by Colmerauer, 1972, as cited in Covington et al., 1988, p. 2) To answer questions that are posed to the system, an *inference engine* (a program) is used to search a knowledge base. Knowledge is most frequently represented using first-order predicate calculus, production rules, semantic networks, and frames. For example, a knowledge base might include the facts: Larry is a parent of Gary and David. This might be represented in Prolog as

1. parent(larry, gary), and
2. parent(larry, david).

(Versions of Prolog often reserve the use of capitals for variables.) If one were to be able to interrogate about whether or not a person was a child of Larry, the additional facts

1. child(gary, larry), and
2. child(david, larry),

or the rule

1.  child(X, Y) :-
        parent(Y, X).

could be included (:- denotes "if"). The computer has no intrinsic understanding of the relationships "parent" or "child." It simply has codings (termed *functors*) that relate "gary," "david," and "larry."

With the existence of such a knowledge base, it becomes possible to query the system about the relationship between two people. For example, if one wanted to know whether or not "david" was the parent of "gary," one could enter

? - parent(david, gary).

The inference engine would then search the knowledge base of rules and facts and fail to validate "parent(david, gary)" and therefore would reply, "no." More general questions could be asked, such as

? - parent(larry, X).

where X is a variable. The inference engine would then search the knowledge base, attempting to match the variable to any name it could find (in this case, either "gary" or "david").

Although these examples are extremely simple, it is not difficult to imagine more complex relationships programmed in a knowledge base. The elements in the knowledge base need not be facts, but may be conjectures with degrees of confidence assigned by the human expert. The knowledge base may contain conditional statements (production rules), such as, "IF *premise* THEN *conclusion*" or "IF *condition* WITH *certainty greater than x* THEN *action*." Through the successive inclusion of broad-ranging truths to very specific knowledge about a limited domain, a versatile knowledge base and query system can be created.

DENDRAL, a chemistry program that processed mass spectral and nuclear magnetic response data to provide information regarding the molecular structure of unknown compounds, was one of the first such systems. The program was started in the mid-1960s and was subsequently refined and extended by several researchers (e.g., Feigenbaum et al., 1971; Lindsay et al., 1980). MYCIN (Shortliffe, 1974; Adams, 1976; Buchanan and Shortliffe, 1985), a program to diagnose bacterial infections in hospital patients, was an outgrowth of the "knowledge-based" DENDRAL project. Other examples of well-known knowledge-based systems can be found in

Bennett and Hollander (1981), Barr and Feigenbaum (1981), and Lenat (1983).

The expert system PROSPECTOR was developed by the Stanford Research Institute to aid exploration geologists in the search for ore deposits (Duda et al., 1978). Work on the system continued until 1983 (Waterman, 1986, p. 49). Nine different mineral experts contributed to the database; it contains over 1,000 rules and a taxonomy of geological terms with more than 1,000 entries. The following sequence represents an example of PROSPECTOR receiving information from a geologist:

"1:   THERE ARE DIKES

     (Dike) (5)

  2:   THERE ARE CRETACEOUS DIORITES
     (Cretaceous diorites) (5)

  3:   THERE IS PROBABLY SYENODIORITE
     (Monzonite) (3)

  4:   THERE MIGHT BE SOME QUARTZ MONZONITE
     (Quartz-monzonite) (2)"

(Waterman, 1986, p. 51). The values in parentheses represent the degree of certainty associated with each statement (–5 indicates complete certainty of absence while +5 indicates complete certainty of existence). The nouns in parentheses represent the internally stored name for the substance described. Through subsequent questioning of the human expert by the expert system, the program is able to offer a conjecture such as

My certainty in (PCDA) [Type-A porphyry copper deposit] is now: 1.683

followed by a detailed listing of the rules and facts that were used to come to this conclusion.

In 1980, PROSPECTOR was used to analyze a test drilling site near Mount Tolman in eastern Washington that had been partially explored. PROSPECTOR processed information regarding the geological, geophysical, and geochemical data describing the region and predicted the existence of molybdenum in a particular location (Campbell et al., 1982). "Subsequent drilling by a mining company confirmed the prediction as to where ore-grade molybdenum mineralization would be found and where it would not be found" (Waterman, 1986, p. 58).

Waterman (1986, pp. 162–199) described the construction of an expert system and discussed some potential problems. For example, the number of rules required for a given application may grow very large. "PUFF, an expert system that interprets data from pulmonary function tests, had to have its number of rules increased from 100 to 400 just to get a 10 percent increase in performance" (Waterman, 1986, p. 182). PUFF required five person-years to construct. There are no general techniques for assessing a system's completeness or consistency. Nevertheless, despite the procedural difficulties associated with constructing expert systems, useful programs have been created to address a wide range of problems in various domains including medicine, law, agriculture, military sciences, geology, and others (Waterman, 1986, p. 205). Building expert systems has now become routine (Barr et al., 1989, p. 181).

### 1.3.4  A Criticism of the Expert Systems or Knowledge-Based Approach

There is some question whether or not the research in expert or knowledge-based systems truly advances the field of artificial intelligence. Dreyfus and Dreyfus (1984, 1986) claimed that when a beginner is first introduced to a new task, such as driving a car, he or she is taught specific rules to follow (e.g., maintain a two-second separation between yourself and the car in front of you). But as the beginner gains experience, less objective cues are used. "He listens to the engine as well as looks at his speedometer for cues about when to shift gears. He observes the demeanor as well as the position and speed of pedestrians to anticipate their behavior. And he learns to distinguish a distracted or drunk driver from an alert one" (Dreyfus and Dreyfus, 1984). It is difficult to believe that the now-expert driver is relying on rules in making these classifications. "Engine sounds cannot be adequately captured by words, and no list of facts about a pedestrian at a crosswalk can enable a driver to predict his behavior as well as can the experience of observing people crossing streets under a variety of conditions" (Dreyfus and Dreyfus, 1984). They asserted that when a human expert is interrogated by a "knowledge-engineer" to assimilate rules for an expert system, the expert is "forced to regress to the level of a beginner and recite rules he no longer uses . . . there is no reason to believe that a heuristically programmed computer accurately replicates human thinking" (Dreyfus and Dreyfus, 1984).

Other problems occur in the design of expert systems. Human experts, when forced to verbalize rules for their behavior, may not offer a consistent set of explanations. There may be inherent contradictions in their rules. In addition, different experts will differ on the rules that should be employed. The question of how to handle these inconsistencies remains open and is often handled in an ad hoc manner by knowledge-engineers who do not have expertise in the field of application. Simply finding an expert can be troublesome, for most often there is no objective measure of "expertness." And even when an expert is found, there is always the chance that the expert will simply be wrong. History is replete with incorrect expertise (e.g., a geocentric solar system, and see Cerf and Navasky, 1984). Moreover, expert systems often generate preprogrammed behavior. Such behavior can be *brittle*, in the sense that it is well optimized for its specific environment, but incapable of adapting to any changes in the environment.

Consider the hunting wasp, *Sphex flavipennis*. When the female wasp must lay its eggs, it builds a burrow and hunts out a cricket, which it paralyzes with three injections of venom (Gould and Gould, 1985). The wasp then drags the cricket into the burrow, lays the eggs next to the cricket, seals the burrow, and flies away. When the eggs hatch, the grubs feed on the paralyzed cricket. Initially, this behavior appears sophisticated, logical, and thoughtful (Wooldridge, 1968, p. 70). But upon further examination, limitations of the wasp's behavior can be demonstrated. Before entering the burrow with the cricket, the wasp carefully positions its paralyzed prey with its antennae just touching the opening of the burrow and "then scoots inside, 'inspects' its quarters, emerges, and drags the captive inside" (Gould and Gould, 1985). As noted by French naturalist Jean Henri Fabré, if the cricket is moved just slightly while the wasp is busy in its burrow, upon emerging the wasp will replace the cricket at the entrance and again go inside to inspect the burrow. "No matter how many times Fabré moved the cricket, and no matter how slightly, the wasp would never break out of the pattern. No amount of experience could teach it that its behavior was wrongheaded: its genetic inheritance had left it incapable of learning that lesson" (Gould and Gould, 1985).

The wasp's instinctive program is essentially a rule-based system that is crucial in propagating the species, unless the weather happens to be a bit breezy. "The insect, which astounds us, which terrifies us with its extraordinary intelligence, surprises us, the next moment, with its stupidity, when confronted with some simple fact that happens to lie outside its ordinary practice" (Fabré, cited in Gould and Gould, 1985). Genetically hard-coded behavior is inherently brittle. Similarly, an expert system chess program might do very well, but if the rules of the game were changed, even slightly, by perhaps allowing the king to move up to two squares at a time, the expert system might no longer be expert. This brittleness of domain-specific programs has been recognized for many years (Samuel, 1959).

### 1.3.5  Fuzzy Systems

Another procedural problem associated with the construction of a knowledge base is that when humans describe complex environments, they do not typically speak in absolutes. Linguistic descriptors of real-world circumstances are not precise but rather are "fuzzy." For example, when one describes the optimum behavior of an investor interested in making money in the stock market, the adage is "buy low, sell high." But how low is "low?" And how high is "high?" It is unreasonable to suggest that if the price of the stock climbs to a certain precise value in dollars per share, then it is high; yet if it were only $0.01 lower, it would not be high. Useful descriptions need not be of a binary or crisp nature.

Zadeh (1965) introduced the notion of "fuzzy sets." Rather than describing elements as being either in a given set or not, membership in the set was viewed as a matter of degree ranging over the interval [0, 1]. A membership of 0.0 indicates that the element absolutely is not a member of the set, and a membership of 1.0 indicates that the element absolutely is a member of the set. Intermediate values indicate degrees of membership. The choice of the appropriate membership function to describe elements of a set is left to the researcher.

Negoita and Ralescu (1987, p. 79) note that descriptive phrases such as "numbers approximately equal to 10" and "young children" are not tractable by methods of classic set theory or probability theory. There is an undecidability about the membership or nonmembership in a collection of such objects, and there is nothing random about the concepts in question. A classic set can be represented precisely as a binary valued function $f_A$: $X \rightarrow \{0, 1\}$, the *characteristic function*, defined as

$$f_A(x) = \begin{cases} 1, & \text{if } x \in A; \\ 0, & \text{otherwise.} \end{cases}$$

The collection of all subsets of $X$ (the power set of $X$) is denoted

$$P(X) = \{A | A \text{ is a subset of } X\}.$$

In contrast, a fuzzy subset of $X$ is represented by a *membership function:*

$$u : X \rightarrow [0, 1].$$

The collection of all fuzzy subsets of $X$ (the fuzzy power set) is denoted by $F(X)$:

$$F(X) = \{u | u : X \rightarrow [0, 1]\}.$$

It is natural to enquire as to the effect of operations such as union and intersection on such fuzzy sets. If $u$ and $v$ are fuzzy sets, then

$$(u \text{ or } v)(x) = \max[u(x), v(x)]$$
$$(u \text{ and } v)(x) = \min[u(x), v(x)].$$

Other forms of these operators have been developed (Yager, 1980; Dubois and Prade, 1982; Kandel, 1986, pp. 143–149). One form of the complement of a fuzzy set, $u : X \rightarrow [0, 1]$ is

$$u^c(x) = 1 - u(x).$$

Other properties of fuzzy set operations, such as commutativity, associativity, and distributivity, as well as other operators such as addition, multiplication, and so forth, may be found in Negoita and Ralescu (1987, pp. 81–93).

It is not difficult to imagine a *fuzzy system* that relates fuzzy sets in much the same manner as a knowledge-based system. The range of implementation and reasoning methodologies is much richer in fuzzy logic. The rules are simply fuzzy rules describing memberships in given sets rather than absolutes. Such systems have been constructed and Bezdek and Pal (1992) give a comprehensive review of efforts in fuzzy systems from 1965.

### 1.3.6 Perspective on Methods Employing Specific Heuristics

Human experts can only give dispositions or rules (fuzzy or precise) for problems in their domain of expertise. There is a potential difficulty when such a system is required to address problems for which there are no human experts. Schank (1984, p. 34) states, definitively, "Expert systems are horribly misnamed, since there is very little about them that is expert . . . while potentially useful, [they] are not a theoretical advance in our goal of creating an intelligent machine." He continues:

> The central problem in AI has little to do with expert systems, faster programs, or bigger memories. The ultimate AI breakthrough would be the creation of a machine that can learn or otherwise change as a result of its own experiences . . . like most AI terms, the words "expert system" are loaded with a great deal more implied intelligence than is warranted by their actual level of sophistication. . . . Expert systems are not innovative in the way the real experts are; nor can they reflect on their own decision-making processes.

This generalization may be too broad. Certainly, both expert and fuzzy systems can be made very flexible. They can generate new functional rules that were not explicitly stated in the original knowledge base. They can be programmed to ask for more information from human experts if they are unable to reach any definite (or suitably fuzzy) conclusion in the face of current information. Yet one may legitimately question whether the observed "intelligence" of the system should really be attributed to the system, or merely to the programmer who implemented knowledge into a fixed program. Philosophically, there appears to be little difference between such a hard-wired system and a simple calculator. Neither is intrinsically intelligent.

The widespread acceptance of the Turing Test has both focused and constrained research in artificial intelligence in two regards: (1) the imitation of human behavior and (2) the evaluation of artificial intelligence solely on the basis of behavioral response. But, "Ideally, the test of an effective understanding system is not the realism of the output it produces, but rather the validity of the method by which that output is produced" (Schank, 1984, p. 53). Hofstadter (1985, p. 525) admitted to being an "unabashed pusher of the validity of the Turing Test as a way of operationally defining what it would be for a machine to genuinely think." But he also cogently wrote while playing devil's advocate: "I'm not any happier with the Turing Test as a test for thinking machines than I am with the Imitation Game [the Turing Test] as a test for femininity" (Hofstadter, 1985, p. 495). Certainly, even if a man could imitate a woman, perfectly, he would still be a man. Imitations are just that: imitations. It is important to define and program mechanisms that generate intelligent behavior. Artificial intelligence should not seek to merely solve problems, but should rather seek to solve the problem of how to solve problems.

## 1.4 NEURAL NETWORKS

A human may be described as an intelligent problem-solving machine.
Singh (1966, p. 1) suggested that "the search for synthetic intelligence must
begin with an inquiry into the origin of natural intelligence, that is, into the
working of our own brain, its sole creator at present." The idea of constructing an artificial brain or *neural network* has been proposed many times
(e.g., McCulloch and Pitts, 1943; Rosenblatt, 1957, 1962; Samuel, 1959;
Block, 1963; and others).

The brain is an immensely complex network of neurons, synapses,
axons, dendrites, and so forth (Figure 1-2), a "mammoth automatic tele-
phone exchange" (Singh, 1966, p. 129). Through detailed modeling of these
elements, a simulated network that is capable of diverse behaviors may be
constructed. The human brain comprises at least $2 \times 10^{10}$ neurons, each
possessing about 10,000 synapses distributed over each dendritic tree with

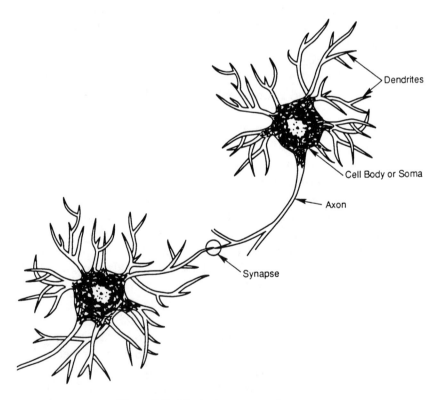

**Figure 1-2**   The basic structure of a neuron.

an average number of synapses on the axon of one neuron again being about 10,000 (Block, 1963; Palm, 1982, p. 10). Modeling the precise structure of this connection scheme would appear beyond the capabilities of foreseeable methods. Fortunately, this may not be necessary.

Rather than deduce specific replications of the human brain, models may be employed. Among the first such artificial neural network designs was the *perceptron* (Rosenblatt, 1957, 1958, 1960, 1962). A perceptron (Figure 1-3) consists of three types of units: sensory units, associator units, and response units. A stimulus will activate some sensory units. These sensory units in turn activate, with varying time delays and connection strengths, the associator units. These activations may be positive (excitatory) or negative (inhibitory). If the weighted sum of the activations at an associator unit exceeds a given threshold, the associator unit activates and sends a pulse, again weighted by a connection strength, onto the response units. There is obvious analogous behavior of units and neurons, of connections and axons and dendrites. The characteristics of the stimulus-response (input-output) of the perceptron describe its behavior.

Earlier work by Hebb (1949) indicated that neural networks could learn to recognize patterns by weakening and strengthening the connections between neurons. Rosenblatt (1957, 1960, 1962) and others (e.g., Keller, 1961; Kesler, 1961; Block, 1962; Block et al., 1962) studied the effects of changing the connection strengths in a perceptron by various rules (Rumelhart and McClelland, 1986, p. 155). Block (1962) indicated that when the

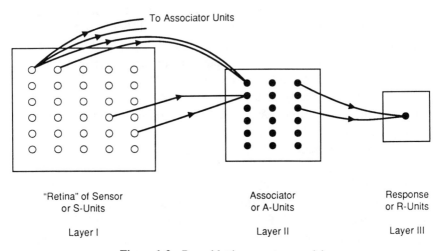

**Figure 1-3**    Rosenblatt's perceptron model.

perceptron was employed on some simple pattern recognition problems, the behavior of the machine degraded gradually with the removal of association units. That is, the perceptrons were robust, not brittle. Rosenblatt (1962, p. 28) admitted that his perceptrons were "extreme simplifications of the central nervous system, in which some properties are exaggerated and others suppressed." But he also noted that the strength of the perceptron approach lay in the ability to analyze the model.

Minsky and Papert (1969) studied the computational limits of perceptrons with one layer of modifiable connections. They demonstrated that such processing units were not able to calculate mathematical functions such as parity or the topological function of connectedness without using an absurdly large number of predicates (Rumelhart and McClelland, 1986, p. 111). But these limitations do not apply to networks of perceptrons that consist of multiple layers of perceptrons, nor does their analysis address networks with recurrent feedback connections (rather than simple feedforward connections, although any perceptron with feedback can be approximated by an equivalent but larger feedforward network). Nevertheless, Minsky and Papert (1969, pp. 231–232) speculated that the study of multilayered perceptrons would be "sterile" in the absence of an algorithm to usefully adjust the connections of such architectures.

Minsky and Papert (1969, p. 4) offered, "We have agreed to use the name 'perceptron' in recognition of the pioneer work of Frank Rosenblatt," but Block (1970) noted that "they study a severely limited class of machines from a viewpoint quite alien to Rosenblatt's." While Block (1970) recognized the mathematical prowess of Minsky and Papert, he also replied, "Work on the four-layer *Perceptrons* has been difficult, but the results suggest that such systems may be rich in behavioral possibilities." Block (1970) admitted the inability of simple perceptrons to perform functions such as parity checking and connectedness, but remarked, "Human beings cannot perceive the parity of large sets . . . nor connectedness." The recognition of more common objects such as faces was viewed as a more appropriate test.

Block questioned prophetically, "Will the formulations or methods developed in the book have a serious influence on future research in pattern recognition, threshold logic, psychology, or biology; or will this book prove to be only a monument to the mathematical virtuosity of Minsky and Papert? We shall have to wait for a few years to find out" (Block 1970).

Minsky and Papert's speculation that efforts with multilayered perceptrons would be sterile served in part to restrict funding and thus research efforts in neural networks during the 1970s and early 1980s. The criticisms by Minsky and Papert (1969) were passionate and persuasive. Papert (1988) admitted, "Yes, there was *some* hostility in the energy behind the research reported in *Perceptrons*, and there is *some* degree of annoyance at the way the new [resurgence in neural network research] has developed; part of our drive came, as we quite plainly acknowledged in our book, from the fact that funding and research energy were being dissipated on what still appear to me . . . to be misleading attempts to use connectionist methods in practical applications." Subsequent to Minsky and Papert (1969), neural network research was continued by Grossberg (1976, 1982), Amari (1967, 1971, 1972, and many others), Kohonen (1984), and others, but to a lesser degree than that conducted on knowledge-based systems. A resurgence of interest grew in the mid-1980s following further research by Hopfield (1982), Hopfield and Tank (1985), Rumelhart and McClelland (1986), Mead (1989), and others (Simpson, 1990, pp. 136–145, provides a concise review of efforts in neural networks; also, see Hecht-Nielsen, 1990).

It is now well known that multiple layers of perceptrons with variable connection strengths, bias terms, and nonlinear sigmoid functions can approximate arbitrary measurable mapping functions. In fact, universal function approximators can be constructed with a single hidden layer of squashing units and an output layer of linear units (Cybenko, 1989; Hornik et al., 1989; Barron, 1993). The application of such structures to pattern recognition problems is now routine. But as noted, such structures are simply mapping functions. Functions are not intrinsically intelligent. The crucial problem then becomes training such functions to yield the appropriate stimulus-response. There are several proposed methods to discover a suitable set of weights and bias terms, given an overall topological structure and a set of previously classified patterns (e.g., Werbos, 1974; Hopfield, 1982; Rumelhart and McClelland, 1986; Arbib and Hanson, 1990; Levine, 1991).

Currently, the method most often employed (i.e., back propagation) is based on a simple gradient descent search of the error response surface determined by the set of weights and biases. But this method is likely to discover suboptimal solutions because the response surface is a general nonlinear function and may possess many local optima. Moreover, a gradient descent algorithm is inherently no more intelligent than any other deterministic algorithm. Conceptually, the back propagation routine is little different from the addition of two integers.

There does not appear to be any evidence to suggest that biologic neural networks alter connection strengths via methods similar to gradient-based search. If the bottom-up approach to neural networks is to lead to artificially intelligent machines, the intelligence must come in the search for the appropriate structure and parameters of the particular mapping function. "Learning models which cannot adaptively cope with unpredictable changes in a complex environment have an unpromising future as models of mind and brain" (Grossberg, 1987). Models of self-organizing networks (e.g., Grossberg, 1987, and others) appear more broadly useful as explanations of biologic nervous systems.

## 1.5  DEFINITION OF INTELLIGENCE

If one word were to be used to describe research in artificial intelligence, that word might be *fragmented*. Opinions as to the cause of this scattered effort are varied. Atmar (1976) remarked:

> Perhaps the major problem is our viewpoint. Intelligence is generally regarded as a uniquely human quality. And yet we, as humans, do not understand ourselves, our capabilities, or our origins of thought. In our rush to catalogue and emulate our own staggering array of behavioral responses, it is only logical to suspect that investigations into the primal causative factors of intelligence have been passed over in order to more rapidly obtain the immediate consequences of intelligence.

Minsky (1991), on the other hand, assigns blame to attempts at unifying theories of intelligence: "There is no one best way to represent knowledge or to solve problems, and the limitations of current machine intelligence largely stem from seeking unified theories or trying to repair the deficiencies of theoretically neat but conceptually impoverished ideological positions."

A prerequisite to embarking upon research in artificial intelligence should be a definition of the term *intelligence*. As noted above (Atmar, 1976), many definitions of intelligence have relied on this property being uniquely human (e.g., Singh, 1966, p.1) and often reflect a highly anthropocentric view. Schank (1984, p. 49) stated:

> No question in AI has been the subject of more intense debate than that of assessing machine intelligence and understanding. People unconsciously

feel that calling something other than humans intelligent denigrates humans and reduces their vision of themselves as the center of the universe. Dolphins are intelligent. Whales are intelligent. Apes are intelligent. Even dogs and cats are intelligent.

Certainly other living systems can be described as being intelligent, without ascribing specific intelligence to any individual member of the system. Any proposed definition of intelligence should not rely on comparisons to individual organisms.

In contrast to Staugaard's comments (1987, p. 23), Minsky has offered the following definition of intelligence (1985, p. 71): "Intelligence . . . means . . . the ability to solve hard problems." But how hard does a problem have to be? Who is to decide which problem is hard? All problems are hard until you know how to solve them, at which point they become easy. Finding the slope of a polynomial at any specific point is very difficult, unless you are familiar with derivatives, in which case it is trivial. Such a definition would appear problematic.

For an organism, or any system, to be intelligent, it must make decisions. Any decision may be described as the selection of how to allocate the available resources. And an intelligent system must face a range of decisions, for if there were only one possible decision, there would really be no decision at all. Moreover, decision making requires a goal. Without the existence of a goal, decision making is pointless. The intelligence of such a decision-making entity becomes a meaningless quality.

This argument begs the question, "Where do goals come from?" Consider biologically reproducing organisms. They exist in a finite arena; as a consequence, there is competition for the available resources. Natural selection is inevitable in any system of self-replicating organisms that fill the available resource space. Selection stochastically eliminates those variants that do not acquire sufficient resources. Thus, while evolution as a process is purposeless, the first purposeful goal imbued into all living systems is survival. Those variants that do not exhibit behaviors that meet this goal are stochastically culled. The genetically preprogrammed behaviors of the survivors (and thus the goal of survival) are reinforced in every generation through intense competition.

Such a notion has been suggested many times. For example, Carne (1965, p. 3) remarked, "Perhaps the basic attribute of an intelligent organism is its capability to learn to perform various functions within a changing environment so as to survive and to prosper." Atmar (1976) offered, "Intelligence is that property in which the organism senses, reacts to, learns from, and subsequently adapts its behavior to its present environment in order to better promote its own survival."

Note that any automaton whose behavior (i.e., stimulus-response pairs that depend on the state of the organism) is completely prewired (e.g., a simple hand-held calculator or the hunting wasp previously described) cannot learn anything. Nor can it make decisions. Such systems should not be viewed as intelligent. But this should not be taken as a contradiction to the statement that "the genetically preprogrammed behaviors of the survivors (and thus the goal of survival) are passed along to future progeny." Behaviors in all biota, individuals or populations, are dependent on underlying genetic programs. In some cases, these programs mandate specific behaviors; in others, they create nervous systems capable of adapting behavior of the organism based on its experiences.

But the definition of intelligence should not be restricted to biological organisms. Intelligence is a property of purpose-driven decision makers. It applies equally well to humans, colonies of ants, robots, social groups, and so forth. Thus, more generally, following Fogel (1964; Fogel et al., 1966, p. 2), intelligence may be defined as *the capability of a system to adapt its behavior to meet its goals in a range of environments.* For species, survival is a necessary goal in any given environment; for a machine, both goals and environments may be imbued by the machine's creators.

## 1.6 INTELLIGENCE, THE SCIENTIFIC METHOD, AND EVOLUTION

Ornstein (1965) argued that all learning processes are adaptive. The most important aspect of such learning processes is the "development of implicit or explicit techniques to accurately estimate the probabilities of future events." Similar notions have been offered by Atmar (1976, 1979). When faced with a changing environment, the adaptation of behavior becomes little more than a shot in the dark if the system is incapable of predicting future events. Ornstein (1965) suggested that as predicting future events is the "forte of science," it is sensible to examine the scientific method for useful cues in the search for effective learning techniques.

The scientific method (Figure 1-4) is an iterative process that facilitates the gaining of new knowledge about the underlying processes of

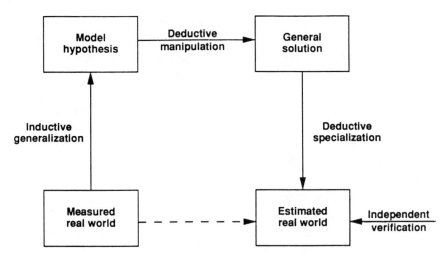

**Figure 1-4**   The scientific method.

an observable environment. Unknown aspects of the environment are estimated. Data are collected in the form of previous observations or known results and combined with newly acquired measurements. After the removal of known erroneous data, a class of models of the environment that is consistent with the data is generalized. This process is necessarily inductive. The class of models is then generally reduced by parametrization, a deductive process. The specific hypothesized model (or models) is then tested in its ability to predict future aspects of the environment. Models that prove worthy are modified, extended, or combined to form new hypotheses that carry on a "heredity of reasonableness" (Fogel, 1964). This process is iterated until a sufficient level of credibility is achieved. "As the hypotheses correspond more and more closely with the logic of the environment they provide an 'understanding' that is demonstrated in terms of improved goal-seeking behavior in the face of that environment" (Fogel et al., 1966, p. 111). It appears reasonable to seek methods to mechanize the scientific method in an algorithmic formulation so that a machine may carry out the procedure and similarly gain knowledge about its environment and adapt its behavior to meet goals.

The scientific method can be used to describe a process of human investigation of the universe, or of learning processes in general. Atmar (1976), following Weiner (1961), proposed that there are "three distinct organization forms of intelligence: phylogenetic, ontogenetic and sociogenetic, which are equivalent to one another in process, each containing a quantum unit of mutability and a reservoir of learned behavior." Individuals of most species are capable of learning ontogenetically (self-arising within the individual). The minimum unit of mutability is the proclivity of a neuron to fire. The reservoir of learned behavior becomes the entire "collection of engrams reflecting the sum of knowledge the organism possesses about its environment" (Atmar, 1976). Sociogenetic learning (arising within the group) is the basis for a society to acquire knowledge and communicate (Wilson, 1971; Atmar, 1976). The quantum unit of mutability is the "idea," while "culture" is the reservoir of learned behavior.

But phylogenetic learning (arising from within the lineage) is certainly the most ancient, and the most commonly exhibited, form of intelligence. The quantum unit of mutability is the nucleotide base pair, and the reservoir of learned behavior is the genome of the species. The recognition of evolution as an intelligent learning process is a recurring idea (Cannon, 1932; Turing, 1950; Fogel, 1962; and others). Fogel et al. (1966, p. 112) developed a correspondence between natural evolution and the scientific method. In nature, individual organisms serve as hypotheses concerning the logical properties of their environment. Their behavior is an inductive inference concerning some as yet unknown aspects of that environment. Validity is demonstrated by their survival. Over successive generations, organisms become successively better predictors of their surroundings.

Minsky (1985, p. 71) disagreed, claiming that evolution is not intelligent "because people also use the word 'intelligence' to emphasize swiftness and efficiency. Evolution's time rate is so slow that we don't see it as intelligent, even though it finally produces wonderful things we ourselves cannot yet make." But time does not enter into the definition of intelligence offered above, and it need not. Atmar (1976) admits that "the learning period [for evolution] may be tortuously long by human standards, but it is real, finite, and continuous." And evolution can proceed quite rapidly (e.g., viruses). Units of time are a human creation. The simulation of the evolutionary process on a computer need not take billions of years. Successive generations can be iterated very quickly. Metaphorically, the videotape of evolution can be played at fast forward with no alteration of the basic algorithm. Arguments attacking the speed of the process (as opposed to the rate of learning) are without merit.

There is obvious value in plasticity. Organisms that can adapt to changes in the environment at a greater rate than through direct physical modifications will tend to outcompete less mutable organisms. Thus the evolutionary benefit of ontogenetic learning is obvious. Sociogenetic learning is even more powerful as the communicative group possesses even greater plasticity in behavior, a more durable memory, and a greater range of possible mutability (Atmar, 1976). But both ontogenetic learning and sociogenetic learning are "tricks" of phylogenetic learning, invented through the randomly driven search of alternative methods of minimizing behavioral surprise to the evolving species.

If the evolutionary process is accepted as being fundamentally analogous to the scientific method, then so must the belief that this process can be mechanized and programmed on a computing machine. Evolution, like all other natural processes, is a mechanical procedure operating on and within the laws of physics and chemistry (Fogel, 1964; Fogel et al., 1966; Wooldridge, 1968, p. 25; Atmar, 1976, 1979, 1991; Mayr, 1988, pp. 148–159). If the scientific method is captured in an algorithm, then so must induction be captured as an intrinsic part of that algorithm.

Fogel et al. (1966, p. 122) noted that induction had been presumed to require creativity and imagination, but through the simulation of evolution, induction can be reduced to a routine procedure. Such notions have a propensity to generate pointed responses. Lindsay (1968) wrote in criticism of Fogel et al. (1966), "The penultimate indignity is a chapter in which the scientific method is described as an evolutionary process and hence mechanizable with the procedures described." People unconsciously feel that calling something not human "intelligent" denigrates humans (Schank, 1984, p. 49; cf. Pelletier, 1978, pp. 240–241). Yet wishing something away does not make it so. Wooldridge (1968, p. 129) stated:

> In particular, it must not be imagined that reduction of the processes of intelligence to small-step mechanical operations is incompatible with the apparently spontaneous appearance of new and original ideas to which we apply such terms as "inspiration," "insight," or "creativity." To be sure, there is no way for the physical methods . . . to produce full-blown thoughts or ideas from out of the blue. But it will be recalled that there is a solution for this problem. The solution is to deny that such spontaneity really exists. The argument is that this is an example of our being led astray by attributing too much reality to our subjective feelings—that the explanation of the apparent freedom of thought is the incompleteness of our consciousness and our resulting lack of awareness of the tortuous . . . nature of our thought processes.

Hofstadter (1985, p. 529) went further:

Having creativity is an automatic consequence of having the proper representation of concepts in a mind. It is not something you add on afterward. It is built into the way concepts are. To spell this out more concretely: If you have succeeded in making an accurate model of *concepts*, you have thereby also succeeded in making a model of the creative process, and even of consciousness.

Creativity and imagination are part of the invention of evolution just as are eyes, opposable thumbs, telephones, and calculators.

The process of evolution can be described as four essential processes: self-reproduction, mutation, competition, and selection (Mayr, 1988; Hoffman, 1989; and many others). The self-reproduction of germline DNA and RNA systems is well known. In a positively entropic universe (as dictated by the second law of thermodynamics), the property of mutability is guaranteed; error in information transcription is inevitable. A finite arena guarantees the existence of competition. Selection becomes the natural consequence of the excess of organisms that have filled the available resource space (Atmar, 1979). The implication of these very simple rules is that evolution is a procedure that can be simulated and used to generate creativity and imagination mechanically.

## 1.7 EVOLVING ARTIFICIAL INTELLIGENCE

It is natural to conclude that by simulating the evolutionary learning process on a computer, the machine can become intelligent, that it can adapt its behavior to meet goals in a range of environments. "Intelligence is a basic property of life" (Atmar, 1976). It has occurred at the earliest instance of natural selection and has pervaded all subsequent living organisms. In many ways, life is intelligence, and the processes cannot be easily separated.

Numerous opinions about the proper goal for artificial intelligence research have been expressed. But intuitively, intelligence must be the same process in living organisms as it is in machines. The "artificial" is not nearly as important as the "intelligence." "Artificial Intelligence is the study of intelligent behavior. Its ultimate goal is a theory of intelligence that accounts for the behavior of naturally occurring intelligent entities and that guides the creation of artificial entities capable of intelligent behavior" (Genesereth and Nilsson, 1987). Evolutionary processes account for such intelligent behavior and can be simulated and used for the creation of intelligent machines.

## REFERENCES

Adams, J. B. (1976). "A Probability Model of Medical Reasoning and the MYCIN Model," *Mathematical Biosciences*, Vol. 32, pp. 177–186.

Amari, S.-I. (1967). "A Theory of Adaptive Pattern Classifiers," *IEEE Trans. of Elec. Comp.*, Vol. EC-16, pp. 299–307.

Amari, S.-I. (1971). "Characteristics of Randomly Connected Threshold-Element Networks and Network Systems," *Proc. of the IEEE*, Vol. 59:1, pp. 35–47.

Amari, S.-I. (1972). "Learning Patterns and Pattern Sequences by Self-Organizing Nets of Threshold Elements," *IEEE Trans. Comp.*, Vol. C-21, pp. 1197–1206.

Arbib, M. A., and A. R. Hanson (1990). *Vision, Brain, and Cooperative Computation*. Cambridge, MA: MIT Press.

Atmar, J. W. (1976). "Speculation on the Evolution of Intelligence and Its Possible Realization in Machine Form." Sc.D. diss., New Mexico State University, Las Cruces.

Atmar, J. W. (1979). "The Inevitability of Evolutionary Invention." Unpublished manuscript.

Atmar, W. (1991). "On the Role of Males," *Animal Behaviour*, Vol. 41, pp. 195–205.

Barr, A., and E. A. Feigenbaum (1981). *The Handbook of Artificial Intelligence*, Vol. 1. San Mateo, CA: William Kaufmann.

Barr, A., P. R. Cohen, and E. A. Feigenbaum (1989). *The Handbook of Artificial Intelligence*, Vol. 4. Reading, MA: Addison-Wesley.

Barron, A. R. (1993). "Universal Approximation Bounds for Superpositions of a Sigmoidal Function," *IEEE Trans. Info. Theory,* Vol. 39:3, pp. 930–945.

Bennett, J. S., and C. R. Hollander (1981). "DART: An Expert System for Computer Fault Diagnosis," *Proc. of IJCAI-81,* pp. 843–845.

Bernstein, A., V. De, M. Roberts, T. Arbuckle, and M. A. Belsky (1958). "A Chess Playing Program for the IBM 704," *Proc. West Jut. Comp. Conf.,* Vol. 13, pp. 157–159.

Bezdek, J. C., and S. K. Pal (1992). *Fuzzy Models for Pattern Recognition: Models that Search for Structures in Data*. Piscataway, NJ: IEEE Press.

Block, H. D. (1962). "The Perceptron: A Model for Brain Functioning," *Rev. Mod. Phys.,* Vol. 34, pp. 123–125.

Block, H. D. (1963). "Adaptive Neural Networks as Brain Models," *Proc. of Symp. Applied Mathematics,* Vol. 15, pp. 59–72.

Block, H. D. (1970). "A Review of 'Perceptrons: An Introduction to Computational Geometry,' " *Information and Control,* Vol. 17:5, pp. 501–522.

Block, H. D., B. W. Knight, and F. Rosenblatt (1962). "Analysis of a Four Layer Series Coupled Perceptron," *Rev. Mod. Phys.,* Vol. 34, pp. 135–142.

Buchanan, B. G., and E. H. Shortliffe (1985). *Rule-Based Expert Systems: The MYCIN Experiments of the Stanford Heuristic Programming Project*. Reading, MA: Addison-Wesley.

Campbell, A. N., V. F. Hollister, R. O. Duda, and P. E. Hart (1982). "Recognition of a Hidden Mineral Deposit by an Artificial Intelligence Program," *Science*, Vol. 217, pp. 927–929.

Cannon, W. D. (1932). *The Wisdom of the Body*. New York: Norton and Company.

Carne, E. B. (1965). *Artificial Intelligence Techniques*. Washington, DC: Spartan Books.

Cerf, C., and V. Navasky (1984). *The Experts Speak: The Definitive Compendium of Authoritative Misinformation*. New York: Pantheon Books.

Charniak, E., and D. V. McDermott (1985). *Introduction to Artificial Intelligence*. Reading, MA: Addison-Wesley.

Countess of Lovelace (1842). "Translator's Notes to an Article on Babbage's Analytical Engine." In *Scientific Memoirs*, Vol. 3, edited by R. Taylor, pp. 691–731.

Covington, M. A., D. Nute, and A. Vellino (1988). *Prolog Programming in Depth*. Glenview, IL: Scott, Foresman.

Cybenko, G. (1989). "Approximations by Superpositions of a Sigmoidal Function," *Math. Contr. Signals, Syst.*, Vol. 2, pp. 303–314.

Dreyfus, H., and S. Dreyfus (1984). "Mindless Machines: Computers Don't Think Like Experts, and Never Will," *The Sciences*, November/December, pp. 18–22.

Dreyfus, H., and S. Dreyfus (1986). "Why Computers May Never Think Like People," *Tech. Review*, January, pp. 42–61.

Dubois, D., and H. Prade (1982). "A Class of Fuzzy Measures Based on Triangular Norms—A General Framework for the Combination of Uncertain Information," *Int. J. of General Systems*, Vol. 8:1.

Duda, R., P. E. Hart, N. J. Nilsson, P. Barrett, J. G. Gaschnig, K. Konolige, R. Reboh, and J. Slocum (1978). "Development of the PROSPECTOR Consultation System for Mineral Exploration," SRI Report, Stanford Research Institute, Menlo Park, CA.

Feigenbaum, E. A., B. G. Buchanan, and J. Lederberg (1971). "On Generality and Problem Solving: A Case Study Involving the DENDRAL Program." In *Machine Intelligence 6*, edited by B. Meltzer and D. Michie. New York: American Elsevier, pp. 165–190.

Fogel, L. J. (1962). "Autonomous Automata," *Industrial Research*, Vol. 4, pp. 14–19.

Fogel, L. J. (1964). "On the Organization of Intellect." Ph.D. diss., UCLA.

Fogel, L. J., A. J. Owens, and M. J. Walsh (1966). *Artificial Intelligence through Simulated Evolution*. New York: John Wiley.

Genesereth, M. R., and N. J. Nilsson (1987). *Logical Foundations of Artificial Intelligence*. Los Altos, CA: Morgan Kaufmann.

Gould, J. L., and C. G. Gould (1985). "An Animal's Education: How Comes the Mind to be Furnished?" *The Sciences*, Vol. 25:4, pp. 24–31.

Greenblatt, R., D. Eastlake, and S. Crocker (1967). "The Greenblatt Chess Program," *FJCC*, Vol. 31, pp. 801–810.

Grossberg, S. (1976). "Adaptive Pattern Classification and Universal Recoding: Part I. Parallel Development and Coding of Neural Feature Detectors," *Biological Cybernetics*, Vol. 23, pp. 121–134.

Grossberg, S. (1982). *Studies of Mind and Brain*. Dordrecht, Holland: Reidel.

Grossberg, S. (1987). "Competitive Learning: From Interactive Activation to Adaptive Resonance," *Cognitive Science*, Vol. 11, pp. 23–63.

Hebb, D. O. (1949). *The Organization of Behavior*. New York: John Wiley.

Hecht-Nielsen, R. (1990). *Neurocomputing*. Reading, MA: Addison-Wesley.

Hoffman, A. (1989). *Arguments on Evolution: A Paleontologist's Perspective*. New York: Oxford Univ. Press.

Hofstadter, D. R. (1985). *Metamagical Themas: Questing for the Essence of Mind and Pattern.* New York: Basic Books.

Hopfield, J. J. (1982). "Neural Networks and Physical Systems with Emergent Collective Computational Abilities," *Proc. Nat. Acad. of Sciences,* Vol. 79, pp. 2554–2558.

Hopfield, J. J., and D. Tank (1985). " 'Neural' Computation of Decision in Optimization Problems," *Biological Cybernetics,* Vol. 52, pp. 141–152.

Hornik, K., M. Stinchcombe, and H. White (1989). "Multilayer Feedforward Networks Are Universal Approximators," *Neural Networks,* Vol. 2, pp. 359–366.

Jackson, P. C. (1985). *Introduction to Artificial Intelligence,* 2nd ed. New York: Dover.

Kandel, A. (1986). *Fuzzy Expert Systems.* Boca Raton, FL: CRC Press.

Keller, H. B. (1961). "Finite Automata, Pattern Recognition and Perceptrons," *J. Assoc. Comput. Mach.,* Vol. 8, pp. 1–20.

Kesler, C. (1961). "Preliminary Experiments on Perceptron Applications to Bubble Chamber Event Recognition." Cognitive Systems Research Program, Rep. No. 1, Cornell University, Ithaca, NY.

Kohonen, T. (1984). *Self-Organization and Associative Memory.* Berlin: Springer-Verlag.

Lenat, D. B. (1983). "EURISKO: A Program that Learns New Heuristics and Domain Concepts," *Artificial Intelligence,* Vol. 21, pp. 61–98.

Levine, D. S. (1991). *Introduction to Neural and Cognitive Modeling.* Hillsdale, NJ: Lawrence Erlbaum.

Levy, D. N. L., and M. Newborn (1991). *How Computers Play Chess.* New York: Computer Science Press.

Lindsay, R. K. (1968). "Artificial Evolution of Intelligence," *Contemp. Psych.,* Vol. 13:3, pp. 113–116.

Lindsay, R. K., B. G. Buchanan, E. A. Feigenbaum, and J. Lederberg (1980). *Applications of Artificial Intelligence for Organic Chemistry: The DENDRAL Project.* New York: McGraw-Hill.

Mayr, E. (1988). *Toward a New Philosophy of Biology: Observations of an Evolutionist.* Cambridge, MA: Belknap Press.

McCarthy, J., P. J. Abrahams, D. J. Edwards, P. T. Hart, and M. I. Levin (1962). *LISP 1.5 Programmer's Manual.* Cambridge, MA: MIT Press.

McCulloch, W. S., and W. Pitts (1943). "A Logical Calculus of the Ideas Immanent in Nervous Activity," *Bull. Math. Biophysics*, Vol. 5, pp. 115–133.

Mead, C. (1989). *Analog VLSI and Neural Systems*. Reading, MA: Addison-Wesley.

Minsky, M. L. (1985). *The Society of Mind*. New York: Simon and Schuster.

Minsky, M. L. (1991). "Logical Versus Analogical or Symbolic versus Connectionist or Neat versus Scruffy," *AI Magazine*, Vol. 12:2, pp. 35–51.

Minsky, M. L., and S. Papert (1969). *Perceptrons*. Cambridge, MA: MIT Press.

Negoita, C. V., and D. Ralescu (1987). *Simulation, Knowledge-Based Computing, and Fuzzy Statistics*. New York: Van Nostrand Reinhold.

Newell, A., J. C. Shaw, and H. A. Simon (1958). "Chess Playing Programs and the Problem of Complexity," *IBM J. of Res. & Dev.*, Vol. 4:2, pp. 320–325.

Newell, A., and H. A. Simon (1963). "GPS: A Program that Simulates Human Thought." In *Computers and Thought*, edited by E. A. Feigenbaum and J. Feldman. New York: McGraw-Hill, pp. 279–293.

Ornstein, L. (1965). "Computer Learning and the Scientific Method: A Proposed Solution to the Information Theoretical Problem of Meaning," *J. of the Mt. Sinai Hosp.*, Vol. 32:4, pp. 437–494.

Palm, G. (1982). *Neural Assemblies: An Alternative Approach to Artificial Intelligence*. Berlin: Springer-Verlag.

Papert, S. (1988). "One AI or Many?" In *The Artificial Intelligence Debate: False Starts, Real Foundations,* edited by S. R. Braubard. Cambridge, MA: MIT Press.

Pelletier, K. R. (1978). *Toward a Science of Consciousness*. New York: Dell.

Rich, E. (1983). *Artificial Intelligence*. New York: McGraw-Hill.

Rosenblatt, F. (1957). "The Perceptron, a Perceiving and Recognizing Automaton." Project PARA, Cornell Aeronautical Lab. Rep., No. 85-640-1, Buffalo, NY.

Rosenblatt, F. (1958). "The Perceptron: A Probabilistic Model for Information Storage and Organization in the Brain," *Psychol. Rev.*, Vol. 65, p. 386.

Rosenblatt, F. (1960). "Perceptron Simulation Experiments," *Proc. IRE*, Vol. 48, pp. 301–309.

Rosenblatt, F. (1962). *Principles of Neurodynamics: Perceptrons and the Theory of Brain Mechanisms*. Washington, DC: Spartan Books.

Rumelhart, D. E. and J. L. McClelland (1986). *Parallel Distributed Processing: Explorations in the Microstructures of Cognition*, Vol. 1. Cambridge, MA: MIT Press.

Samuel, A. L. (1959). "Some Studies in Machine Learning Using the Game of Checkers," *IBM J. of Res. and Dev.*, Vol. 3:3, pp. 210–229.

Samuel, A. L. (1963). "Some Studies in Machine Learning Using the Game of Checkers." In *Computers and Thought*, edited by E. A. Feigenbaum and J. Feldman. New York: McGraw-Hill, pp. 71–105.

Schank, R. C. (1984). *The Cognitive Computer: On Language, Learning, and Artificial Intelligence*. Reading. MA: Addison-Wesley.

Schildt, H. (1987). *Artificial Intelligence Using C*. New York: McGraw-Hill.

Shannon, C. E. (1950). "Programming a Computer for Playing Chess," *Philosophical Magazine*, Vol. 41, pp. 256–275.

Shortliffe, E. H. (1974). "MYCIN: A Rule-Based Computer Program for Advising Physicians Regarding Antimicrobial Therapy Selection." Ph.D. diss., Stanford University.

Simpson, P. K. (1990). *Artificial Neural Systems: Foundations, Paradigms, Applications and Implementations*. New York: Pergamon Press.

Singh, J. (1966). *Great Ideas in Information Theory, Language and Cybernetics*. New York: Dover.

Staugaard, A. C. (1987). *Robotics and AI: An Introduction to Applied Machine Intelligence*. Englewood Cliffs, NJ: Prentice Hall.

Swade, D. D. (1993). "Redeeming Charles Babbage's Mechanical Computer," *Scientific American*, Vol. 268, No. 2, February, pp. 86–91.

Turing, A. M. (1950). "Computing Machinery and Intelligence," *Mind*, Vol. 59, pp. 433–460.

Turing, A. M. (1953). "Digital Computers Applied to Games." In *Faster than Thought*, edited by B. V. Bowden. London: Pittman, pp. 286–310.

Waterman, D. A. (1986). *A Guide to Expert Systems*. Reading, MA: Addison-Wesley.

Weiner, N. (1961). *Cybernetics*, Part 2. Cambridge, MA: MIT Press.

Werbos, P. (1974). "Beyond Regression: New Tools for Prediction and Analysis in the Behavioral Sciences." Ph.D. diss., Harvard University.

Wilson, E. O. (1971). *The Insect Societies*. Cambridge, MA: Belknap Press.

Wooldridge, D. E. (1968). *The Mechanical Man: The Physical Basis of Intelligent Life.* New York: McGraw-Hill.

Yager, R. R. (1980). "A Measurement–Informational Discussion of Fuzzy Union and Intersection," *IEEE Trans. Syst. Man Cyber.*, Vol. 10:1, pp. 51–53.

Zadeh, L. (1965). "Fuzzy Sets," *Information and Control*, Vol. 8, pp. 338–353.

# 2

# Natural Evolution

## 2.1 THE NEO-DARWINIAN PARADIGM

A revolution in biological thought, and indeed in human philosophy, was begun when Charles Darwin and Alfred Russel Wallace each presented their evidence for the theory of evolution before the Linnean Society of London on July 1, 1858. The position that their theories and observations have come to occupy in biology cannot be exaggerated. Dobzhansky has remarked, "Nothing in biology makes sense except in the light of evolution" (Dobzhansky et al., 1977, frontispiece). And Mayr (1963, p. 1) has said, "There is no area of biology in which [evolution] has not served as an ordering principle." Classic Darwinian evolutionary theory, combined with the selectionism of Weismann and the genetics of Mendel, has now become a rather universally accepted set of arguments known as the neo-Darwinian paradigm (Fisher, 1930; Wright, 1931; Haldane, 1932; Dobzhansky, 1937; Huxley, 1942; Mayr, 1942; Simpson, 1944; Rensch, 1947; Stebbins, 1950).

Neo-Darwinism asserts that the history of the vast majority of life is fully accounted for by only a very few statistical processes acting on and within populations and species (Hoffman, 1989, p. 39). These processes are reproduction, mutation, competition, and selection. Reproduction is an obvious property of all life. But similarly as obvious, mutation is guaranteed in any system that continuously reproduces itself in a positively entropic universe. Competition and selection become the inescapable consequences of any expanding population constrained to a finite arena. Evolution is then the result of these fundamental interacting stochastic processes as they act on populations, generation after generation (Huxley, 1963; Wooldridge, 1968, p. 25; and others).

The questions that arise if evolution is to be accurately emulated for engineering purposes are many. (1) What is truly being optimized by evolution? (2) How extensive is that optimization? (3) To whom do the benefits of optimization accrue: to the individual gene, to the individual (and its genome), or to the species as a whole? (4) What is the true nature of the gene? (5) What is the significance of neutral mutations in evolution? (6) What are the benefits of sex and sexual selection? Evolutionary mechanisms create a complex web of interacting effects that cannot be easily partitioned or disentangled (Hoffman, 1989, pp. 32–33), but the physics that governs the evolutionary process may be quite simple and expressible by a rather small set of rules.

## 2.2 THE GENOTYPE AND THE PHENOTYPE: THE OPTIMIZATION OF BEHAVIOR

Living organisms can be viewed as a duality of their genotype (the underlying genetic coding) and their phenotype (the manner of response contained in the behavior, physiology and morphology of the organism). Lewontin (1974) illustrated this distinction by specifying two state spaces: a populational genotypic (informational) space $\mathbf{G}$ and a populational phenotypic (behavioral) space $\mathbf{P}$. Four functions map elements in $\mathbf{G}$ and $\mathbf{P}$ to each other (Figure 2-1). Atmar (1992) modified these functions to be

$$f_1: \mathbf{I} \times \mathbf{G} \rightarrow \mathbf{P},$$

$$f_2: \mathbf{P} \rightarrow \mathbf{P},$$

$$f_3: \mathbf{P} \rightarrow \mathbf{G},$$

$$f_4: \mathbf{G} \rightarrow \mathbf{G}.$$

The function $f_1$, *epigenesis*, maps the element $g_1 \in \mathbf{G}$ into the phenotypic space $\mathbf{P}$ as a particular collection of phenotypes $p_1$ whose development is modified by its environment, an indexed set of symbols $(i_1, \ldots, i_k) \in \mathbf{I}$,

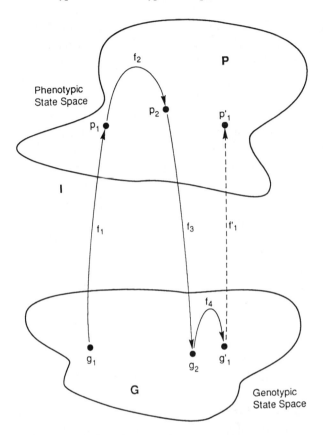

**Figure 2-1**    The evolution of a population within a single generation. Evolution can be viewed as occurring as a succession of four mapping functions (*epigenesis, selection, genotypic survival,* and *mutation*) relating the genotypic information state space and the phenotypic behavioral state space.

where **I** is the set of all such environmental sequences. The function $f_2$, *selection*, maps phenotypes $p_1$ into $p_2$. As natural selection only operates on the phenotypic expressions of the genotype (Mayr, 1960, p. 24, 1970, p. 131; Hartl and Clark, 1989, p. 431), the underlying coding $g_1$ is not involved in function $f_2$. The function $f_3$, *genotypic survival*, describes the effects of selection and migration processes on **G**. Function $f_4$, *mutation*, maps the representative codings $g_2 \in$ **G** to the point $g'_1 \in$ **G**. This function represents the "rules" of mutation and recombination, and encompasses all genetic changes. With the creation of the new population of genotypes $g'_1$, one generation is complete. Evolutionary adaptation occurs over successive iterations of these mappings.

The neo-Darwinian argument asserts that natural selection is the predominant mediating evolutionary force that prevails in shaping the phenotypic characters of organisms in the vast majority of situations encountered in nature (Mayr, 1988; Hoffman, 1989; Brunk, 1991; Wilson, 1992, p. 75; and others). It is strictly an a posteriori process that rewards current success (Mayr, 1988, p. 43) primarily through the statistical culling of inappropriate individuals. Selection acts in the face of phenotypic variation. Parents and their offspring typically demonstrate at least a general resemblance in their phenotypic traits (Hartl and Clark, 1989, p. 430). Their behaviors may in fact be virtually identical, that is, reproduction may be very nearly replication (Hoffman, 1989, p. 24). But phenotypic variation is always observed within populations and species and is largely the result of mutation and recombination (if applicable), environmental constraints placed on an individual's development, and replicative errors of the genome. The interaction between the species and its environment (which includes other organisms) determines the relative success (differential reproduction) or failure (genetic death) of the species.

Selection is often viewed as leading to the maintenance or increase of populations' "fitness," where fitness is defined as the ability to survive and reproduce in a specific environment (Hartl and Clark, 1989, p. 147). It has been asserted that although fitness cannot be directly measured, "its distribution in a population can be roughly estimated in any given environmental context on the basis of ecology and functional morphology of the organisms. Hence it is an empirically testable biological proposition" (Hoffman, 1989, p. 29). Atmar (1994) indicated that a singular measure of evolutionary fitness is the appropriateness of the species' behavior in terms of its ability to anticipate its environment. The quantitative ability to perform suitable prediction and elicit appropriate response yields a measure of fitness.

In contrast, Fisher (1930) defined fitness in terms of the gene as the per capita rate of increase (of a genotype, based on the average effect of gene substitutions, e.g., Fisher, 1930, pp. 30–34). But such a definition is problematic in light of the pleiotropic and polygenic nature of the genotype. *Pleiotropy* is the effect that a single gene may simultaneously affect several phenotypic traits. *Polygeny* is the effect that a single phenotypic characteristic of an individual may be determined by the simultaneous interaction of many genes (Figure 2-2). Assigning fitness to individual genes implicitly ignores their interactions, or describes them only on the average, and often assumes a one-gene/one-trait model of the relationship between the

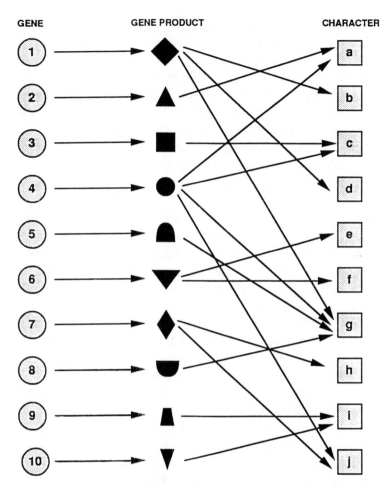

**Figure 2-2**   The effects of pleiotropy and polygeny. *Pleiotropy* is the effect where a single gene affects multiple phenotypic characters. *Polygeny* is the effect where a single phenotypic character is affected by multiple genes. (After Mayr, 1963, p. 265.)

genotype and the phenotype. Although such a reductionist simplification is mathematically tractable and has been extensively analyzed (e.g., Fisher, 1930), it is not broadly useful in predicting or assessing the adaptation of behaviors. Such efforts have been labeled "beanbag genetics" (Mayr, 1959, 1963, p. 263, 1988, p. 149; cf. Haldane, 1964). Bonner (1988, p. 24) suggested "evolution can no longer be looked at solely as changes in gene frequencies within populations."

The one-gene/one-trait model of evolutionary genetics is an over-simplification. Naturally evolved systems are extensively pleiotropic and highly polygenic. The importance of these profound genetic interactions on evolved structures has long been argued by Wright (1931), Simpson (1949, p. 224), Dobzhansky (1970), Stanley (1975), Mayr (1959, 1963, 1982, 1988), Dawkins (1986, p. 296), Hartl and Clark (1989, pp. 7, 149, 430, 501, 503–504), and others. Further, selection acts on collections of interactive phenotypic traits, not on singular traits in isolation. The appropriateness of an organism's holistic functional behavior in light of the physics of its environment is the sole quality that is optimized through selection.

The fundamental characteristics of diverse environments are often profoundly similar, and convergent evolution is the general outcome. The compound image-forming eye has been invented at least three times during the course of evolution: in mollusks, arthropods, and vertebrates (Salvini-Plawen and Mayr, 1977, indicated that simple light-sensitive organs have been evolved 40 to 65 times independently). The most common ancestor of these three taxa could have occurred no later than 450 million years ago and more probably 550 to 600 million years ago (Atmar, pers. comm.; Marshall, pers. comm.). But in all three cases, a profoundly similar informational neurophysiology has been invented, although slightly differently realized. In vertebrates, the neural connections lay on top of the retinal surface. In mollusks, they occur behind the eye as they do in arthropods. But in all three, a network of collateralized synaptic connections occur in a series of amacrine, horizontal, and bipolar cells that generate edge enhancement, motion detection, and modulatable light sensitivities in strikingly similar manners (Atmar, 1979). The convergent functional behavior of these independently evolved constructions leads to the conclusion that the invention of such a functional structure is exceedingly probable. Although there are obvious differences in the implementation of the eye arrangements, their functional behavior is profoundly similar. The physical and historical constraints woven into the mechanisms and process of the construction of a cell appear to predestine the evolution of a particular image-forming eye (Atmar, 1979).

Similarly, the invention of flight has occurred repeatedly. Gliding has been invented independently in fish, amphibians, reptiles, and mammals. Self-sustained flight has evolved independently in pterosaurs, birds, mammals, and insects (Bonner, 1988, p. 169). Other forms of flight have been invented in insects, arachnids, and plants. Young spiders, in which the young are transported over great distances by means of a parachute produced from silken thread, have been documented to drift over 400 miles (Sheppard, 1975). Plants similarly use airborne transportation to facilitate the dispersal of their seeds. In some cases, seeds have evolved an airfoil (e.g., *Zanonia macrocarpa*; Fogel, pers. comm.). The underlying genetic structures for these independently evolved phenotypic characteristics are diverse, yet the functionalities are notably similar.

Even ethologies are often profoundly convergent. During displays of aggression, animals as varied as Australian crayfish, baboon spiders, toads, wolves, and black-headed gulls all assume postures that make them appear larger to their adversaries. These behaviors include the raising of body hair, standing on hind legs in an upright manner, and spreading of the forelegs or claws (Keeton, 1980, pp. 517–518). Bonner (1988, p. 64; 1993, pp. 39–59) suggested that something as fundamental as multicellularity must also have been independently invented multiple times throughout the course of evolutionary history.

Pleiotropy and polygeny preclude the possibility of singular genes for these complex effects. While it is possible to alter specific traits through single gene mutations, this does not indicate a gene "for" that particular trait. By analogy, it is possible under the right circumstances to change a single card in a poker hand and to alter a flush (five cards of one suit) into a straight (five cards in ascending order). But that does not indicate that the single changed card is a "card for a straight." There are no individual genes for specific behaviors, such as "making oneself appear big," in natural evolved systems.

## 2.3 IMPLICATIONS OF WRIGHT'S ADAPTIVE TOPOGRAPHY: OPTIMIZATION IS EXTENSIVE YET INCOMPLETE

Wright (1932) offered the concept of the adaptive topography to describe the fitness of individuals and to serve to illustrate the manner in which evolution may proceed into novel adaptive zones. This concept has since become central to evolutionary theory. Individual (or populational) genotypes map into their respective phenotypes, which are in turn mapped onto the adaptive topography (Figure 2-3). Each peak corresponds with a fitness-optimized phenotype and, by consequence, one or more optimized genotypes. Evolution probabilistically proceeds up the slopes of the topog-

**Figure 2-3** Evolution on an inverted adaptive topography. A landscape is abstracted to represent the fitness of alternative phenotypes and, as a consequence, alternative genotypes. Rather than viewing individuals or populations as maximizing fitness and thereby climbing peaks on the landscape, a more intuitive perspective may be obtained by inverting the topography. Populations proceed down the slopes of the topography toward valleys of minimal predictive error.

raphy toward peaks as selection culls inappropriate phenotypic variants. But no natural topography is stable. Rather, the topography changes shape over time as a function of extrinsic environmental dynamics and organism-environment interactions. As the topography shifts, the allelic balance in the population changes as the result of selection on the distribution of phenotypes.

The adaptive topography is a virtually continuous function because the range of phenotypic expression may also be regarded as virtually continuous (Hartl and Clark, 1989, p. 7). Boundary conditions, however, define the limits of possible evolutionary changes. Although not all genetic changes are possible (or are of infinitesimally small probability), the range of phenotypic expression can vary widely due to the multiple, nonlinear, and additive effects of gene products. Complex, indistinguishably different behaviors may be coded for by very different genetic programs. This indistinguishability, to a great degree, makes the structure of the genetic program generally irrelevant. Selection directly acts only on the phenotype.

Atmar (1979), Templeton (1982), Raven and Johnson (1986, p. 400), and others suggested that it is more appropriate to view the adaptive landscape from an inverted position. The peaks become troughs, "minimized prediction error entropy wells" (Atmar, 1979). Such a viewpoint is intuitively appealing. Searching for peaks depicts evolution as a slowly advancing, tedious, uncertain process. Moreover, there appears to be certain fragility to an evolving phyletic line; an optimized population might be expected to quickly fall off the peak under slight perturbations. But the inverted topography leaves an altogether different impression. Populations advance rapidly, falling down the walls of the error troughs.

Selection pressures are never wholly abated in nature. Indeed, the more normal circumstance is that selection pressures remain generally intense and drive phenotypes as close to an optimum as possible, given the initial and boundary conditions. "The picture emerging of natural selection at the level of the individual . . . is one of exuberance, power, and a potential for quickness" (Wilson, 1992, p. 92). But the environment is not static. It changes, and species' optimizations lag behind those changes, evolving toward new optima on the adaptive topography. It is impossible for a species to be perfectly adapted to its environment because of this flux in organism-environment interaction. Moreover, phenotypic characteristics take on a historical quality as adaptations to past environments may serve to restrict the potential for advancing into novel adaptive zones. While some phenotypic characteristics are deeply ingrained in the developmental sequence of the organism, other adaptations are maintained by a constant pressure of selection, without which they would degenerate due to random genetic drift.

All populations continually undergo selection for adaptations to the current environment. "Evolution is opportunistic, and natural selection makes use of whatever variation it encounters" (Mayr, 1988, p. 153). "Natural selection does not work like an engineer. It works like a tinkerer" (Jacob, 1977). The "baggage" of selection for adaptations to past environments imposes constraints on available current behaviors. Evolution simultaneously leads both to "organs of extreme perfection" (Darwin, 1859) and to global suboptimality. Functionally critical behaviors may be expected to be extremely well optimized. Behaviors that are less critical may be expected to vary to a greater degree.

## 2.4 THE EVOLUTION OF COMPLEXITY: MINIMIZING SURPRISE

A general trend of evolution is the generation of organisms of increasing complexity. Simon (1962) defined complexity as that situation when "given the properties of the parts and the laws of their interaction, it is not a trivial matter to infer the properties of the whole," while Bonner (1988, p. 98) has described the complexity of a system not only in terms of the number of interacting parts, but also in terms of their differences in structure and function. These differences often lead to divisions of labor in biological systems (e.g., number of cell types). Bonner (1988) emphasized these sorts of interactions, along with hierarchies of size, as being most fundamentally important. But there are special problems in examining systems of such extraordinary complexity. "Each organic system is so rich in feedbacks, homeostatic devices, and potential multiple pathways that a complete description is quite impossible. Thus, a prediction of its productions is also impossible. Furthermore, the analysis of such a system would require its destruction and thus preclude the completion of the analysis" (Mayr, 1982, p. 49). In examining the fossil record and the estimated sequence of organisms, the "inescapable conclusion [is] that the earliest forms were simple and small, and that as evolution has progressed there appeared increasingly complex and larger plants and animals" (Bonner, 1988, p. 161).

Increasing complexity is required to advance the quality of prediction of environmental events. The environment can be viewed as an $n$th-order, nonstationary stochastic process where the previous $n$ symbols (e.g., the motion of the sun across the sky) influence or are associated with the probability of the occurrence of the next symbol. Should the correlation of certain strings of symbols be high, then it is to be expected that the evolving phyletic line will come to optimally predict ever longer symbol strings; uncorrelated sources will tend to be ignored in favor of more certain portents of future events. If the universe were completely uncorrelated in its symbol strings of increasing length, optimal prediction would degenerate to just the most likely symbol. But the universe is not uncorrelated, and the languagelike characteristics of phenotypic behaviors incorporated into an evolving phyletic line are readily apparent.

There is enormous complexity in living systems, in a cell, an organ, an individual, a population, a species, or an ecosystem. "Living systems are characterized by elaborate feedback mechanisms unknown in their precision and complexity in any inanimate system" (Mayr, 1982, p. 53). Complexity in the phenotype is not random, but rather is well organized. Such complexities have been documented at various levels ranging from multicellularity to animal behavior (Bonner, 1988). Complexity does not persist for its own sake but rather is maintained as "entities at one level are compounded into new entities at the next higher level—cells into tissues, tissues into organs, and organs into functional systems" (Mayr, 1988, p. 14). Increased complexity allows for a greater range of potential behaviors and thus provides a competitive advantage.

## 2.5  SEXUAL REPRODUCTION

The term *sex* derives from the Latin *secare*, to cut or divide something that was originally whole. The exchange of genetic information is fundamental to the cutting and dividing of DNA that takes place during sexual reproduction. This exchange takes many forms: bacterial conjugation, transduction via viral transport, and the more familiar recombination that occurs in plants and animals. But sex requires finding a mate, either by happenstance, active search, or attraction. Further, the behaviors that are associated with attracting mates often make individuals more vulnerable to predators. Yet the benefits of sexuality must outweigh these costs, for the great majority of known species have a sexual phase in their life cycle.[1]

Diploid organisms have two copies of each chromosome in every somatic cell, with one copy being contributed from each parent. The total

---

[1]Wilson (1992, p. 134) places the number of *known* species at 1,413,000, with 751,000 of these being insects, 248,400 being higher plants, and 281,000 being other animals. Virtually all these have a sexual phase in their life cycle. Yet Wilson also comments that vast arrays of species remain to be found in bacteria, fungi, and other groups, and he estimates that there are somewhere between 10 and 100 million species on the planet. The majority of species are yet undiscovered. How common sex is for the undiscovered species remains to be observed.

number of chromosomes in the cells of most eukaryotes (organisms with fully nucleated cells) varies between 10 and 50 but can exceed 1,000 in some polyploid plants. During recombination, haploid (nonredundant) gametes are fused to form new diploid cells.

A reduction division is then required for this infusion to generate a stable number of chromosomes in the sexually reproducing lineage. This division is termed *meiosis*. In this process, each chromosome from both parents is duplicated. A crossing-over between homologous chromosomes may occur in which segments of the chromosome are exchanged. The rate of crossing-over varies widely from species to species and between sexes. Male fruit flies (*Drosophila* sp.) exhibit no crossing-over at all, while in mammals the rate of crossing-over is about 30 percent higher in females (Gould and Gould, 1989, p. 34). During meiosis, a reduction division occurs in which one of the two homologous chromosomes is sorted into each cell. If crossing-over does take place, it occurs predominantly during this first meiotic division. The chromatids then undergo a second reduction division such that each gamete receives a potentially hybrid combination of each pair of homologous chromosomes from each parent.

In contrast, sexual reproduction operates in a different manner. Sexual reproduction offers a significant ability for a species to generate genetic diversity and, as a consequence, phenotypic diversity. The overt functional advantage of sexual recombination to an evolving species is the significantly increased rate of exploration of the genotypic/phenotypic state space, as compared with clonal parthenogenesis, especially in changing environments. Recombination will ultimately tend to expose a wide variety of individual genotypes to various environmental conditions. The number of such genetic combinations is, for all practical purposes, unlimited. It is presumed that each offspring receives each chromosome from each parent in a random manner. In humans, $2^{23}$ distinct zygotes can be produced from only two parents by simply considering the possible combinations.

Errors are inevitable during this reshuffling of information. The species' genetic program carried in every cell of every individual's body is not recently evolved, nor is it simple. Rather, it is ancient at the extreme and enormously complex. Maintaining the fidelity of the genetic information is critical. The enzyme complex that transcribes the chromosome appears to error check the nucleotide chain being replicated, replacing the appropriate base to the complementary strand as replication proceeds. Further error checking ("proofreading") is accomplished by checking for mismatches. But there are also many environmental sources of mutational variation.

These may result in deletions, substitutions, insertions, and inversions of sections of DNA, all forms of entropic informational decay. Mutations that affect both strands of DNA are difficult to repair because a reference copy is generally used as a guide. Such randomization of genetic information will quickly fail to produce competitive phenotypes. A lack of competitive phenotypes implies severe costs to the species unless information maintenance mechanisms are invoked to maintain the functionality of the genotype (Atmar, 1991).

Three potential advantages of recombination have been identified (Crow, 1988): (1) greater efficiency for adjusting to a changing environment, (2) bringing together independently created beneficial mutations, and (3) removing deleterious mutations. The relative importance of these factors remains under debate, although there appears to be broad agreement that removing deleterious mutations is a fundamental attribute of recombinatory mechanisms (e.g., Crow, 1988; Bernstein et al., 1988; Bell, 1988). Bernstein et al. (1988) have argued that endogenous repair was the original function for which recombination served. Bell (1988) suggested that a second method for repair is to subject each individual to stringent tests of performance and to eliminate those that fail to attain a tolerable degree of achievement (exogenous repair). Under this view, recombination serves to expose genetic defects to the culling force of selection. There is less agreement that recombination is maintained because it can bring together favorable mutations (Crow, 1988), and certainly the relevance of recombination for adjusting to changing environments (Bell, 1988) must depend on the degree to which the organism's environment is in flux.

## 2.6  SEXUAL SELECTION

Sexual reproduction allows for *sexual selection*. This term refers to the process by which males and females of a species determine or "select" their mates. These processes often involve prolonged demonstrations of vigor between members of the species, typically the males. Male-male competition has been viewed as an important source of sexual selection since Darwin (1859). He concluded that the result of these encounters was not generally death to the vanquished, but "few or no offspring" (Gould and Gould, 1989, p. 86). A genetic death is equally as real as a physiological death in purging a defect from the germline.

Males in many species have evolved specific attributes that appear designed solely for male-male competition. Antlers, for example, are used primarily in intraspecies competition but otherwise appear poorly constructed for predator defense. The enlarged claw of male crabs (especially fiddler crabs, in which the pincer may constitute one-third of the crab's total body weight) is similarly observed only in mature males and is not required for survival. Rather, the claw is used in wrestling matches between males and for attracting females.

Aggressive behavior is typical of virtually all males and can be triggered by specific stimuli. In experiments with stickleback fish, Tinbergen (1951, pp. 27–28) indicated that males are more aggressive toward decoys with a red coloration but no visual resemblance to a fish than towards anatomically correct, colorless decoys. Similar results have been described by Lack (1946, pp. 144–147) in which male robins threatened a pile of red feathers more readily than a stuffed young male that lacked a red breast. Male sexual maturation is often accompanied by these sex-specific characters that incite aggressive behavior in other males.

There are numerous examples of male-male competition in a great variety of diverse species (Gould and Gould, 1989, pp. 85–265). A male stag beetle has overdeveloped horns and an enlarged mandible that appear specialized for intraspecies fighting. Combat between male stalk-eyed flies in Australia includes a ritual in which the males line up eye-to-eye and apparently determine which individual has a wider-set pair of eyes. Male salmon returning from the sea to spawn develop a hooked jaw that aids in fights with other males. As the males die shortly after spawning, the problems in feeding caused by the hooked jaw are of no consequence. Male elephant seals, due to the very limited breeding ground, are under intense sexual selection, and high mortality rates are not uncommon.

Demonstrations of male vigor appear to be a principal component of the evolutionary process that exposes and expurgates significant genetic errors from germline DNA. Those males that prove themselves "fragile" through prolonged competition do not mate. Males have often become a sacrificial component of a reproductive subpopulation. Sexual selection may be viewed as operating as a gene defect filter by continually testing the male germline for vigor (Maynard Smith, 1988, p. 177; Atmar, 1991), and such male-male competition serves to cull genetic defects from the breeding deme prior to reproduction.

## 2.7 ASSESSING THE BENEFICIARY OF EVOLUTIONARY OPTIMIZATION

Evolution is an optimization process (Mayr, 1988, p. 105). Selection statistically eliminates suboptimal phenotypes. Although the purposes of many of the evolved behaviors are transparent, the underlying reason for, and the ultimate beneficiary of, these behaviors has remained an open question that has undergone considerable debate. There are at least three commonly stated and plausible hypotheses: The benefits of optimization accrue to (1) the individual gene, (2) the individual's genome, or (3) the reproducing population.

If evolution is expected to lead to perfected genes, the nature of the gene must be explained. The early work of Morgan with *Drosophila* led to the conception of the gene as the smallest unit of recombination. "Two characters were regarded as determined by different genes if they could be recombined, and as determined by the same gene if they could not be recombined" (Keeton, 1980, p. 656). Early on, genes were conceptualized as particles linearly arranged on chromosomes. Recombination was explained by a crossing-over mechanism that broke the chromosomes apart at points between these ordered particles and reassembled appropriate chromosomal segments.

Currently, a gene is commonly defined as the genetic information necessary to promote the synthesis of one polypeptide chain (Raven and Johnson, 1986, p. G-12). But it is also known that in eukaryotes, a gene and any given segment of DNA are rarely colinear. "Any 'single' gene, in the sense of a single continuously read passage of DNA text, is not stored in one place" (Dawkins, 1986, p. 174). Because of the complex and interwoven informational mappings, Lewin (1983) suggested that a gene should be redefined as one polypeptide/one gene, reversing the previous definition, allowing the functional product to define the gene. Because selection acts immediately only on the phenotype, and only by consequence on the underlying genotype, it would seem far more prudent to emphasize the functionality of the cohesive genotype rather than its apparent structure.

The danger lies in the promotion of an atomistic "beanbag" perspective of evolution that has led to proposals of "selfish genes" (Dawkins, 1976, 1982). But there is an obvious problem with the proposition that individual genes are the units of selection: Individual genes cannot be assigned a meaningful fitness value in isolation. The phenotypic impact of any single gene varies as a pleiotropic and polygenic function of all other genes and as a function of the environment. Selection cannot take place in the absence of competition, and only through competition is relative fitness assessed.

Only a small percentage of the eukaryotic genotype actually codes for expressible behavior (Lewin, 1986; Mayr, 1988). The great majority of human DNA is untranslated (Lewin, 1986; Brunk, 1991). It is somewhat unreasonable, therefore, to speak of evolution producing a set of optimized genes when much of the genome is "junk" (Lewin, 1986). Moreover, assigning absolute fitness to genes leads "to an overvaluation of additive gene effects . . . [and] invariably [leads] to unrealistic results" (Mayr, 1982, p. 41). Mayr (1982, p. 400) has criticized such an explanation as meaningless because "it tells us nothing about the multiplication of species nor, more broadly, about the origin of organic diversity."

A second alternative would assert that evolution operates such that benefit accrues to the individual or its genome. But if the individual is the beneficiary of optimization, then that benefit does not persist long, as an individual's life span is minute in any evolutionary sense and its genetic legacy is rapidly washed away in an infinite sequence of sexual divisions and fusions. If evolution were truly to act to optimize individual genotypes, then far greater rates of clonal parthenogenesis must be expected than are observed. Once the best possible genotype was found, the optimum strategy under this physics would be to copy it endlessly. But the overwhelming majority of species are sexual. Further, if the individual acts solely for its own benefit, then many observed altruistic behaviors appear paradoxical.

Hamilton (1964), and earlier Haldane (1932), suggested that an explanation of apparent altruism could come in the form of *kin selection*. This argument asserts that selection operates on the level of individuals so as to increase the frequency of genetic representation of an individual in future generations. Brothers and sisters are often viewed as sharing half of their genes, on the average, so they would be more apt to act altruistically toward each other than toward more distant relations from the same species or toward completely distinct species. Sacrificing oneself for three brothers is viewed as a "selfish" act of propagating more copies of one's own genes into future generations.

This explanation has been criticized by Sober (1992) because, due to the effects of selection, siblings almost never share only half of their genes. "A population in which natural selection has destroyed lots of variation may be such that all individuals are very similar to each other, and full sibs are even more so (Dawkins, 1979)" (Sober, 1992). Nevertheless, this mechanism (a relatedness of $r = \frac{1}{2}$ between siblings or otherwise as appropriate) is used to explain the apparent altruism of the members of sexually sterile castes, for instance in social insects (bees, ants) in which these workers exist solely to serve the hive or colony and never to reproduce themselves (Hartl and Clark, 1989, p. 563). Kin selection is seen as maximizing *inclusive fitness*, the probability that a specific genetic representation will be copied into future generations.

Despite wide-ranging support for this idea (Bonner and May, 1981; Dawkins, 1982, pp. 193–194; and others), the argument is open to criticism. Selection is now no longer truly acting on the individual as a whole, but rather on fractions of the genotype pool. Specifically, selection is viewed as acting to increase the chances that the largest possible fraction of an individual genotype will be multiplied and will increase in frequency (Hoffman, 1989, p. 138). The individual is dissolved into fractions of genetic representation that are supposed to be acting in support of their own reproduction. As a unit of selection, the individual "dissolves into vagueness" (Hoffman, 1989, p. 140). The argument ultimately reduces to viewing individual genes as independent units affecting the phenotype of individuals. But as has been well documented by Mayr (1970, pp. 162–185), there is a unity to the genotype. "No gene has a fixed selective value; the same gene may confer high fitness on one genetic background and be virtually lethal on another" (Mayr 1970, p. 184). That is, the fraction of similarity between two individual genotypes may be absolutely irrelevant. Two individuals may differ in but a single gene out of thousands or tens of thousands, yet this difference may be associated with a lethal defect. It is insufficient simply to maximize the fraction of genetic representation in future generations. The fraction not represented is absolutely crucial to the realized phenotypic effect.

If evolution is to be viewed as a process such that advantage accrues to individuals, it is reasonable to ask, "Is it . . . evolutionarily to each parent's advantage to form a monogamous pair bond and make a large investment in the young?" (Keeton, 1980, p. 544). The question implicitly assumes that some benefit for creating offspring accrues to the parents. But that benefit must be identified. The argument presupposes that each parent has an interest in leaving offspring, typically the greatest possible number of offspring. But individuals must compete for survival with other members of the population, and the most intense competition comes from members of the same species that are, essentially, behaviorally identical. An overabundance of the species is a real threat to all members of the species because available resources are ultimately limited. The fundamental reproductive drive becomes an explanation after the fact if individuals are to be viewed as the ultimate beneficiaries of evolutionary invention. "Animals sometimes behave in a way that makes no sense from the point of view of maximizing individual fitness" (Hartl and Clark, 1989, p. 560).

Evolution is a learning process. Phylogenetic learning (i.e., learning arising from within the species) is the most commonly exhibited and most ancient form of intelligence. Through mutation and selection there is an obvious optimization of behavior. As described in Chapter 1, Atmar (1976), following Weiner (1961), proposed phylogenetic, ontogenetic, and sociogenetic learning to be equivalent processes, each containing a quantum unit of mutability and a reservoir of learned behavior. In phylogenetic learning, the quantum unit of mutability is a single nucleotide base pair. The reservoir of learned behavior is the species' genome. From such a perspective, the unit of selection is the individual, but the ultimate beneficiary of evolutionary invention is the species, or at least the reproducing population.

The notion that individuals forgo certain possible benefits "for the good of the species" has become associated with the term *group selection*, which was strongly advocated by Wynne-Edwards (1962). This argument asserts that competition for survival occurs between entire groups of individuals and that groups replace individuals as the unit of selection while speciation replaces individual reproduction.

Group selectionist explanations have fallen out of favor with many evolutionary biologists following counterarguments by Williams (1966) and Maynard Smith (1976). Even Mayr (1970, p. 115), who has commented that reproductive populations benefit from selection, remarked that "all attempts to establish group selection as a significant evolutionary process are unconvincing." Hoffman (1989, p. 137) relates a good example, and even though the following quote is lengthy, it is worth repeating:

John Maynard Smith (1976) made a very simple but powerful argument to this effect. Consider a population the members of which have been conditioned by group selection to forgo some potential advantages to their individual offspring and to cooperate with each other for the sake of their common welfare. If such a population is invaded by an immigrant that still acts exclusively for the sake of its own offspring—to increase as much as possible the fraction of the population its progeny will constitute in future generations—it shall certainly do better in reproducing within this population than its more altruistic members. Provided therefore that these behaviors have a genetic background and are inheritable, an assumption shared by the theory of group selection, the selfish individuals will soon outcompete the altruists in the population. In the nonhuman world, altruistic behaviors should therefore occur at best temporarily, until selfishness takes over again.

Thus, group selection cannot be the solution to the dilemma that the phenomena of apparent altruism poses to the genetic theory of evolutionary forces.

To escape the apparent paradox that altruistic behavior poses, many biologists have adopted Hamilton's (1964) kin selection.

But the argument by Maynard Smith (1976) has an implicit assumption that restricts its application. The assumption is that the conditions of the experiment remain constant. That is, altruistic (and therefore mutually cooperative) individuals will continue to adopt this policy, even when encountering the selfish individuals. Under such conditions, Maynard Smith's (1976) conclusions are correct: Selfish individuals would certainly outcompete altruistic individuals and would quickly come to dominate the population. If there is no mechanism for the altruists and selfish actors to identify other members of the population as either altruists or selfish actors, and if behavior is genetically preprogrammed into each individual, then intense competition is the likely result (e.g., Lysenko's clusters of oak trees; see Hoffman, 1989, p. 137).

But suppose that the individuals in the population evolve mechanisms that allow them to recognize other individuals as either altruistic or selfish. Further suppose that individuals can vary their policies based on these recognitions. There are several expected results under these new conditions. The first is that altruists would not only continue to cooperate amongst themselves (enhancing the benefits to the group), but they would also ostracize selfish individuals. Another likely outcome is that some of the altruists would instead adopt selfish policies and, at least for some time, continue to be recognized for their previous altruistic behavior and thereby take advantage of other altruists by fooling them into cooperating. Further, some selfish individuals would adopt behaviors associated with altruists, thereby fooling other altruists into cooperating only to take advantage of them at a later time. Whether or not mutual cooperation or selfishness rise to dominate the population then becomes a question of evolutionary dynamics: How quickly can recognition and deception mechanisms be evolved? In fact, there may be no stable result. But the observed evidence indicates that recognition mechanisms are pervasive in evolved organisms and that behavior does vary in light of the recognition of expected encounters, so the easy analysis of Maynard Smith (1976) simply does not apply to the real circumstance and may be dismissed.

What cannot be so easily dismissed is the idea of groups replacing individuals as the unit of selection. It is clear that individuals compete for existence. When a pack of wolves bring down a deer, there can be no doubt that selection acted against the individual deer. The term *group selection* serves to discredit the idea that groups are the ultimate beneficiaries of selection. There is no logical necessity for the unit of selection to correspond directly to the unit for which adaptations serve to benefit (cf. Williams, 1966, p. 92; Dawkins, 1982, p. 81; Maynard Smith, 1988, pp. 54, 186). Instead, the reproductive population can be seen as the beneficiary of selection acting against individuals, culling inappropriate (i.e., self-defeating) individual behaviors.

Previously paradoxical or anomalous behaviors are more easily explained when optimization is viewed as accruing to the reproducing population. Sexual recombination serves to verify allelic combinations rapidly and exhaustively. Those that are nonviable are quickly sieved from the population. Sexual selection, and more specifically male-male contest, serves as a secondary genetic error expurgation mechanism; the viability of the species' germline is enhanced through the aggressive competition between sexually mature males (Atmar, 1991). It is not unreasonable to expect that individuals of certain populations will become sacrificial, never mate, and only serve to protect those individuals that reproduce.

Just as the individual's fitness is a function of its entire cohesive genetic composition—and no genetic structure can be measured in isolation—the population's fitness is a function of the entire cohesive set of behaviors of its individuals. When the appropriateness of individuals' behavior is viewed outside of the context of the species, behaviors often appear inexplicable or even irrational. These observations, however, can generally be reconciled when attention is focused on the reproductive population as a whole.


## 2.8 CHALLENGES TO NEO-DARWINISM

The neo-Darwinian view of evolution has not gone unchallenged. The question of whether microevolution (evolution within populations and species) can account for evolution on a larger scale has been debated at length. Goldschmidt (1940) believed that the genetical forces postulated by neo-Darwinists were not sufficiently powerful to create new species and

argued that macromutations ("hopeful monsters") are requisite to speciation. In distinct contrast, Simpson (1944) instead argued that all historical
biological phenomena are brought about by the same evolutionary forces
acting at all levels; Simpson's perspective has prevailed for more than four
decades. Recently, there have once again been claims that the traditional
neo-Darwinian view does not explain the observed evidence of evolution,
and alternative hypotheses have been proposed.

### 2.8.1  Neutral Mutations and the
### Neo-Darwinian Paradigm

Kimura (1983) proposed that most changes in gene frequencies (a
common definition of evolution) are of no selective value, but are in fact
neutral. It had previously been believed that "there is no evidence for the
existence of genes that remain selectively 'neutral' " (Mayr, 1963, p. 159).
Recent research has in fact established that many changes at the molecular
level are entirely neutral. Those who were predisposed to believe that genes
are the targets of selection were therefore left an opening to argue less
emphasis on natural selection. Such models have been criticized as over-
emphasizing the importance of individual genes (Mayr, 1982, p. 102; and
others). If the individual as a whole is taken as the target of selection, then
numerous neutral genes, or even potentially harmful genes, can be carried
as "hitchhikers," as long as the individuals survive selection due to other
expressed characteristics. Although the neutral theory was originally
thought to be in conflict with neo-Darwinism, in fact, the mere existence of
neutral mutations does not violate the neo-Darwinian paradigm (Brunk,
1991). At best, it only offers a mechanism of phenotypic variation that is
not directly attributable to the intense selection pressures commonly associated with natural selection.

### 2.8.2  Punctuated Equilibrium

*Punctuated equilibrium*, offered by Eldredge and Gould (1972), is
perhaps the most well known novel hypothesis. They proposed that the
fossil record accurately reflects periods of extremely (geologically) rapid
morphological change associated with speciation, followed by prolonged
periods of stasis. This is in contrast to the hypothesis of *phyletic gradualism*,
which asserts that morphological transformations are the result of the
accumulation of small changes occurring over long periods of time, with

the apparent gaps in the fossil record being the result of incomplete data. Punctuated equilibrium has received various interpretations, ranging from it being a "minor gloss" on neo-Darwinism (Dawkins, 1986, p. 250) to it being a "revolt against the principle of continuity" (Rieppel, 1987).

Hoffman (1989, p. 100) characterized two versions of punctuated equilibrium: *weak* and *strong*. The weak version asserts that the evolution of species does not proceed for long in the same direction, nor does so with a constant rate, but rather varies in both direction and rate. This is no challenge to neo-Darwinism, as the neo-Darwinian paradigm certainly predicts a variation in the rates and directions of evolution as populations enter novel adaptive zones. Indeed, these variations have been documented by Simpson (1944, 1953). The strong version of punctuated equilibrium, which may be viewed as somewhat extreme, argues that gradual phenotypic change is negligible in the evolution of species, with the gaps between successive species being dominant. Hoffman (1989, p. 105) described the problems of validating this version with evidence in the fossil record, which is not at all complete and is subject to enormous variation. Moreover, there is evidence of a continuous range of evolutionary rates, rather than the distinctly bimodal distribution that would be expected under the strong version (Gingerich, 1983).

Some advocates of punctuated equilibrium have proposed that there are fundamental differences between *microevolution* (within a species) and *macroevolution* (generation of new species) (Stanley, 1979). Macroevolution has been described as requiring macromutations, mutations that introduce large effects in the phenotype, with the result being "rectangular evolution" (Stanley, 1975). Gould (1980) apparently supported a "potential saltational origin for the essential features of key adaptations. Why may we not imagine that gill arch bones of an ancestral agnathan moved forward in one step to surround the mouth and form proto-jaws?" Yet more recently, Gould and Eldredge (1993) indicated that the interpretations of punctuated equilibrium as saltational theory are "misunderstandings . . . that misread geological abruptness as true suddenness" and do not support such a view.

Although attention was originally focused on the apparent rapid change associated with punctuations in the paleontological record, it has now turned to the apparent stasis of many species (Gould and Eldredge, 1993). The argument asserts that because species often maintain stability even during times of dramatic climatic change (e.g., glacial cycling), stasis must be viewed as an active phenomenon rather than merely a passive response to unaltered environments. Mayr (1988, p. 468) admitted that "I agree with Gould that the frequency of stasis in fossil species revealed by recent analysis was unexpected by most evolutionary biologists," but also argued that prolonged stasis is not in contention with neo-Darwinism, for any major morphological restructuring would require a drastic interference to the cohesion of the genotype and would be selected against quite vigorously (Mayr, 1988, p. 434). Punctuated equilibrium as offered in Gould and Eldredge (1993) does not present a challenge to the basic structure of neo-Darwinism. The patterns of prolonged stasis and rapid morphological change are consistent with neo-Darwinism, even if they are not fully anticipated by it.

## 2.9 SUMMARY

The notion of Darwinian evolution is essentially quite simple. In fact, Gould (1977, p. 11) and Mayr (1988, p. 117) have described the principle of evolution as "simplicity itself," and yet this apparently obvious principle was resisted for three-quarters of a century after being proposed by Darwin and Wallace. Mayr (1988, p. 117) speculated that the reasons for the resistance were: (1) Darwin was unable to explain the source of phenotypic variations, (2) Darwin was unable to prove the occurrence of natural selection, (3) a probabilistic theory was unpalatable in a time when the universe was viewed as being deterministic, and (4) scientific thought was essentialist, viewing the population solely in terms of an average behavior and regarding variation as nothing but errors around the mean values (Mayr, 1982, p. 47). The selection that is so critical to Darwin's evolution is untenable in the absence of a populational view.

Evolution most aptly refers to changes in adaptation and diversity, and not directly to changes in gene frequencies. Gene frequencies persist only as a result of selection on the phenotype. The genetic variation of individuals is largely a chance phenomenon, primarily a product of recombination and "ultimately of mutation" (Mayr, 1988, p. 532). Selection is probabilistic, and its primary target is the individual. Sexual reproduction allows for the rapid phenotypic exploration of an underlying genetic theme. It also allows for additional error correction mechanisms (e.g., sexual selection). Nonetheless, the specific mechanisms involved in recombination are unimportant from an optimization perspective, except for the manner in which they affect individual phenotypes.

The individual is the target of selection, but the species, or minimally, the reproducing population, is the ultimate genetic reservoir of all learned behavior. It is an evolutionary element that can have a measurable fitness and possess a degree of permanence. The notion that the species is the ultimate beneficiary of evolutionary optimization has been proposed by Mayr (1963, 1988), Conrad (1990), Atmar (1991), and others. But Hecht and Hoffman (1986) and many others appear to view the process of optimization accruing to the species as an alternative to individual selection, rather than the result of individual selection. Yet if all individuals are viewed as acting in their own best interest, many of the observed behaviors appear paradoxical. Arguments identifying the teleonomic (purpose-driven) (Mayr, 1988, p. 45) behavior of individuals as benefiting their respective species appear more appropriate and concise. Arguments that attribute such behaviors to a desire to pass along an individual's genetic structure may appear somewhat contrived.

Lindsay (1968) commented, "The theory of evolution is not typical of scientific theories. Rather than prescribing a specific process or formula it merely provides a plausibility argument involving a couple of general principles and gains broad acceptance by virtue of the lack of plausible alternatives." But the neo-Darwinian paradigm, the modern synthesis of evolutionary thought, lays out a well-defined process that extends beyond a mere plausibility argument. Individuals reproduce sufficiently well so as to expand to fill the available resource space. Errors during genetic replication result in individual phenotypic variation. Furthermore, due to the nature of the genetic program, these phenotypic variations are heritable. Competition results from the inevitable excess population and leads to stochastic selection against those individuals that are less well adapted to the present environment. Randomness is the propellant of the evolutionary process; the adaptive topography is its primary determinant. Darwinian evolution is no more than the inevitable consequence of competing information-reproducing systems operating within a finite arena in a positively entropic universe (Atmar, 1992).

## REFERENCES

Atmar, J. W. (1976). "Speculation on the Evolution of Intelligence and Its Possible Realization in Machine Form." Sc.D. diss., New Mexico State University, Las Cruces.

Atmar, J. W. (1979). "The Inevitability of Evolutionary Invention." Unpublished manuscript.

Atmar, W. (1986). Personal communication, AICS Research, Inc.

Atmar, W. (1991). "On the Role of Males," *Animal Behaviour,* Vol. 41, pp. 195–205.

Atmar, W. (1992). "On the Rules and Nature of Simulated Evolutionary Programming." In *Proc. of the First Ann. Conf. on Evolutionary Programming,* edited by D. B. Fogel and W. Atmar. La Jolla, CA: Evolutionary Programming Society, pp. 17–26.

Atmar, W. (1994). "Notes on the Simulation of Evolution," *IEEE Trans. on Neural Networks,* Vol. 5:1, pp. 130–148.

Bell, G. (1988). "Uniformity and Diversity in the Evolution of Sex." In *The Evolution of Sex: An Examination of Current Ideas,* edited by R. E. Michod and B. R. Levin. Sunderland, MA: Sinauer, pp. 126–138.

Berstein, H., F. A. Hopf, and R. E. Michod (1988). "Is Meotic Recombination an Adaptation for Repairing DNA, Producing Genetic Variation, or Both?" In *The Evolution of Sex: An Examination of Current Ideas,* edited by R. E. Michod and B. R. Levin. Sunderland, MA: Sinauer, pp. 139–160.

Bonner, J. T. (1988). *The Evolution of Complexity by Means of Natural Selection.* Princeton, NJ: Princeton University Press.

Bonner, J. T. (1993). *Life Cycles: Reflections of an Evolutionary Biologist.* Princeton, NJ: Princeton University Press.

Bonner, J. T., and R. M. May (1981). Introduction to *The Descent of Man, and Selection in Relation to Sex,* by C. Darwin. Princeton, NJ: Princeton University Press (reprint).

Brunk, C. F. (1991). "Darwin in an Age of Molecular Revolution," *Contention,* Vol. 1:1, pp. 131–150.

Conrad, M. (1990). "The Geometry of Evolution," *BioSystems,* Vol. 24, pp. 61–81.

Crow, J. F. (1988). "The Importance of Recombination." In *The Evolution of Sex: An Examination of Current Ideas,* edited by R. E. Michod and B. R. Levin. Sunderland, MA: Sinauer, pp. 56–73.

Darwin, C. (1859). *On the Origin of Species by Means of Natural Selection or the Preservations of Favored Races in the Struggle for Life.* London: John Murray.

Dawkins, R. (1976). *The Selfish Gene.* Oxford: Clarendon Press.

Dawkins, R. (1979). "Twelve Misunderstandings of Kin Selection," *Zeitschrift für Tierpsychologie*, Vol. 51, pp. 184–200.

Dawkins, R. (1982). *The Extended Phenotype.* Oxford: Oxford University Press.

Dawkins, R. (1986). *The Blind Watchmaker.* Oxford: Clarendon Press.

Dobzhansky, T. (1937). *Genetics and the Origins of Species.* New York: Columbia University Press.

Dobzhansky, T. (1970). *Genetics of the Evolutionary Processes.* New York: Columbia University Press.

Dobzhansky, T., F. J. Ayala, G. L. Stebbins, and J. W. Valentine (1977). *Evolution.* San Francisco: W. H. Freeman.

Eldredge, N., and S. J. Gould (1972). "Punctuated Equilibria: An Alternative to Phyletic Gradualism." In *Models of Paleobiology*, edited by T. J. M. Schopf. San Francisco: W. H. Freeman, pp. 82–115.

Fisher, R. A. (1930). *The Genetical Theory of Natural Selection.* Oxford: Clarendon Press.

Fogel, G. B. (1993). Personal communication, UCLA.

Gingerich, P. D. (1983). "Rates of Evolution: Effects of Time and Temporal Scaling," *Science*, Vol. 222, pp. 159–161.

Goldschmidt, R. (1940). *The Material Basis of Evolution.* New Haven, CT: Yale University Press.

Gould, J. L., and C. G. Gould (1989). *Sexual Selection.* New York: Scientific American Library.

Gould, S. J. (1977). *Ever Since Darwin: Reflections in Natural History.* New York: W. W. Norton.

Gould, S. J. (1980). "Is a New and General Theory of Evolution Emerging?" *Paleobiology,* Vol. 6, pp. 119–130.

Gould, S. J., and N. Eldredge (1993). "Punctuated Equilibrium Comes of Age," *Nature*, Vol. 366, November 18, pp. 223–227.

Haldane, J. B. S. (1932). *The Causes of Evolution.* London: Longman.

Haldane, J. B. S. (1964). "A Defense of Beanbag Genetics," *Perspectives in Biology and Medicine*, Vol. 7, pp. 343–359.

Hamilton, W. D. (1964). "The Genetical Evolution of Social Behavior: I and II," *J. Theor. Biol.*, Vol. 7, pp. 1–52.

Hartl, D. L., and A. G. Clark (1989). *Principles of Population Genetics,* 2nd ed. Sunderland, MA: Sinauer.

Hecht, M. K., and A. Hoffman (1986). "Why Not Neodarwinism? A Critique of Paleobiological Challenges," *Oxford Surv. Evol. Biol.*, Vol. 3, pp. 1–47.

Hoffman, A. (1989). *Arguments on Evolution: A Paleontologist's Perspective.* New York: Oxford University Press.

Huxley, J. S. (1942). *Evolution: The Modern Synthesis.* London: Allen and Unwin.

Huxley, J. (1963). "The Evolutionary Process," In *Evolution as a Process*, edited by J. Huxley, A. C. Hardy, and E. B. Ford. New York: Collier Books, pp. 9–33.

Jacob, F. (1977). "Evolution and Tinkering," *Science,* Vol. 196, pp. 1161–1166.

Keeton, W. T. (1980). *Biological Science*, 3rd ed. New York: W. W. Norton.

Kimura, M. (1983). *The Neutral Theory of Molecular Evolution.* Cambridge, England: Cambridge University Press.

Lack, D. L. (1946). *The Life of the Robin.* London: H. F. and G. Whiterby.

Lewin, B. (1983). *Genes.* New York: John Wiley.

Lewin, R. (1986). " 'Computer Genome' Is Full of Junk DNA," *Science*, Vol. 232, pp. 577–578.

Lewontin, R. C. (1974). *The Genetic Basis of Evolutionary Change.* New York: Columbia University Press.

Lindsay, R. K. (1968). "Artificial Evolution of Intelligence," *Contemp. Psychology*, Vol. 13:3, pp. 113–116.

Marshall, C. (1993). Personal communication, UCLA.

Maynard Smith, J. (1976). "Group Selection," *Quart. Rev. Biol.*, Vol. 51, pp. 277–283.

Maynard Smith, J. (1988). *Did Darwin Get It Right?: Essays on Games, Sex, and Evolution.* New York: Chapman and Hall.

Mayr, E. (1942). *Systematics and the Origin of Species.* New York: Columbia University Press.

Mayr, E. (1959). "Where are We?" *Cold Spring Harbor Symp. Quant. Biol.,* Vol. 24, pp. 409–440.

Mayr, E. (1960). "The Evolution of Life." Panel in *Evolution after Darwin: Issues in Evolution,* Vol. 3, edited by S. Tax and C. Callender. Chicago: University of Chicago Press.

Mayr, E. (1963). *Animal Species and Evolution.* Cambridge, MA: Belknap Press.

Mayr, E. (1970). *Populations, Species, and Evolution.* Cambridge, MA: Belknap Press.

Mayr, E. (1982). *The Growth of Biological Thought: Diversity, Evolution, and Inheritance.* Cambridge, MA: Belknap Press.

Mayr, E. (1988). *Toward a New Philosophy of Biology: Observations of an Evolutionist.* Cambridge, MA: Belknap Press.

Raven, P. H., and G. B. Johnson (1986). *Biology.* St. Louis: Times Mirror/Moseby College.

Rensch, B. (1947). *Neuere Probleme der Abstammungslehre.* Stuttgart: Ferdinand Enke.

Rieppel, O. (1987). "Punctuational Thinking at Odds with Leibniz and Darwin," *N. Jb. Geol. Paleont. Abh.*, Vol. 174, pp. 123–133.

Salvini-Plawen, L. V., and E. Mayr (1977). "On the Evolution of Photoreceptors and Eyes," *Evolutionary Biology*, Vol. 10, pp. 207–263.

Sheppard, P. M. (1975). *Natural Selection and Heredity*, 4th ed. London: Hutchinson.

Simon, H. A. (1962). "The Architecture of Complexity," *Proc. Amer. Phil. Soc.*, Vol. 106, pp. 467–482.

Simpson, G. G. (1944). *Tempo and Mode in Evolution.* New York: Columbia University Press.

Simpson, G. G. (1949). *The Meaning of Evolution: A Study of the History of Life and Its Significance for Man.* New Haven, CT: Yale University Press.

Simpson, G. G. (1953). *The Major Features of Evolution.* New York: Columbia University Press.

Sober, E. (1992). "The Evolution of Altruism: Correlation, Cost, and Benefit," *Biology and Philosophy*, Vol. 7, pp. 177–187.

Stanley, S. M. (1975). "A Theory of Evolution above the Species Level," *Proc. Nat. Acad. Sci.*, Vol. 72:2, pp. 646–650.

Stanley, S. M. (1979). *Macroevolution—Pattern and Process.* San Francisco: W. H. Freeman.

Stebbins, G. L. (1950). *Variation and Evolution in Plants.* New York: Columbia University Press.

Templeton, A. R. (1982). "Adaptation and the Integration of Evolutionary Forces." In *Perspectives in Evolution,* edited by R. Milkman. Sunderland, MA: Sinauer, pp. 15–31.

Tinbergen, N. (1951). *The Study of Instinct.* Oxford: Oxford University Press.

Weiner, N. (1961). *Cybernetics*, Part 2, Cambridge, MA: MIT Press.

Williams, G. C. (1966). *Adaptation and Natural Selection: A Critique of Some Current Evolutionary Thought.* Princeton, NJ: Princeton University Press.

Wilson, E. O. (1992). *The Diversity of Life.* New York: W. W. Norton.

Wooldridge, D. E. (1968). *The Mechanical Man: The Physical Basis of Intelligent Life.* New York: McGraw-Hill.

Wright, S. (1931). "Evolution in Mendelian Populations," *Genetics,* Vol. 16, pp. 97–159.

Wright, S. (1932). "The Roles of Mutation, Inbreeding, Crossbreeding, and Selection in Evolution." In *Proc. 6th Int. Cong. Genetics,* Vol. 1. Ithaca, NY, pp. 356–366.

Wynne-Edwards, V. C. (1962). *Animal Dispersion in Relation to Social Behavior.* London: Oliver and Boyd.

# 3

# Computer Simulation
# of Natural Evolution

## 3.1 EARLY SPECULATIONS AND
## SPECIFIC ATTEMPTS

The idea of generating machine learning through simulated evolution has been proposed many times. Cannon (1932) pictured natural evolution as a learning process, very little different in mechanism or consequence than an individual undergoes, proceeding by random trial and error. Turing (1950) recognized "an obvious connection between [machine learning] and evolution." Friedman (1959) speculated that a simulation of mutation and selection would be able to design "thinking machines" and specifically remarked that chess-playing programs could be designed by such a method. Campbell (1960), following earlier work (Campbell, 1956a, 1956b), offered the conjecture that "in all processes leading to expansions of knowledge, a blind-variation-and-selective-survival process is involved." The first attempts at the formal application of evolutionary theory to practical engineering problems appeared in the areas of statistical process control, machine learning, and function optimization.

### 3.1.1 Box: Evolutionary Operation

Box and colleagues (1957, 1960, 1966; Box and Hunter, 1959; Box and Chanmugam, 1962; Box and Draper, 1969) advocated a technique called *evolutionary operation* (EVOP) that was applied to a manufacturing plant as a management process, implemented through the votes of a committee of technical managers. EVOP has been successfully applied to a wide variety of manufacturing processes, although it saw its earliest use in the chemical industry (Hunter, 1958, 1960; Koehler, 1958a, 1958b; Barnett, 1960). Under EVOP, the plant is viewed as an evolving species. The quality of the product advances through random mutations and selection as determined by the committee (Box and Draper, 1969, pp. 8–9). EVOP is still mentioned occasionally in literature on the optimization of manufacturing processes, but the method was never implemented in autonomous computer simulation.

### 3.1.2 Friedberg: A Learning Machine

Friedberg (1958; Friedberg et al., 1959) focused attention on gradually improving a machine language computer program, which itself coded for a program, by choosing instructions that were most often associated with a successful result. The number of possible programs for the selected tasks was very large, forbidding an exhaustive search for the best program. The hope was for similar programs to be clustered so as to receive similar judgment. Toward this goal, every program having a specific instruction in a certain location was termed to be in a *class*. Each contending program belonged to as many different classes as there were locations for instructions. The learning procedure, in evaluating the performance of two non-overlapping classes of programs, compared instructions occupying the same location. Friedberg devised a scoring technique that was supposed to classify good and bad instructions appropriately.

Scoring was only made with respect to single instructions, mainly due to the enormous computer time and storage required to evaluate pairs or higher-ordered combinations of instructions. A program called Herman (not an acronym) simulated a computer processing a set of 64 instructions $(I_0, \ldots, I_{63})$ each comprised of 14 bits. Every combination of 14 bits (two bits for the operation code and two six-bit data and/or instruction addresses) was an executable instruction, and every sequence of 64 instructions was a performable program. An external program called the Teacher caused

Herman to be performed successively over many trials and examined Herman's memory to determine if a desired task had been performed successfully in that trial. Success or failure enabled a third program, the Learner, to evaluate the different instructions that appeared in Herman.

Before each new trial, random bits were placed in specific memory locations as inputs, with the others remaining as they were from the previous trial. The program was started at $I_0$ and terminated upon execution of $I_{63}$. The Teacher then examined the contents of preselected data locations (outputs) and determined whether or not the bits in these locations satisfied a chosen relationship with the bits placed in the input locations at the beginning of the trial. If the program had not terminated after executing 64 instructions, a failure was declared. Only success or failure was indicated to the Learner.

As there were $2^{14}$ different instructions that could possibly occupy a single location $I_k$, it was impossible to monitor the performance of each of these given the available computer architecture. Instead, two instructions (initially chosen at random) were "on record" for each location $I_k$, so that there were 128 instructions on record in total. For each $I_k$, one of the two instructions on record was "active" and the other was "inactive." In any trial, the program executed by Herman consisted of the 64 active instructions. The Learner altered the program by two methods: (1) It frequently interchanged the two instructions on record for a single location based on their association with successful results (i.e., their class score), and (2) it occasionally made a random change by removing one of the 128 instructions from the record and replacing it with a new 14-bit number. A random change was made after every 64th failure. Random changes were timed with a given number of failures so as to make alterations infrequent when the program was performing optimally.

The results of several experiments indicated that the learning program evolved programs that would output identical or complementary bits to the input, or lower-order bits of the sum of two input bits, but did not achieve success in generating more complicated functions of the input, such as a logical AND. Friedberg et al. (1959) indicated that the length of time required to adapt the program was longer than the expected time required by a completely random search. Changes in systematic order based on success or failure led to a reasonable chance that the process would cycle, creating duplicate programs every 128 failures. Updating Herman at random showed significant improvement but still only approached the efficiency of a completely random search.

To facilitate more efficient learning, Friedberg et al. (1959) suggested a hill-climbing search. The given problem was to be partitioned into parts, with the more difficult parts dealt with first. This approach was called Ramsy. The Teacher ordered the parts in terms of difficulty. If the program failed on a given run, all the participating (i.e., active) instructions were replaced by new random instructions. If the program succeeded, all the participants became *bound*, and the next part of the problem was under-taken. Bound instructions were exempted from subsequent replacement unless no participants could be replaced after a failing run because all were bound. Under such conditions, Ramsy was initialized with new instructions and learning was restarted.

Experiments in learning typical logical operators, including AND, EXCLUSIVE-OR, and so forth, were conducted. Ramsy performed better than completely random chance techniques, but its primary drawback was a tendency to become stuck as successive parts of the problem were encountered. This precluded the method from learning solutions to complex programming problems. Friedberg (1958) originally described the research as showing "limited success," but admitted after experiments with Ramsy that "where we should go from here is not entirely clear" (Friedberg et al., 1959).

While Friedberg et al. (1959) did not explicitly claim to be simulating natural evolution, that is the generally accepted interpretation (Jackson, 1974). Dunham and North, coauthors of Friedberg et al. (1959), indicated their belief that simulated evolution is "more powerful than commonly recognized" and cited success in evolving bit manipulators and in laying out the wiring of a 1,400-terminal black box (Dunham et al., 1963). These successes were not given much attention by the artificial intelligence community.

### 3.1.3 Bremermann's Experiments

Bremermann (1958) remarked that the "principle of evolution . . . is most useful as a key to the understanding of creative thinking and learning" and recognized evolution as an optimization process. Optimization is ac-complished by searching over a response surface that indicates the fitness of each possible arrangement of the available genotype. Bremermann (1958) chose a binary encoding of the genotype; an individual was defined as a string of symbols from $\{0, 1\}$. The response surface was defined by the number of bits in an individual that differed from a target bit string. Thus each bit independently contributed to the overall fitness of the individual without regard to other bits. For these conditions, Bremermann (1958) determined that the mutation rate (i.e., the probability of flipping a bit) that achieves the most rapid improvement is obtained when the mutation is such that "in the average in each generation in each individual one bit is changed." But such a response surface is atypical of real-world adaptive topographies that are pervasively determined by interactive effects (i.e., pleiotropy and polygeny).

Bremermann (1962) considered the problem of minimizing a real-valued fitness function $f(x_1, \ldots, x_n)$, where $x_i \in \mathbf{R}$. Simple functions were selected in order to provide for a more tractable analysis of the evolutionary process. Linear systems of equations were considered, with the goal being to evolve a solution vector $\mathbf{x}$ that minimized $\|A\mathbf{x} - \mathbf{b}\|_2$, where $A$ is an $n \times n$ matrix and $\mathbf{b}$ is an $n \times 1$ column vector. The elements $x_i$ were claimed to be analogous to an organism's genes. If only one of these elements was mutated at a time, the evolutionary process led quickly "to a stable point . . . [which] need not even be a saddle point [of the fitness function]" (Bremermann, 1962). For this evolutionary scheme to succeed, multiple elements had to be altered simultaneously, leading to a combinatorial explosion of possibilities. Bremermann (1962) suggested that each element could be given a probability of changing, but he commented that such a mechanism would be extremely slow to overcome stagnation.

Experiments indicated that:

> Depending upon the step size we reach a point of stagnation which may or may not be near the solution. For well conditioned systems (ratio of the largest to smallest eigenvalue close to one) and with some previous knowledge about the range of variables and for $n$ not large . . . the method gets us in a few minutes machine time close to the solution. For badly conditioned systems the process gets trapped at a point of stagnation. . . . A reduction in the step size results in further progress but after a while the process gets trapped again (Bremermann, 1962).

This was later termed the *trap phenomenon* (Bremermann and Rogson, 1964).

It appears that this trap phenomenon was subsequently misinterpreted. Ashby (1968) asserted that in general dynamic systems, as the system is made larger (i.e., with more components to be optimized), the response curve changes from a steady slope to a step function. But the response surface in question here remains a quadratic function regardless of the dimensionality. A gradient technique would find the globally optimal solution. The stagnation points that Bremermann encountered were not local optima, but rather points on the outside of elliptical contour lines of the multidimensional parabolic surface such that the fixed-length movement along a coordinate axis always resulted in a new point that resided on a higher-contour ellipse (Figure 3-1).

Bremermann conjectured that sexual mating overcomes the situation where asexual evolution is stagnant. Mating schemes that combined elements of solutions in pairs and greater collections, by linear superposition and by random combinations, were tried. "None of these schemes, however, gave any spectacular results" (Bremermann, 1962). Attention was turned to linear programming problems, and again the results were undesirable. Random changes to only single components resulted in rapid stagnation. Further, the combination of two independently discovered stagnation points ("sexual recombination") also stagnated on problems of modest size (eight variables). Bremermann was genuinely disappointed with the lack of success, and this investigation has been described as "Bremermann's disappointment" (Atmar, 1979).

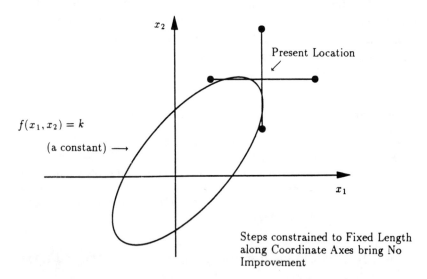

**Figure 3-1**   The ellipse represents a contour on the response surface being searched. The present location is at a point higher than this contour, but no improvement can be made by walking in a direction that is aligned with the coordinate axes for the specified fixed length. A reduction in the step size could be made to attain an improvement, but an equivalent ellipse would exist such that no further gains could be made with this reduced step.

Subsequent investigation (Bremermann and Rogson, 1964) indicated that evolving in random directions, rather than along the axes of the coordinate system, provided for a better search in linear programming problems. A fixed mutation size of high or low length was added to each component of the evolving solution vector. The superiority of this search scheme is to be expected. A much greater range of phenotypic expression is available to the evolving solution. Further improvements could have been expected if the step size had been made a continuous random variable (e.g., Gaussian). Extensions of this direction-based form of stochastic search with rotating coordinates are detailed in Wilde (1964, pp. 151–155; Wilde and Beightler, 1967, pp. 307–313).

Bremermann et al. (1965, 1966; Bremermann, 1967, 1968, 1973) tested other transformations such as majority mating and crossing over pairs of independently discovered solutions. No definite benefit was obtained. On the basis of the requirements for multiple "gene" mutation, Bremermann (1967) conjectured that many biological species are at a genetic stagnation point, rather than at an optimum.

### 3.1.4  Reed, Toombs, and Barricelli: Assessing Crossing Over

Barricelli (1954) offered some of the very first simulations to use evolutionary principles, pursuing the same general procedures as many current efforts in artificial life (cf. Langton, 1989). This early research was continued in Barricelli (1957, 1962a, 1962b), and Reed et al. (1967) later conducted a series of evolutionary gaming experiments that centered around a simplified game of poker. There were two players and each received only one card. There were two types of cards, high and low. Three types of bets were allowed: pass, low bet, and high bet. A pass bet cost two units, a low bet cost three units, and a high bet cost seven units. If the two opponents bet differently, the highest bet always won. If the bets were the same, the higher hand won. In the event of a tie, no units were exchanged.

The betting strategies were defined in terms of the probabilities of betting "pass" with a low hand ($L_p$), betting "pass" with a high hand ($H_P$), betting "low" with a low hand ($L_L$), and betting "low" with a high hand ($H_L$). The remaining probabilities are simply functions of these terms. In addition, four mutational parameters were associated with each strategy (Reed et al., 1967). These controlled the manner in which the strategies would be perturbed. Generating a new solution by crossing over was handled by selecting each element from either parent with a 50 percent probability. Experiments were conducted in which 50 parents were maintained at each generation. Evaluation of the parents and offspring (one per parent) was made over 20 trials of the game.

Reed et al. (1967) concluded that "under conditions simulating polygenic control of quantitative characters, crossing does not enhance the speed of selective adaptation . . . the breeding characteristic spreads less rapidly or not at all." Additional experiments were conducted in which the effects of the genetic structure were nonpolygenic. Under these conditions, "crossing greatly enhances the speed of selective adaptation, particularly if interactions between the expressions of different hereditary factors is avoided" (Reed et al., 1967). As noted previously, however, it is precisely this interactivity among genetic effects (polygeny and pleiotropy) that predominates in living systems.

### 3.1.5  Observations

The inability to rapidly discover suitable computer programs as evidenced in Friedberg (1958; Friedberg et al., 1959) received considerable criticism. Minsky (1961) wrote an unfavorable review of this research, calling it "a comparable failure. . . . The machine did learn to solve some extremely simple problems. But it took on the order of 1,000 times longer than pure chance would expect." In retrospect, this assessment is an exaggeration; the performance of Herman was on the order of 10 times longer than pure chance would expect. Moreover, Ramsy consistently outperformed random search. Minsky (1961) did agree that "in the last section of [Friedberg et al. (1959)] we see some real success obtained by breaking the problem into parts and solving them sequentially." Unfortunately, the relative successes of Friedberg et al. (1959) were overshadowed by the criticism of the earlier research (Friedberg, 1958).

Ramsy had a tendency to have all its instructions bound (i.e., fixated) without being able to solve the problem at hand completely. In effect, the program had climbed to the top of a locally optimal hill without reaching the global optimum solution. Minsky attributed this problem to what he termed the "Mesa phenomena" (Minsky and Selfridge, 1961). "In changing just one instruction at a time the machine had not taken large enough steps in its search through the program space" (Minsky, 1961). This criticism would be appropriate for Herman, but not for Ramsy, which altered all its unbound program instructions after every failure.

The efforts of Friedberg (1958; Friedberg et al., 1959) were limited to a population size of one parent. The intrinsic benefits of a parallel search were not obtained. The limited success obtained by Friedberg was also due in part to the difficulties in determining the worth of highly interactive separate program instructions.

Bremermann's conjecture that a single bit was analogous to a gene is questionable. A single bit in a bit string may be more analogous to a single nucleotide. The crossing over and other mating schemes resembled the form of such genetic operations, but not their function. The resulting effect was merely that of a large-scale mutation, and not that of sexual recombination.

This effect was also evident in Reed et al. (1967). Under polygenic conditions, crossing over provided no benefit to evolutionary optimization (Reed et al., 1967; Barricelli, cited in Bossert, 1967). This was due to the relatively large behavioral change that occurred when such interactive components were broken apart and reassembled without regard to the context in which they were evolved. Reed et al. (1967) did, however, employ polyphyletic search and indirectly included stochastic selection. Each solution was evaluated over 20 Monte Carlo trials. No arrangement for probabilistic survival was incorporated in Friedberg (1958; Friedberg et al., 1959) or Bremermann (1962, 1967, 1968, 1973).

## 3.2  FOGEL: EVOLUTIONARY PROGRAMMING

L. Fogel conceived of using simulated evolution on a population of contending algorithms to develop artificial intelligence and explored this possibility of *evolutionary programming* in a series of studies (Fogel, 1962a, 1962b, 1962c, 1963, 1964; Fogel and Walsh, 1964; Fogel et al., 1965a, 1965b, 1966; and others). Intelligent behavior was viewed as requiring the composite ability to: (1) predict one's environment, coupled with (2) a translation of the predictions into a suitable response in light of the given goal. For the sake of generality, the environment was described as a sequence of symbols taken from a finite alphabet. The evolutionary problem was defined as evolving an algorithm that would operate on the sequence of symbols thus far observed in such a manner so as to produce an output symbol that is likely to maximize the algorithm's performance in light of both the next symbol to appear in the environment and a well-defined payoff function. Finite state machines provided a useful representation for the required behavior.

A finite state machine is a transducer that can be stimulated by a finite alphabet of input symbols, that can respond in a finite alphabet of output symbols, and that possesses some finite number of different internal states. The corresponding input-output symbol pairs and next-state transitions for each input symbol, taken over every state, specify the behavior of any finite state machine, given any starting state. For example, a three-state machine is shown in Figure 3-2. The alphabet of input symbols are elements of the set $\{0, 1\}$, whereas the alphabet of output symbols are elements of the set $\{\alpha, \beta, \gamma\}$ (input symbols are shown to the left of the virgule, output symbols are shown to the right). The finite state machine transforms a sequence of input symbols into a sequence of output symbols. Table 3-1 indicates the response of the machine to a given string of symbols, presuming that the machine is found in state C. It is presumed that the machine acts when each input symbol is perceived and the output takes place before the next input symbol arrives.

Fogel proposed evolutionary programming to operate on finite state machines in the following manner. A population of finite state machines is exposed to the environment, that is, the sequence of symbols that have been observed up to the current time. For each parent machine, as each input symbol is offered to the machine, each output symbol is compared with the next input symbol. The worth of this prediction is then measured with respect to the given payoff function (e.g., all-none, absolute error, squared

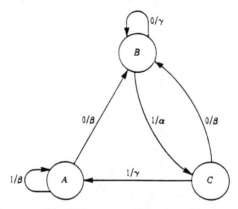

**Figure 3-2**  A three-state finite machine. Input symbols are shown to the left of the virgule. Output symbols are to the right of the virgule. Unless otherwise specified, the machine is presumed to start in state "A." (After Fogel et al., 1966, p. 12.)

| Present State | C | B | C | A | A | B |
|---|---|---|---|---|---|---|
| Input Symbol | 0 | 1 | 1 | 1 | 0 | 1 |
| Next State | B | C | A | A | B | C |
| Output Symbol | $\beta$ | $\alpha$ | $\gamma$ | $\beta$ | $\beta$ | $\alpha$ |

**Table 3-1**    The response of the finite state machine (shown in Figure 3-2) to a string of symbols. In this example, the machine starts in state C.

error, or any other expression of the meaning of the symbols). After the last prediction is made, a function of the payoff for each symbol (e.g., average payoff per symbol) indicates the fitness of the machine.

Offspring machines are created by randomly mutating each parent machine. Each parent produces a single offspring (simply for convenience). There are five possible modes of random mutation that naturally result from the description of the machine: change an output symbol, change a state transition, add a state, delete a state, or change the initial state. The deletion of a state and change of the initial state are only allowed when the parent machine has more than one state. Mutations are chosen with respect to a probability distribution, which is typically uniform. The number of muta-tions per offspring is also chosen with respect to a probability distribution (e.g., Poisson) or may be fixed a priori. These offspring are then evaluated over the existing environment in the same manner as their parents. Other mutations, such as majority logic mating operating on three or more machines, were proposed in Fogel et al. (1966) but not implemented.

The machines that provide the greatest payoff are retained to become parents of the next generation. Typically, half the total machines are saved so that the parent population remains at a constant size. This process is iterated until an actual prediction of the next symbol (as yet unexperienced) in the environment is required. The best machine generates this prediction, the new symbol is added to the experienced environment, and the process is repeated. Fogel (1964; Fogel et al., 1966) used "nonregressive" evolution. To be retained, a machine had to rank in the top half of the population. Saving lesser-adapted machines was discussed as a possibility (Fogel et al., 1966, p. 21) but not incorporated.

There is an inherent versatility in such a procedure. The payoff function can be arbitrarily complex and can possess temporal components; there is no requirement for the classical squared error criterion or any other smooth function. Further, it is not required that the predictions be made with a one-step look ahead. Forecasting can be accomplished at an arbitrary length of time into the future. Multivariate environments can be handled, and the environmental process need not be stationary because the simulated evolution will adapt to changes in the transition statistics.

Fogel et al. (1964, 1966) described a series of experiments in which successively more difficult prediction tasks were presented to the evolutionary program. These included simple two-symbol cyclic sequences, more complex eight-symbol cyclic sequences degraded by random noise, sequences of symbols generated by other finite state machines, nonstationary sequences, and sequences taken from Flood (1962).

For example, a nonstationary sequence of symbols was generated by classifying each of the increasing integers as being prime (symbol 1) or nonprime (symbol 0). Thus the environment consisted of the sequence 01101010001 . . . , where each symbol depicts the primeness of the positive integers 1, 2, 3, 4, 5, 6, 7, 8, 9, 10, 11, . . . , respectively. Testing for primeness is straightforward, but predicting whether or not the next integer will be prime based on the sequence of observed primes and nonprimes appeared nontrivial. The payoff function for prediction was all or none, that is, one point for each correct prediction, zero points for each error, modified by subtracting 0.01 multiplied by the number of states of the machine. This penalty for complexity was provided to maintain parsimonious machines in light of the limited memory of the available computer (IBM 704).

Figure 3-3 shows the cumulative percentage of correct predictions in the first 200 symbols. After the initial fluctuation (due to the small sample size), the prediction score increased to 78 percent at the 115th symbol and then essentially remained constant until the 200th prediction. At this point, the best machine possessed four states. At the 201st prediction, the best machine possessed three states, and at the 202nd prediction, the best machine possessed only one state with both output symbols being 0. After 719 symbols, the process was halted with the cumulative percentage of correct predictions reaching 81.9 percent. The asymptotic worth of this machine would be 100 percent correct because the prime numbers become increasingly infrequent and the machine continued to predict "nonprime."

The goal was then changed to offer a greater payoff for predicting a rare event. Correctly predicting a prime was worth one plus the number of

**Figure 3-3**    The cumulative percentage of correct predictions in the first 200 prime numbers. (From Fogel et al., 1966, p. 37.)

nonprimes that preceded it. Similarly, correctly predicting a nonprime was worth one plus the number of primes that preceded that nonprime. During the first 150 symbols there were 30 correct predictions of primes, 37 incorrect predictions (false alarms), and five missed primes. From the 151st symbol to the 547th there were 65 correct predictions of primes and 67 false alarms. That is, of the first 35 primes, five were missed; of the next 65 primes, none was missed. Fogel et al. (1966) indicated that the evolutionary algorithm learned to recognize numbers that are divisible by two or three as being nonprime. Some recognition that numbers divisible by five are nonprime was also evidenced. Fogel (1968) later remarked that the evolutionary program had successively discovered "cyclic properties within the environment . . . in essence, the equivalent of first recognizing that numbers divisible by two are not prime, etc. In other words, the program was synthesizing a definition of primeness without prior knowledge of the nature of primeness *or* an ability to divide. Clearly the evolutionary program would never be a perfect predictor, but that is to be expected." No finite state machine can represent the algorithm for generating prime numbers.

Fogel (1962b, 1966) considered the problem of designing conscious automata. Consciousness was viewed as self-referential modeling. To be conscious, "the entity must include within itself an ability to develop various models of itself, to examine these models upon request, to select a suitable model in the light of the inquiry and to display that model to the observer upon request" (Fogel, 1966). Such modeling was made through the use of evolving finite state models of evolving finite state predictors coupled with the environment.

Fogel and Burgin (1969) used evolutionary programming for gaming (coevolution). A series of two-person zero-sum gaming experiments was conducted. Evolutionary programming was able to discover the globally best strategy in simple games involving a small number of possible plays (e.g., four) and outperform human subjects in more complicated circumstances. Extensions addressed nonzero-sum games such as pursuit-evasion. Evolutionary programming was used to guide an interceptor toward a moving target in three dimensions. As the target was generally allowed greater maneuverability, the success of the interceptor depended on an ability to predict the target's position at some future time without a priori knowledge of its dynamics. Burgin (1969) provided further description of the two-person zero-sum gaming experiments.

The time-varying nature of the adaptive topography in the cited experiments (1962–1970) aids in the prevention of evolutionary stagnation. After each prediction, the newly observed symbol is added to the experienced sequence. The fitness of the evolving machines reflects the payoff from the last prediction. The adaptive topography changes. Machines that perform poorly on the last prediction are mapped onto a higher position on the error surface, while machines that offer good predictions have a corresponding lower error score. Because the adaptive topography is in continual flux, the problems associated with evolutionary stagnation on a static topography are considerably reduced.

Complexity of the representation is increased as the evolving finite state machines discover regularities in the experienced sequence. A larger number of states provides for a greater degree of expressible behavior (i.e., possible sequences). This complexity has other advantages as well. Neutral mutations (e.g., addition of a state that is unexpressed when the machine is driven by the observed environment) may serve as an informational buffer, reducing the chance that random mutation will change expressed states. Further, the change in, say, a single output symbol is likely to have less phenotypic (behavioral) impact on a 20-state machine than on a two-state machine, assuming that the change is expressed. Increasing the number of states has the effect of reducing the step size of the search, allowing for fine-tuning the evolving structure to the bottom of a minimal error trough.

Additional evolutionary programming experiments in sequence prediction were performed by Lutter and Huntsinger (1969). Evolutionary modeling was able to rapidly relearn environments that had been previously experienced, even after radical environmental change. The sequence of finite state machines had built in a memory of the previous sequences. Burgin (1974) offered a comparison of evolutionary system identification to quasilinearization and indicated that evolutionary programming was well suited for modeling systems described by nonlinear differential equations in light of nontraditional payoff functions. Dearholt (1976) successfully used evolutionary classification techniques on samples of electrocardiograms depicting common heart diseases.

Initial reviews of the evolutionary programming method were favorable. Feigenbaum (1963) described the process as building "complex Markovian models." Kleyn (cited in Fogel et al., 1965a) described the process as an "excellent and novel approach to a learning or self organizing system." But Solomonoff (1966) remarked "the method of Fogel et al. should not be regarded in its present state as being particularly good for working any but the simplest problems." Solomonoff described evolutionary programming mainly as a simple hill-climbing process using a single parent machine to evolve a single offspring machine. Little emphasis was placed on the parallel use of multiple machines as was actually performed. This description persisted in subsequent reviews (e.g., Holland, 1975, p. 163; Kieras, 1976; Rada, 1981; Lenat, 1983).

Solomonoff (1966) had a number of other criticisms. He commented that "a relatively minor [difficulty] is the penalty for complexity of machine that is incorporated into the 'score' that the machine makes on a prediction run." Fogel et al. (1966) generally set such penalty terms to be proportional to the number of states. Solomonoff (1966) suggested that the appropriate penalty term "is by no means arbitrary, but can be computed—in some cases with exactness. Use of any other penalty function will result, on the average, in poorer predictions."

Such criticism is well directed, but unfortunately it is often difficult to compute the exact penalty term. Mallows (1973), Akaike (1974), Rissanen (1978), Barron (1984), and others have suggested procedures for assessing the trade-off between the goodness of fit of a model and the number of its associated degrees of freedom. Assumptions such as the environmental noise being stationary and Gaussian are typically required. But Fogel et al. (1966) were specifically interested in nonstationary, non-Gaussian environments, and the appropriate choice for a penalty for overfitting the observed data remains debatable (Fogel, 1991a). Further, the penalty terms in both Akaike's information criterion (Akaike, 1974) and the minimum description length principle (Rissanen, 1978) are essentially proportional to the degrees of freedom of the model, as was the penalty term employed by Fogel et al. (1966).

Solomonoff was concerned that the simulated evolution did not contain overt mechanisms corresponding to observed genetic processes such as crossover, inversion, and so forth. He commented that such mechanisms tend to "push synergistic genes together on the chromosome," defining synergistic as "two things are 'synergistic' if their occurrence together produces more beneficial effect than the sum of the benefits they give when they occur separately." (Solomonoff, 1966). But such a view requires assigning a fitness to individual genes. As discussed in Chapter 2, this is an inappropriate perspective.

Solomonoff (1966) described research in simulated evolution to be "very limited in both quantity and quality." He further speculated that "while it is possible to develop machines to solve simple problems by mutating a few states at a time, this process is far too slow to obtain solutions to complex problems" (Solomonoff, 1966). No firm description of what was meant by slow or complex was offered. He did, however, encourage further research in the area.

To make a preliminary assessment of the lack of complexity attributed by Solomonoff (1966), the size of the available state space of possible solutions can be computed. Atmar (1976) calculated that the number of possible configurations for a finite state machine given $n$ states, $a$ input symbols, and $b$ output symbols is given by

$$N = (n^a b^a)^n.$$

Table 3-2 indicates the number of possible machines for $n \leq 10$ and input/output alphabets of 1, 2, 3, 4, and 8 symbols. Fogel et al. (1966) conducted experiments in which the environment was taken to be a binary sequence and the maximum number of states for any machine was set at 25. Therefore, the size of the state space was $(25^2 2^2)^{25} = (5^{100})(2^{50})$. The state

|         | $\alpha/\beta = 1$ | $\alpha/\beta = 2$ | $\alpha/\beta = 3$ | $\alpha/\beta = 4$ | $\alpha/\beta = 8$ |
|---------|------------|------------|------------|------------|------------|
| $n = 1$  | 1 | 4 | 27 | 256 | $1.7 \times 10^7$ |
| $n = 2$  | 4 | 256 | 46,656 | $1.7 \times 10^7$ | $1.8 \times 10^{19}$ |
| $n = 3$  | 27 | 46,656 | $3.9 \times 10^9$ | $9.0 \times 10^{12}$ | $1.3 \times 10^{33}$ |
| $n = 4$  | 256 | $1.7 \times 10^7$ | $9.0 \times 10^{12}$ | $1.9 \times 10^{19}$ | $1.5 \times 10^{48}$ |
| $n = 5$  | 3,125 | $1.0 \times 10^{10}$ | $4.4 \times 10^{17}$ | $1.1 \times 10^{26}$ | $1.2 \times 10^{64}$ |
| $n = 6$  | 46,656 | $9.0 \times 10^{12}$ | $4.0 \times 10^{22}$ | $1.3 \times 10^{33}$ | $5.0 \times 10^{80}$ |
| $n = 7$  | $8.2 \times 10^5$ | $1.1 \times 10^{16}$ | $5.8 \times 10^{27}$ | $3.3 \times 10^{40}$ | $7.9 \times 10^{97}$ |
| $n = 8$  | $1.7 \times 10^7$ | $1.8 \times 10^{19}$ | $1.3 \times 10^{33}$ | $1.5 \times 10^{48}$ | $3.9 \times 10^{115}$ |
| $n = 9$  | $3.9 \times 10^9$ | $3.9 \times 10^{22}$ | $4.4 \times 10^{38}$ | $1.1 \times 10^{56}$ | $1.2 \times 10^{126}$ |
| $n = 10$ | $1.0 \times 10^{10}$ | $1.1 \times 10^{26}$ | $2.1 \times 10^{44}$ | $1.2 \times 10^{64}$ | $1.8 \times 10^{152}$ |

**Table 3-2**   The number of possible finite state machines given $n$ states and $\alpha = \beta$ input-output symbols.

space becomes immensely large, even when restricted to relatively small machines.

Subsequent reviews were mixed. Brody and Lindgren (1968) remarked, "although such simulation of evolution by computer . . . has thus far dealt with only relatively simple problems, the method appears to offer an extremely powerful tool." Lutter and Huntsinger (1969) felt that evolutionary programming was especially suited to interpret continuous data from a stochastic process and hoped "to encourage the use of these techniques, especially in control applications." But Michie (1970) wrote: "The idea of getting a computer to write its own program has appeared and disappeared several times in the past two decades. Early attempts, inspired by the example of biological evolution, were based on generating program symbols randomly, conserving the more successful sequences. Such an approach is now considered naive. . . ." Other positive comments were offered by Atmar (1976), and more critical general comments were offered by Chandrasekaran and Recher (1974), Jackson (1974), and Rada (1981).

Lenat (1983) put forth a strong criticism:

The early (1958–1970) researchers in automatic programming were confident that they could succeed by having programs randomly mutate into desired new ones. This hypothesis was simple, elegant, aesthetic, and incorrect. The amount of time necessary to synthesize or modify a program was seen to increase exponentially with its length. Switching to a higher-level language ... merely chipped away somewhat at the exponent, without muffling the combinatorial nature of the process. All the attempts to get programs to "evolve" failed miserably, casualties of the combinatorial explosion.

But this claim that the amount of time necessary to evolve a solution increases exponentially with its length is unsubstantiated in the literature. Investigations by Ambati et al. (1991) and Fogel (1993a) indicate the contrary.

Perhaps the most pointed criticism of Fogel et al. (1966) was offered by Lindsay (1968). Lindsay commented that a random search "is ... the most inefficient method of problem solving" and cited the failure of Friedberg (1958) as evidence. He proceeded to claim, incorrectly, that the evolutionary search of Fogel et al. (1966) was no better than a completely random search and concluded by proclaiming the work of Fogel et al. (1966) to be "fustian" that "may unfortunately alienate many psychologists from the important work being done in artificial intelligence ..." (Lindsay, 1968). Readers interested in a more careful analysis of the criticisms of early evolutionary programming are referred to Fogel (1991a, 1992).

Only limited work in evolutionary programming was performed from 1976 to 1985 (e.g., Atmar, 1976; Takeuchi, 1980). More recently, the technique has been applied to diverse combinatorial optimization problems. Rather than use finite state machines, representations are chosen based on the problem at hand and mutation operations are constructed that maintain a strong behavioral linkage between each parent and its progeny. The procedure has been applied, for example, to path planning problems (Fogel, 1988, 1993a, 1993b; McDonnell and Page, 1990; Fogel and Fogel, 1990; McDonnell et al., 1992; Page et al., 1992), the training and design of neural networks (Fogel et al., 1990; McDonnell and Waagen, 1994; Angeline et al., 1994), automatic control (Sebald and Schlenzig, 1994), gaming (Fogel, 1991b, 1993c), and general function optimization (Fogel and Atmar, 1990; Fogel and Stayton, 1994). The potential benefits of parallelizing evolutionary programming have been initially examined by Duncan (1993) and Nelson (1994). The most recent efforts can be found in Fogel and Atmar (1992, 1993) and Sebald and Fogel (1994).

## 3.3 RECHENBERG AND SCHWEFEL: EVOLUTION STRATEGIES

Another approach to simulating evolution was independently adopted by Rechenberg (1965) and Schwefel (1965), who have been collaborating in Germany since the early 1960s. They addressed continuous function optimization problems. The most simple method can be implemented as follows:

1.  The problem is defined as finding the real-valued $n$-dimensional vector $\mathbf{x}$ that is associated with the extremum of a functional $F(\mathbf{x}): \mathbf{R}^n \to \mathbf{R}$. Without loss of generality, let the procedure be implemented as a minimization process.

2.  An initial population of parent vectors, $\mathbf{x}_i$, $i = 1, \ldots, P$, is selected at random from a feasible range in each dimension. The distribution of initial trials is typically uniform.

3.  An offspring vector, $\mathbf{x}_i'$ is created from each parent $\mathbf{x}_i$, $i = 1, \ldots,$ $P$, by adding a Gaussian random variable with zero mean and preselected standard deviation to each component of $\mathbf{x}$.

4.  Selection then determines which of these vectors to maintain by ranking the errors $F(\mathbf{x}_i)$ and $F(\mathbf{x}_i')$, $i = 1, \ldots, P$. The $P$ vectors that possess the least error become the new parents for the next generation.

5.  The process of generating new trials and selecting those with least error continues until a sufficient solution is reached or the available computation is exhausted.

In this model, the components of a trial solution are viewed as behavioral traits of an individual, not as genes along a chromosome (cf. Bremermann, 1962). A genetic source for these phenotypic traits is presumed, but the nature of the linkage is not detailed. It is assumed that whatever genetic transformations occur, the resulting change in each behavior will follow a Gaussian distribution with zero mean difference and some standard deviation. Specific genetic alterations can affect many phenotypic characteristics due to pleiotropy and polygeny (Figure 2-2). It is therefore appropriate to vary all the components of a parent simultaneously in the creation of a new offspring.

The original efforts in evolution strategies (Rechenberg, 1965; Schwefel, 1965) examined the preceding algorithm but focused on a single parent–single offspring search. This was termed a (1+1)–ES in that a single offspring is created from a single parent and both are placed in competition for survival with selection eliminating the poorer solution. When viewed as a practical optimization algorithm, there were two main drawbacks to this approach: (1) The constant standard deviation (step size) in each dimension made the procedure slow to converge on optimal solutions, and (2) the brittle nature of a point-to-point search made the procedure susceptible to stagnation at local minima (although the procedure can be shown to asymptotically converge to the global optimum vector **x**; Solis and Wets, 1981).

Rechenberg (1973) defined the expected convergence rate of the algorithm as the ratio of the average distance covered toward the optimum and the number of trials required to achieve this improvement. For a quadratic function,

$$F(\mathbf{x}) = \sum_{i=1}^{n} x_i^2, \tag{3-1}$$

where **x** is an $n$-dimensional vector of reals and $x_i$ denotes the $i$th component of **x**, Rechenberg (1973) demonstrated that the optimum expected convergence rate is given when $\sigma \approx 1.224r/n$, where $\sigma$ is the standard deviation of the zero mean Gaussian perturbation, $r$ denotes the current Euclidean distance from the optimum, and there are $n$ dimensions. Thus, for this simple function the optimum convergence rate is obtained when the average step size is proportional to the square root of the error function and inversely proportional to the number of variables. Additional analyses have been conducted on other functions, and the results have yielded similar forms for setting the standard deviation (Bäck et al., 1991) (see Chapter 4).

Schwefel (1981) developed the use of multiple parents and offspring in evolution strategies, following earlier work of Rechenberg (1973) that used multiple parents but only a single offspring. More recently, two approaches have been explored, denoted by $(\mu+\lambda)$–ES and $(\mu,\lambda)$–ES. In the former, $\mu$ parents are used to create $\lambda$ offspring and all solutions compete for survival with the best $\mu$ being selected as parents of the next generation. In the latter, only the $\lambda$ offspring compete for survival and the $\mu$ parents are completely replaced each generation. That is, the life span of every solution is limited to a single generation. Increasing the population size increases the rate of optimization over a fixed number of generations.

To provide a very simple example, suppose it is desired to find the minimum of the function in Eq. 3-1 for $n = 3$. Let the original population consist of 30 parents, with each component initialized in accordance with a uniform distribution over [–5.12, 5.12] (after De Jong, 1975). Let one offspring be created from each parent by adding a Gaussian random variable with mean zero and variance equal to the error score of the parent divided by the square of the number of dimensions ($3^2 = 9$) to each component. Let selection simply retain the best 30 vectors in the population of parents and offspring. Figure 3-4 indicates the rate of optimization of the best vector in the population as a function of the number of generations. The process rapidly converges close to the unique global optimum.

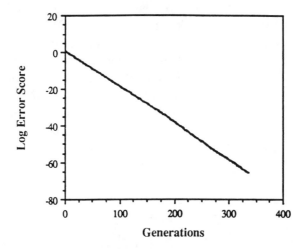

**Figure 3-4**  Using an evolution strategy to find the minimum of a simple three-dimensional quadratic surface. A population of 30 real-valued vectors is maintained at each generation. The curve depicts the rate of optimization of the best vector in the population at each generation. The error score is on a logarithmic scale.

Rather than use a heuristic schedule for reducing the step size over time, Rechenberg introduced the idea of making the distribution of new trials from each parent an additional self-adaptive parameter.[1] In this procedure (detailed in Schwefel, 1981), each solution vector contains not only

---

[1]Rechenberg (pers. comm.) indicated that he first wrote down the idea for self-adaptive parameters in 1967.

the trial vector $\mathbf{x}$ of $n$ dimensions, but a perturbation vector $\sigma$ that provides instructions on how to mutate $\mathbf{x}$ and is itself subject to mutation. For example, if $\mathbf{x}$ is the current position vector and $\sigma$ is a vector of variances corresponding to each dimension of $\mathbf{x}$, then a new solution vector $(\mathbf{x}', \sigma')$ could be created as:

$$\sigma_i' = \sigma_i \cdot \exp(\tau' \cdot N(0, 1) + \tau \cdot N_i(0, 1))$$

$$x_i' = x_i + N(0, \sigma_i')$$

where $i = 1, \ldots, n$, and $N(0,1)$ represents a single standard Gaussian random variable, $N_i(0,1)$ represents the $i$th independent identically distributed (i.i.d.) standard Gaussian, and $\tau$ and $\tau'$ are operator-set parameters affecting global and individual step sizes (Bäck and Schwefel, 1993). In this manner, the evolution strategy can adapt to the width of the error surface on-line and more appropriately distribute trials. This method was extended again (see Schwefel, 1981) to incorporate correlated mutations so that the distribution of new trials could adapt to contours on the error surface (Figure 3-5). Greater consideration to these methods is given in Chapter 4.

Additional extensions included methods for recombining individual solutions in the creation of new offspring. There are many proposed procedures, such as selecting individual components from either of two parents

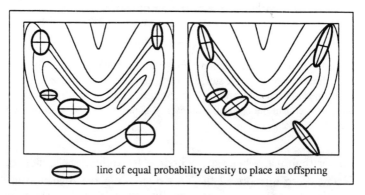

⊕  line of equal probability density to place an offspring

**Figure 3-5**  By implementing correlated mutations across various dimensions, the evolutionary search can adapt to arbitrarily oriented contours on the response surface. The first illustration shows the probability density contours for uncorrelated mutations, while the second indicates the potential for moving more rapidly toward minima when using correlated mutations. (From Bäck et al., 1991.)

at random, averaging individual components from two parents with a given weighting, and so forth (Bäck et al., 1991).

There are strong similarities between evolution strategies and evolutionary programming as applied to real-valued continuous optimization problems. In many cases, the procedures are virtually equivalent, although they were developed independently. The extension to self-adapting independent variances in evolutionary programming was offered in Fogel et al. (1991), with procedures for optimizing the covariance matrix used in generating new trials presented in Fogel et al. (1992). These methods differ from those offered in Schwefel (1981) in that Gaussian perturbations are applied to the self-adaptive parameters instead of lognormal perturbations. Initial comparisons (Bäck et al., 1993; Saravanan and Fogel, 1994) indicate that the procedures in Schwefel (1981) appear to be more robust than those in Fogel et al. (1991). One possible explanation for this is that it is easier for variances of individual terms to transition between small and large values under the methods of Schwefel (1981). Theoretical and empirical comparison between these mechanisms is an open area of research.

Current efforts in evolution strategies are aimed at developing mathematical foundations for the procedures (Bäck et al., 1993; Rudolph, 1994) and investigating their computational complexity theoretically and empirically (Born et al., 1992; Ostermeier, 1992). Efforts have been made to design neural structures (Lohmann, 1992) and apply evolution strategies to system identification (Kuhn and Visser, 1992). Hoffmeister (1991) has examined parallelizing evolution strategies on distributed processing hardware. Recent investigations in evolution strategies can be found in Männer and Manderick (1992) and Davidor et al. (1994).

## 3.4  HOLLAND: GENETIC ALGORITHMS

Holland (1969, 1975) proposed the use of a genetic algorithm as an efficient search mechanism in artificially adaptive systems. This procedure was designed to incorporate specific operators, emphasizing especially crossover and inversion. Crossover was defined (Holland, 1975, p. 98) as taking two coding sequences and exchanging the set of attributes that follow a randomly chosen position. Other crossover operations have been invented and are discussed below. Inversion was defined as taking a random section of code and reversing its indices. The use of genetic operators, specifically crossover, has been termed the distinguishing feature of genetic algorithms (Davis, 1991, p. 17).

Fraser (1968), following considerable earlier development (Fraser, 1957a, 1957b, 1960, 1962, 1967), proposed a procedure quite similar to that presented in Holland (1969, 1975). Fraser proposed that the coding for a given problem be made a string of bits that then undergoes genetic changes through recombination (now commonly known as crossover), inversions, and mutations. The only apparent difference between Fraser's proposal and Holland's is that Holland suggested reproducing each parent in proportion to its relative fitness.

Genetic algorithms are typically implemented as follows.

1. The problem to be addressed is defined and captured in an objective function that indicates the fitness of any potential solution.

2. A population of candidate solutions is initialized subject to certain constraints. Typically, each trial is coded as a vector $\mathbf{x}$, termed a *chromosome*, with elements being described as *genes* and varying values at specific positions called *alleles*. Holland (1975, pp. 70–72) suggested that all solutions should be represented by binary strings. For example, if it were desired to find the scalar value $x$ that maximizes

$$F(x) = -x^2,$$

   then a finite range of values for $x$ would be selected and the minimum possible value in the range would be represented by the string $[0 \ldots 0]$, with the maximum value being represented by the string $[1 \ldots 1]$. The desired degree of precision would indicate the appropriate length of the binary coding.

3. Each chromosome, $\mathbf{x}_i$, $i = 1, \ldots, P$, in the population is decoded into a form appropriate for evaluation and is then assigned a fitness score, $\mu(\mathbf{x}_i)$, according to the objective.

4. Each chromosome is assigned a probability of reproduction, $p_i$, $i = 1, \ldots, P$, so that its likelihood of being selected is proportional to its fitness relative to the other chromosomes in the population. If the fitness of each chromosome is a strictly

positive number to be maximized, this is traditionally accomplished using *roulette wheel selection* (Figure 3-6), although other techniques are available.

5.  According to the assigned probabilities of reproduction, $p_i$, $i = 1$, ..., $P$, a new population of chromosomes is generated by probabilistically selecting strings from the current population. The selected chromosomes generate offspring via the use of specific genetic operators, such as crossover and bit mutation. Crossover is applied to two chromosomes (parents) and creates two new chromosomes (offspring) by selecting a random position along the coding and by splicing the section that appears before the selected position in the first string with the section that appears after the selected position in the second string, and vice versa (Figure 3-7). Other more sophisticated crossover operators have been introduced and are discussed later. Bit mutation simply offers the chance to flip each bit in the coding of a new solution. Typical values for the probabilities of crossover and bit mutation range from 0.6 to 0.95 and 0.001 to 0.01, respectively (De Jong, 1975; Schraudolph and Belew, 1992).

6.  The process is halted if a suitable solution has been found or if the available computing time has expired. Otherwise, the process proceeds to step 3, where the new chromosomes are scored and the procedure iterates.

| No. | String | Fitness | % of Total |
|-----|--------|---------|------------|
| 1 | 01101 | 169 | 14.4 |
| 2 | 11000 | 576 | 49.2 |
| 3 | 01000 | 64 | 5.5 |
| 4 | 10011 | 361 | 30.9 |
| Total | | 1170 | 100.0 |

**Figure 3-6**  Roulette wheel selection in genetic algorithms selects chromosomes for reproduction in proportion to their relative fitness. Essentially, the procedure allocates space on a roulette wheel to each chromosome such that the probability of it being selected varies directly with its fitness. (From Goldberg, 1989, p. 11.)

Crossover Point

Parent #1:   1 1 0 1 | 0 1 1 1 1 0 1          Offspring #1:   1 0 1 0 0 1 1 1 1 0 1

                              →

Parent #2:   1 0 1 0 | 0 0 0 0 1 0 0          Offspring #2:   1 1 0 1 0 0 0 0 1 0 0

**Figure 3-7** The one-point crossover operator is applied to two parents. A crossover point is selected and the two strings that follow that point are exchanged. Other crossover operators that rely on multiple crossover points have been offered.

For example, suppose the task is to find a vector of 100 bits {0, 1} such that the sum of all the bits in the vector is maximized. The objective function could be written as

$$\mu(\mathbf{x}) = \sum_{i=1}^{100} x_i,$$

where $\mathbf{x}$ is a vector of 100 symbols from {0, 1}. Any such vector $\mathbf{x}$ could be scored with respect to $\mu(\mathbf{x})$ and would receive a fitness ranging from zero to 100. Let an initial population of 100 parents be selected completely at random and subjected to roulette wheel selection in light of $\mu(\mathbf{x})$, with the probabilities of crossover and bit mutation being 0.8 and 0.01, respectively. Figure 3-8 shows the rate of improvement of the best vector in the population and the average of all parents, at each generation (one complete iteration of steps 3 to 6) under such conditions. The process rapidly converges on vectors of all 1's.

A number of issues must be addressed when using a genetic algorithm. For example, the suggestion for using binary codings has received considerable criticism (Antonisse, 1989; Vignaux and Michalewicz, 1991; Michalewicz, 1992). To understand the motivation for using bit strings, the notion of schemata must be introduced. Consider a string of symbols from an alphabet **A**. Suppose that some of the components of the string are held fixed while others are free to vary. Define a wild card symbol, # ∉ **A**, that matches any symbol from **A**. A string with fixed and variable symbols defines a schema. Consider the string [01##], defined over the union of {#} and the alphabet **A** = {0, 1}. This set includes [0100], [0101], [0110], and [0111]. Holland (1975, pp. 66–74) recognized that every evaluated string actually offers partial information about the expected fitness of all

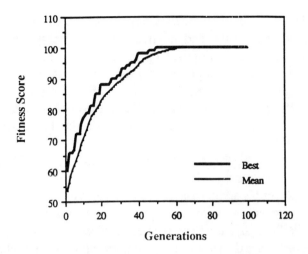

**Figure 3-8**   The results of a genetic algorithm maximizing the number of bits that are set equal to 1 in a 100-bit chromosome. Fitness is simply taken to be the number of 1's in the coding structure. The curves depict the fitness of the best chromosome in the population of 100 such chromosomes as well as the mean fitness of all parents as a function of the number of generations.

possible schemata in which that string resides. That is, if string [0000] is evaluated to have some fitness, then partial information is also received about the worth of sampling from variations in [####], [0###], [#0##], [#00#], [#0#0], and so forth. This characteristic is termed *implicit parallelism*, in that through a single sample, information is gained with respect to many schemata. Holland (1975, p. 71) speculated that it would be beneficial to maximize the number of schemata being sampled, thus providing maximum implicit parallelism, and also proved that this is achieved for $|A| = 2$. Binary strings were therefore suggested as a universal representation.

The use of binary strings is not universally accepted in the genetic algorithm literature, however. Michalewicz (1992, p. 82) indicated that for real-valued numerical optimization problems, floating-point representations outperform binary representations because they are more consistent, more precise, and lead to faster execution. But Michalewicz (1992, p. 75) also claimed that genetic algorithms perform poorly when the state space of possible solutions is extremely large, as required for high-precision numerical optimization of many variables that could take on real-values in a large range. This claim is perhaps too broad. The size of the state space alone does not determine the efficiency of the genetic algorithm, regardless of the choice of representation. Very large state spaces can sometimes be searched quite efficiently, and relatively small state spaces sometimes provide significant difficulties. But it is fair to say that maximizing implicit parallelism will not always provide for optimum performance. Many researchers in genetic algorithms have forgone the bit strings suggested by Holland (1975, pp. 70–72) and have achieved reasonable results for difficult problems (Montana, 1991; Syswerda, 1991; Wright, 1991; Michalewicz, 1992; and others).

Selection in proportion to fitness can be problematic. There are two practical considerations: (1) Roulette wheel selection depends on positive values, and (2) simply adding a large constant value to the objective function can eliminate selection, with the algorithm then proceeding as a purely random walk. Several heuristics have been devised to compensate for these issues. For example, the fitness of all parents can be scaled relative to the mean fitness in the population (Goldberg, 1989, p. 77), or proportional selection can be based on ranking by fitness. Selection based on ranking also eliminates problems with functions that have large offsets.

One mathematical problem with selecting parents to reproduce in proportion to their relative fitness is that this procedure cannot ensure asymptotic convergence to a global optimum (Rudolph, 1994). The best chromosome in the population may be lost at any generation, and there is no assurance that any gains made up to a given generation will be retained in future generations. This can be overcome by employing a heuristic termed *elitist selection* (Grefenstette, 1986) that simply always retains the best chromosome in the population. This procedure guarantees asymptotic convergence (Eiben et al., 1991; Fogel, 1994; Rudolph, 1994), but the specific rates of convergence vary by problem and are generally unknown. Greater consideration to convergence rates is offered in Chapter 4.

Genetic algorithms are distinguished by the emphasis on crossover, with bit mutation serving as a background operator to ensure that all possible alleles can enter the population (Holland, 1975, pp. 110–111). The probabilities commonly assigned to crossover and bit mutation reflect this philosophical view. But the choice of crossover operator is not straightforward.

Holland (1975, p. 160) and others (e.g., Goldberg, 1983; Grefenstette et al., 1985) propose that genetic algorithms work by identifying good "building blocks" and by eventually combining these to get larger building blocks. This idea has become known as the building block hypothesis. The hypothesis suggests that a one-point crossover operator would perform better than an operator that, say, took each bit from either parent with equal probability (uniform crossover), because it could maintain sequences (blocks) of "good code" that are associated with above-average performance and not disrupt their linkage. But this has not always been clearly demonstrated in the literature. Syswerda (1989) conducted function optimization experiments with uniform crossover, two-point crossover, and one-point crossover. Uniform crossover generally provided better solutions with less computational effort. Moreover, it has been noted that sections of code that reside at opposite ends of a chromosome are more likely to be disrupted under one-point crossover than are sections that are near the middle of the chromosome. Holland (1975, pp. 106–109) proposed an inversion operator that would reverse the index position for a section of the chromosome so that linkages could be constructed between arbitrary genes. But inversion has not been found to be useful in practice (Davis, 1991, p. 21). The relevance of the building block hypothesis is presently unclear, but its value is likely to vary significantly by problem.

Premature convergence is another important concern in genetic algorithms. This occurs when the population of chromosomes reaches a configuration such that crossover no longer produces offspring that can outperform their parents, as must be the case in a homogeneous population. Under such circumstances, all standard forms of crossover simply regenerate the current parents. Any further optimization relies solely on bit mutation and can be quite slow. Premature convergence is often observed in genetic algorithm research (De Jong, 1975; Pitney et al., 1990; Bickel and Bickel, 1990; Davis, 1991; and others) because of the exponential reproduction of the best-observed chromosomes coupled with the strong emphasis on crossover. Davis (1991, pp. 26–27) recommends that when the population converges on a chromosome that would require the simultaneous mutation of many bits to improve it, the run is practically completed and either it should be restarted using a different random seed or hill-climbing heuristics should be employed to search for improvements.

One recent proposal for alleviating the problems associated with premature convergence was offered in Schraudolph and Belew (1992). The method, termed *dynamic parameter encoding* (DPE), dynamically resizes the available range of each parameter. Broadly, when a heuristic suggests that the population has converged, the minimum and maximum values for the range are resized to a smaller window and the process is iterated. In this manner, DPE can zoom in on solutions that are closer to the global optimum than provided by the initial precision. Schraudolph (pers. comm.) kindly

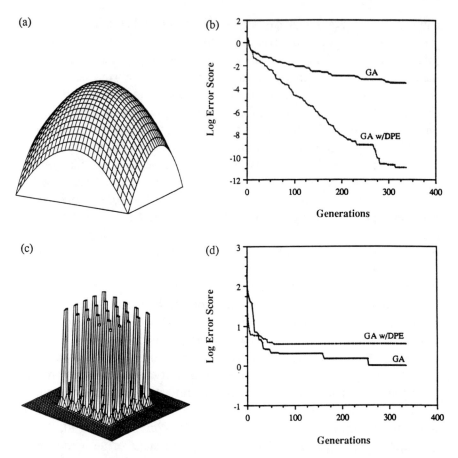

**Figure 3-9**  Results comparing genetic algorithms to genetic algorithms with dynamic parameter encoding. (a) An inverted quadratic function shown in two dimensions. (b) The results of optimization on a three-dimensional quadratic function. Dynamic parameter encoding provides a substantial advantage. (c) An inverted illustration of Shekel's foxholes. (d) The results of optimization on Shekel's foxholes. Dynamic parameter encoding does not appear to improve the efficiency or effectiveness of the genetic search on this function.

provided results from experiments with DPE presented in Schraudolph and Belew (1992). As indicated in Figure 3-9, DPE clearly outperforms the standard genetic algorithm when searching a quadratic bowl, but actually performs worse on a multimodal function (Shekel's foxholes). The effectiveness of DPE is an open, promising area of research. DPE only zooms in, so the initial range of parameters must be set to include the global optimum or it will not be found. But it would be relatively straightforward to include a mechanism in DPE to expand the search window as well as to reduce it. The details of DPE are offered greater consideration in Chapter 4.

Although many open questions remain, genetic algorithms have been used to address diverse practical optimization problems successfully (Holland, 1992a). Current research efforts include: (1) developing a stronger mathematical foundation for the genetic algorithm as an optimization technique (Davis and Principe, 1991; Schraudolph and Belew, 1992; Qi and Palmieri, 1993; Rudolph, 1994), including analysis of classes of problems that are difficult for genetic algorithms (Liepins and Vose, 1991; Whitley, 1991; Hart and Belew, 1991; Forrest and Mitchell, 1993) as well as sensitivity to performance of the general technique to various operator and parameter settings (Vignaux and Michalewicz, 1991; Schaffer and Eshelman, 1991; Spears and De Jong, 1991; Goldberg et al., 1992; Michalewicz, 1992; Kreinovich et al., 1993), (2) comparing genetic algorithms with other optimization methods and examining the manner in which they can be enhanced by incorporating other procedures such as simulated annealing (Mahfoud and Goldberg, 1992; Ingber and Rosen, 1992; Adler, 1993), (3) using genetic algorithms for computer programming and engineering problems (Forrest and Mayer-Kress, 1991; Kristinsson and Dumont, 1992; Krishnakumar and Goldberg, 1992; Koza, 1992), (4) applying genetic algorithms to rule-based classifier systems (Riolo, 1991; Liepins et al., 1991; Abu Zitar and Hassoun, 1993), (5) using genetic algorithms as a basis for artificial life simulations (Jefferson et al., 1991; Holland, 1992b, pp. 186–195), and (6) implementing genetic algorithms on parallel machines (Spiessens and Manderick, 1991; Mühlenbein et al., 1991). The most recent investigations can be found in Forrest (1993).

## 3.5 CONRAD, GALAR, AND RAY: EVOLUTIONARY DYNAMICS

Conrad and colleagues have performed extensive research in simulated evolution and have examined the relationship between evolutionary learning and genetic learning. Conrad (1974) proposed an "evolutionary learning circuits model" in which he hypothesized that the brain harnesses the same types of mechanisms for learning as does evolution. Simulations of neuronal learning systems that adapt through evolutionary changes, in which the time required to learn various pattern recognition tasks increased as a polynomial function of the size of the task, have been conducted by Kampfer and Conrad (1983).

Conrad (1984) focused attention on the flexible nature of biologic systems: "I . . . argue that biological systems are built to be lucky. More precisely, they are built for learning and evolution, but at the cost of giving up programmability." The problems of evolutionary automatic programming were identified as being related to the brittle nature of most current computer programs: "Suppose we alter [a] program by making a single change at random. The common and often painful experience is that the program does not do anything useful. If one waits for some superlanguage to be invented which removes this delicacy one will wait for a very long time. Such a language is theoretically impossible" (Conrad, 1984). Conrad (1984) emphasized the gradual changes that are possible in biological systems and subsequently focused on the trade-off between programmability (i.e., hard-wired behavior) and evolvability (Conrad, 1985, 1987).

Conrad (1981) and Rizki and Conrad (1985) conducted studies of population dynamics. In the latter effort, simulated organisms were given 15 phenotypic traits including temperature optimum, temperature tolerance, rate of energy intake, adult period, mutation rate, and so forth. A pleiotropic/ polygenic coding scheme was utilized (for details, see Rizki and Conrad, 1985). It was concluded that "populations cultured in constant environments usually developed adaptability more rapidly than those cultured in variable environments. . . . However, the situation was reversed when the populations are cultured in the variable environment long enough for them to develop suitable adaptations" (Rizki and Conrad, 1985). Populations were also seen to vary as a result of sensitivity to initial conditions. These properties were attributed to "founder effects" (see Mayr, 1963, for discussion). Additional experiments are reported in Conrad and Rizki (1989).

Conrad (1988) remarked that artificial intelligence as a field has had two major successes: (1) It has clarified and redefined the nature of intelligence, and (2) it has solved specific problems. Certainly artificial intelligence has solved specific problems but, as noted in Chapter 1, the typical definition of intelligence (if one is admitted) is not generally useful. Conrad (1988) did note that the high-level algorithmic approaches (e.g., expert systems) to pattern recognition and other "hard" problems have "run into problems" and suggested that evolution and self-organization techniques can be used to address these tasks. Conrad (1988) speculated that "eventually humans may come to accept programs with a self-organizing capability as not being intrinsically less trustworthy than the programs they design."

More recently, Conrad (1990) argued that evolving systems can adjust their own evolution. This claim does not suggest that systems can completely *direct* their evolution, but rather that they can protect themselves from adverse mutations. Conrad (1990) offered the example of genetic buffering that occurs in DNA. He rightly remarked that "the concept of evolvability is controversial. Some evolutionists argue that natural selection can act only on the properties that are advantageous to the individual . . . [but] . . . evolvability is advantageous to the species" (Conrad, 1990). Conrad (1990) emphasized the success of evolution as being not only attributable to the two-step process of mutation and selection, but also to the adaptation of the organizational structures that undergo transcription and competition. The benefits of such an approach are also reported in experiments by Schwefel (1981) and Fogel et al. (1991, 1992).

Working independently, Galar (1985, 1989) also studied evolutionary dynamics, specifically the impact of emphasizing less-fit individuals in an evolutionary simulation. Through a series of simple experiments, it was demonstrated that "the escapes from evolutionary traps are due to mutations of handicapped individua of intermediary types" (Galar, 1985). That is, it is important to maintain a probabilistic selection mechanism, or at the least, to maintain less-fit solutions at each generation.

Galar (1991) examined the ability of what was described as a "sexually reproducing" small population to overcome saddles in the adaptive landscape. The recombination operation involved differs from that utilized in typical genetic algorithm research. Galar (1991) defined an individual as a set of real-valued "traits." In asexual reproduction, the value of the $j$th virtual trait of the $k$th individual in the population as a descendant from the $r$th individual is given by

$$x(t)_{k,j} = x(t-1)_{r,j} + e,$$

where $t$ represents the generation number and $e$ represents a Gaussian random variable with mean zero and constant variance. In sexual reproduction, the value of the $j$th virtual trait of the $k$th individual in the population that is a descendant of the $r$th couple is given by

$$x(t)_{k,j} = 0.5[x(t-1)_{2r-1,j} + x(t-1)_{2r,j}] + e.$$

Thus the sexual reproduction being studied was actually a "blending" of the traits. Galar (1991) noted that the "transitions [across saddles in the adaptive landscape] of sexual populations are much more difficult [than for asexual populations]. Small populations can cross saddles, but this ability fades with population growth. . . . The main factor is reproduction of the midparental values of traits: even if some individual gets across a saddle, it usually mates with a partner who is still close to the old local optimum. Because of this, randomly mating populations have to cross saddles as a whole." Galar (1991) concluded that the "resulting differences in the waiting time for saddle crossing can be immense, even if the population consists of [only a small number of] individuals."

Another line of investigation into evolutionary dynamics has been emphasized by Ray (1991a, 1991b), who conducted experiments within the framework of an open-ended ecology. Ray (1991a) focused on developing evolutionary simulations that would allow for the study of features fundamental to all evolutionary systems, not just to organic systems. Within that framework, he divised a simulation (Tierra) that competes computer programs written in assembly code. A program was initially made to possess three parts: (1) a self-exam routine that determined the total length of the program, (2) a reproduction loop, and (3) a copy procedure that would be called by the reproduction loop for as many iterations as there were instructions in the program to replicate. The memory, CPU, and computer's operating system formed the physical environment. CPU was allocated to programs in the environment such that shorter programs would replicate faster than longer programs. Programs that generated errors were removed (actually simply deallocated) from the environment based on a function of the number of failed instructions attempted. Failures came about because a mutation operation was employed that randomly altered instructions both in a general background mode where every bit in every program in the simulation was given a small probability of mutation and in a copy mode where additional alterations could be imposed during self-replication.

An 80-instruction handcrafted program that would replicate itself was used to seed the simulation. Over successive generations, the evolutionary dynamics invented a number of interesting programs with different functionalities. Ray (1991a, 1991b) described one class of program as being *parasitic*; that is, it used other programs' copy procedures to replicate its own code, thereby reducing its own program length (it only had a self-exam and reproduction loop). Because these shorter programs required less CPU time to complete replication, they were able to outcomplete their longer *host* programs. Subsequently, *hyperparasites* were created. They allowed the parasites to access their copy procedure but then usurped control of the reproduction loop and used their own reproduction loop to copy themselves instead of the parasites. Other emergent behaviors are described in Ray (1991a, 1991b).

Tierra demonstrates that complex behaviors can arise from evolutionary dynamics operating on relatively simple competing programs. Assessing the functionality of any particular program is tedious because it involves a line-by-line examination of the assembly code of the program and requires an assessment of how it interacted with the other programs or residual code left over from programs that had perished. Nevertheless, Ray (pers. comm.) is working toward implementing parallel processing programs, rather than sequential processing programs, with the hope of understanding important features associated with the evolution of the division of functionality in organisms.

## 3.6  PHILOSOPHICAL DIFFERENCES BETWEEN EVOLUTIONARY AND GENETIC ALGORITHMS

Although the concept of evolution is almost universally accepted, there are diametrically opposed opinions as to what exactly is being evolved. Davis (1991, p. 2) suggests that "evolution is a process that operates on chromosomes rather than on the living beings they encode." In sharp contrast, Mayr (1988, pp. 162–163) suggests that the reductionist definition of evolution as change in gene frequencies "is not only *not* explanatory, but is in fact misleading. Far more revealing is the definition: 'Evolution is change in the adaptation and in the diversity of populations of organisms.' " These perspectives cannot be reconciled. Adopting one or the other leads to very different philosophies of simulating evolution (Fogel, 1993d).

If the philosophy of Davis (1991, p. 2) is followed, simulated evolution operates on a population of strings of symbols (typically taken from the alphabet $\{0, 1\}$) that are analogous to natural chromosomes. The components of these strings are by consequence analogous to genes, with varying symbols at each position analogous to a gene's allelic variants. The operations applied to these strings resemble those found in genetical systems: point mutations, inversions, crossing-over, and so forth. Each abstracted chromosome in the population is assigned a fitness score based on an external objective function that operates on a transformation of the coding string (converting the genotype into a phenotype). These characteristics are common to genetic algorithms.

If emphasis is instead placed on the adaptation and diversity of a population, following Mayr (1988, pp. 162–163), simulated evolution still operates on a population of coding strings, but the components of these strings typically represent abstracted behavioral traits, either those of individuals or entire reproductive populations (species). These components usually take on continuous values and are made to vary with respect to a Gaussian distribution. For some specific applications, the coding strings contain only genetic information (e.g., a computer program) that must operate in a specific environment in order to generate any observed behavior.[2] Mutations are applied to each string such that a strong behavioral link is maintained between each parent and its offspring. The diversity of such new behaviors is again made to follow a Gaussian distribution, often with zero mean difference and relatively small variance. Selection criteria are used to evaluate the behavior of each string and to determine which members of the population to maintain in future generations. These characteristics are common to evolutionary algorithms, such as evolution strategies and evolutionary programming.

Genetic algorithms emphasize the reductionist, bottom-up assembly of building blocks of genes. Fitness is assigned to individual components based on their average performance, and selection is implemented as a differential reproduction that favors above-average building blocks. In

---

[2]Evolutionary algorithms may be applied to both phenotypic or genetic traits. For example, if the task is to find the real-valued vector $\mathbf{x}$ that minimizes a function $F(\mathbf{x})$, then any trial vector may be viewed as a collection of behavioral traits whose appropriateness is measured by $F(\mathbf{x})$. In contrast, if the task is to discover a finite state machine that optimally predicts a sequence of symbols in light of an arbitrary payoff function (Fogel et al., 1966; Atmar, 1976), then the coding structure is purely genetic. Finite state machines have no behavioral expression until they are driven by an environment (a sequence of symbols).

In each case, mutations are applied such that the behavioral change from parent to offspring follows a normal distribution. In the case of real-valued vectors, this can often be accomplished by simply adding a multivariate Gaussian random variable to the vector. For finite state machines, a variety of mutations can be applied (modify an output symbol, change a state transition, add a state, delete a state, change the start state) with respect to a discrete probability mass function (PMF). The PMF is selected such that the distribution of differences between the expressed behavior (generated sequence of symbols) of the mutated machine and its parent can be sufficiently well approximated by a Gaussian.

contrast, evolutionary algorithms reject the notion that meaningful fitness can be assigned to individual genes in isolation and instead emphasize the total cohesive behavior of an individual or reproducing population. Selection is implemented as a culling force that eliminates relatively poor solutions rather than as a promoter that makes additional copies of above-average solutions.

Genetic algorithms emphasize the overt genetic attributes of recombination in various forms of crossing over, whereas evolutionary algorithms simulate the phenotypic effects that such recombinations generate. The application of recombination operations to purely genetic information in evolution strategies is logically sound because this process operates on simulated individuals. The application of recombination in evolutionary programming is a nonissue because each solution is typically viewed as the analog of a species, and there is no sexual communication between species. The proper choice of perspective depends on the human operator's purpose in conducting the experiment.

## 3.7  SUMMARY

Simulated evolution has a long history. Similar ideas and implementations have been independently invented numerous times. Early attempts at automatic programming and simple function optimization were generally unsuccessful due to inappropriate implementation and the omission of fundamental aspects of natural evolution. These aspects are: (1) the incorporation of a population of contending solutions and, to a lesser degree, (2) stochastic selection.

The three current main lines of investigation—genetic algorithms, evolution strategies, and evolutionary programming—share many similarities. Each maintains a population of trial solutions, imposes random changes to those solutions, and incorporates selection to determine which solutions to maintain into future generations and which to remove from the pool of trials. But these methods also have important differences. Genetic algorithms emphasize models of genetic operators as observed in nature, such as crossing-over, inversion, and point mutation, and apply these to abstracted chromosomes. Evolution strategies and evolutionary programming emphasize mutational transformations that maintain behavioral linkage between each parent and its offspring, respectively at the level of the individual or the species. Recombination may be appropriately applied to individuals, but is not applicable for species.

Holland (1975, pp. 16–17) described evolution based on mutation in the absence of genetic operators as being an enumerative search, in large measure equivalent to blindly selecting solutions at random. Such a claim is not correct. There is much recent evidence that the use of macromutations such as crossover are not required for successful adaptation. This follows previous research by Bremermann (1962, 1967, 1968, 1973) and Reed et al. (1967) that indicated that crossover provided no benefit for searching spaces in which the components of the coding for contending solutions were highly interactive.

No model can be a complete description of the true system. Each of these approaches to evolutionary simulation is incomplete. But each has also been demonstrated to be of practical use when applied to difficult optimization problems. The greatest potential for the application of evolutionary optimization to real-world problems will come from their implementation on parallel machines, for evolution is an inherently parallel process. Each parent can be mutated independently and each offspring can be evaluated independently (unless fitness is an explicit function of other members of the population, e.g., Fogel, 1993c, and even then the process can be accelerated through parallelism). Competition and selection can also be parallelized. Recent advances in distributed and parallel processing architectures will result in dramatically reduced execution times for simulations that would simply be impractical on current serial computers.

Natural evolution is a most robust yet efficient problem-solving technique. Evolutionary computation can likewise be made robust. The same procedures can be applied to diverse problems with relatively little reprogramming. Evolutionary systems, be they natural or simulated, are intelligent under the definition proposed in Chapter 1. They adapt their behavior to meet goals in a range of environments. The property of intelligence is not the "end-point of evolutionary search. Rather, intelligence is inseparable from the trial-and-error process itself" (Atmar, 1990).

## REFERENCES

Abu Zitar, R. A., and M. H. Hassoun (1993). "Regulator Control via Genetic Search Assisted Reinforcement." In *Proc. of the Fifth Intern. Conf. on*

*Genetic Algorithms,* edited by S. Forrest. San Mateo, CA: Morgan Kaufmann, pp. 254–262.

Adler, D. (1993). "Genetic Algorithms and Simulated Annealing: A Marriage Proposal." In *IEEE Conference on Neural Networks 1993*, Piscataway, NJ: IEEE, pp. 1104–1109.

Akaike, H. (1974). "A New Look at the Statistical Model Identification," *IEEE Trans. Auto. Control*, Vol. 19:6, pp. 716–723.

Ambati, B. K., J. Ambati, and M. M. Mokhtar (1991). "Heuristic Combinatorial Optimization by Simulated Darwinian Evolution: A Polynomial Time Algorithm for the Traveling Salesman Problem," *Biological Cybernetics*, Vol. 65, pp. 31–35.

Angeline, P. J., G. M. Saunders, and J. B. Pollack (1994). "An Evolutionary Algorithm that Constructs Recurrent Neural Networks," *IEEE Trans. Neural Networks*, Vol. 5:1, pp. 54–65.

Antonisse, J. (1989). "A New Interpretation of Schema Notation that Overturns the Binary Encoding Constraint." In *Proc. of the Third Intern. Conf. on Genetic Algorithms,* edited by J. D. Schaffer. San Mateo, CA: Morgan Kaufmann, pp. 86–91.

Ashby, W. R. (1968). "Contribution of Information Theory to Pathological Mechanisms," *British J. of Psychiatry*, Vol. 114, pp. 1485–1498.

Atmar, J. W. (1976). "Speculation on the Evolution of Intelligence and Its Possible Realization in Machine Form." Sc.D. diss., New Mexico State University, Las Cruces.

Atmar, J. W. (1979). "The Inevitability of Evolutionary Invention." Unpublished manuscript.

Atmar, W. (1990). "Natural Processes Which Accelerate the Evolutionary Search." In *Proc. of the 24th Asilomar Conf. on Signals, Systems, and Computers*, edited by R. R. Chen. Pacific Grove, CA: Maple Press, pp. 1030–1035.

Bäck, T., and H.-P. Schwefel (1993). "An Overview of Evolutionary Algorithms for Parameter Optimization," *Evolutionary Computation*, Vol. 1:1, pp. 1–24.

Bäck, T., F. Hoffmeister, and H.-P. Schwefel (1991). "A Survey of Evolution Strategies." In *Proc. of the Fourth Intern. Conf. on Genetic Algorithms*, edited by R. K. Belew and L. B. Booker. San Mateo, CA: Morgan Kaufmann, pp. 2–9.

Bäck, T., G. Rudolph, and H.-P. Schwefel (1993). "Evolutionary Programming and Evolution Strategies: Similarities and Differences." In *Proc. of the Second Ann. Conf. on Evolutionary Programming*, edited by D. B. Fogel and W. Atmar. La Jolla, CA: Evolutionary Programming Society, pp. 11–22.

Barnett, E. H. (1960). "Introduction to EVOP," *Industr. and Eng. Chem.*, Vol. 52:6, pp. 500–503.

Barricelli, N. A. (1954). "Esempi Numerici di Processi di Evoluzione," *Methodos*, pp. 45–68.

Barricelli, N. A. (1957). "Symbiogenetic Evolution Processes Realized by Artificial Methods," *Methodos*, Vol. 9:35–36, pp. 143–182.

Barricelli, N. A. (1962a). "Numerical Testing of Evolution Theories: I. Theoretical Introduction and Basic Tests," *Acta Biotheoretica*, Vol. 16, pp. 69–98.

Barricelli, N. A. (1962b). "Numerical Testing of Evolution Theories: II. Preliminary Tests of Performance Symbiogenesis and Terrestrial Life," *Acta Biotheoretica*, Vol. 16, pp. 99–126.

Barron, A. R. (1984). "Predicted Squared Error: A Criterion of Automatic Model Selection." In *Self-Organizing Methods in Modeling*, edited by S. J. Farlow. New York: Marcel Dekker, pp. 87–103.

Bickel, A. S., and R. W. Bickel (1990). "Determination of Near-Optimum Use of Hospital Diagnostic Resources Using the 'GENES' Genetic Algorithm," *Comput. Biol. Med.*, Vol. 20:1, pp. 1–13.

Born, J., H.-M. Voigt, and I. Santibanez-Koref (1992). "Alternative Evolution Strategies to Global Optimization." In *Parallel Problem Solving from Nature 2*, edited by R. Männer and B. Manderick. Amsterdam: North-Holland, pp. 187–196.

Bossert, W. (1967). "Mathematical Optimization: Are There Abstract Limits on Natural Selection?" In *Mathematical Challenges to the Neo-Darwinian Interpretation of Evolution*, edited by P. S. Moorhead and M. M. Kaplan. Philadelphia: Wistar Institute Press, pp. 35–46.

Box, G. E. P. (1957). "Evolutionary Operation: A Method for Increasing Industrial Productivity," *Applied Statistics*, Vol. 6, pp. 81–101.

Box, G. E. P. (1960). "Some General Considerations in Process Optimization," *J. Basic Eng.*, March, pp. 113–119.

Box, G. E. P. (1966). "A Simple System of Evolutionary Operation Subject to Empirical Feedback," *Technometrics*, Vol. 8, pp. 19–26.

Box, G. E. P., and J. Chanmugam (1962). "Adaptive Optimization of Continuous Processes," *Indust. and Eng. Chem. Fundamentals*, Vol. 1, pp. 2–16.

Box, G. E. P., and N. R. Draper (1969). *Evolutionary Operation: A Statistical Method for Process Control*. New York: John Wiley.

Box, G. E. P., and J. S. Hunter (1959). "Condensed Calculations for Evolutionary Operation Programs," *Technometrics*, Vol. 1, pp. 77–95.

Bremermann, H. J. (1958). "The Evolution of Intelligence. The Nervous System as a Model of Its Environment." Technical Report No. 1, Contract No. 477(17), Dept. of Mathematics, University of Wash., Seattle, July.

Bremermann, H. J. (1962). "Optimization through Evolution and Recombination." In *Self-Organizing Systems*, edited by M. C. Yovits, G. T. Jacobi, and G. D. Goldstine. Washington DC: Spartan Books, pp. 93–106.

Bremermann, H. J. (1967). "Quantitative Aspects of Goal-Seeking Self-Organizing Systems." In *Progress in Theoretical Biology*, Vol. 1. New York: Academic Press, pp. 59–77.

Bremermann, H. J. (1968). "Numerical Optimization Procedures Derived from Biological Evolution Processes." In *Cybernetic Problems in Bionics,* edited by H. L. Oestreicher and D. R. Moore. New York: Gordon & Breach, pp. 543–562.

Bremermann, H. J. (1973). "On the Dynamics and Trajectories of Evolution Processes." In *Biogenesis, Evolution, Homeostasis,* edited by A. Locker. New York: Springer-Verlag, pp. 29–37.

Bremermann, H. J., and M. Rogson (1964). "An Evolution-Type Search Method for Convex Sets." ONR Tech. Report, Contracts 222(85) and 3656(58), Berkeley, CA, May.

Bremermann, H. J., M. Rogson, and S. Salaff (1965). "Search by Evolution." In *Biophysics and Cybernetic Systems*, edited by M. Maxfield, A. Callahan, and L. J. Fogel. Washington DC: Spartan Books, pp. 157–167.

Bremermann, H. J., M. Rogson, and S. Salaff (1966). "Global Properties of Evolution Processes." In *Natural Automata and Useful Simulations*, edited by H. H. Pattee, E. A. Edlsack, L. Fein, and A.B. Callahan. Washington DC: Spartan Books, pp. 3–41.

Brody, W. M., and N. Lindgren (1968). "Human Enhancement: Beyond the Machine Age," *IEEE Spectrum*, February, pp. 79–93.

Burgin, G. H. (1969). "On Playing Two-Person Zero-Sum Games against Nonminimax Players," *IEEE Trans. on Systems Science and Cybernetics*, Vol. SSC-5:4, pp. 369–370.

Burgin, G. H. (1974). "System Identification by Quasilinearization and Evolutionary Programming," *Journal of Cybernetics*, Vol. 2:3, pp. 4–23.

Campbell, D. T. (1956a). "Adaptive Behavior from Random Response," *Behavioral Science*, Vol. 1, pp. 105–110.

Campbell, D. T. (1956b). "Perception as Substitute Trial and Error," *Psychol. Rev.*, Vol. 63, pp. 330–342.

Campbell, D. T. (1960). "Blind Variation and Selective Survival as a General Strategy in Knowledge-Processes." In *Self-Organizing Systems*, edited by M. C. Yovits and S. Cameron. New York: Pergamon Press, pp. 205–231.

Cannon, W. D. (1932). *The Wisdom of the Body*. New York: Norton and Company.

Chandrasekaran, B., and L. H. Recher (1974). "Artificial Intelligence—A Case for Agnosticism," *IEEE Trans. on Sys., Man, and Cyber.*, Vol. SMC-4:1, pp. 88–94.

Conrad, M. (1974). "Evolutionary Learning Circuits," *J. Theo. Biol.*, Vol. 46, pp. 167–188.

Conrad, M. (1981). "Algorithmic Specification as a Technique for Computing with Informal Biological Models," *BioSystems*, Vol. 13, pp. 303–320.

Conrad, M. (1984). "Microscopic-Macroscopic Interface in Biological Information Processing," *BioSystems*, Vol. 16, pp. 345–363.

Conrad, M. (1985). "On Design Principles for a Molecular Computer," *Comm. of the ACM*, Vol. 28:5, pp. 464–480.

Conrad, M. (1987). "Rapprochement of Artificial Intelligence and Dynamics," *Europ. J. of Oper. Res.*, Vol. 30, pp. 280–290.

Conrad, M. (1988). "Prolegomena to Evolutionary Programming." In *Advances in Cognitive Science: Steps toward Convergence*, edited by M. Kochen and H. M. Hastings. AAAS Selected Symposium, pp. 150–168.

Conrad, M. (1990). "The Geometry of Evolution," *BioSystems*, Vol. 24, pp. 61–81.

Conrad, M., and M. M. Rizki (1989). "The Artificial Worlds Approach to Emergent Evolution," *BioSystems*, Vol. 23, pp. 247–260.

Davidor, Y., H.-P. Schwefel, and R. Männer, eds. (1994). *Parallel Problem Solving from Nature 3*, Berlin: Springer, in press.

Davis, L., ed. (1991). *Handbook of Genetic Algorithms*. New York: Van Nostrand Reinhold.

Davis, T. E., and J. C. Principe (1991). "A Simulated Annealing Like Convergence Theory for the Simple Genetic Algorithm." In *Proc. of the Fourth Intern. Conf. on Genetic Algorithms*, edited by R. K. Belew and L. B. Booker. San Mateo, CA: Morgan Kaufmann, pp. 174–181.

Dearholt, D. W. (1976). "Some Experiments on Generalization Using Evolving Automata." In *Proc. of the 9th Inter. Conf. on System Sciences*, Honolulu, pp. 131–133.

De Jong, K. A. (1975). "The Analysis of the Behavior of a Class of Genetic Adaptive Systems." Ph.D. diss., University of Michigan, Ann Arbor.

Duncan, B. S. (1993). "Parallel Evolutionary Programming." In *Proc. of the Second Annual Conf. on Evolutionary Programming*, edited by D. B. Fogel and W. Atmar. La Jolla, CA: Evolutionary Programming Society, pp. 202–208.

Dunham, B., D. Frisdal, R. Tridshal, and J. H. North (1963). "Design by Natural Selection," *Synthese*, Vol. 15, pp. 254–259.

Eiben, A. E., E. H. Aarts, and K. M. Van Hee (1991). "Global Convergence of Genetic Algorithms: An Infinite Markov Chain Analysis." In *Parallel Problem Solving from Nature*, edited by H.-P. Schwefel and R. Männer. Berlin: Springer, pp. 4–12.

Feigenbaum, E. A. (1963). "Artificial Intelligence Research," *IEEE Trans. on Information Theory*, Vol. IT-9, pp. 248–253.

Flood, M. M. (1962). "Stochastic Learning Theory Applied to Chance Experiments with Cats, Dogs and Men," *Behavioral Science*, Vol. 7:3, pp. 289–314.

Fogel, D. B. (1988). "An Evolutionary Approach to the Traveling Salesman Problem," *Biological Cybernetics*, Vol. 60:2, pp. 139–144.

Fogel, D. B. (1991a). *System Identification through Simulated Evolution: A Machine Learning Approach to Modeling*. Needham, MA: Ginn Press.

Fogel, D. B. (1991b). "The Evolution of Intelligent Decision-Making in Gaming," *Cybernetics and Systems*, Vol. 22, pp. 223–236.

Fogel, D. B. (1992). "Evolving Artificial Intelligence." Ph.D. diss., UCSD.

Fogel, D. B. (1993a). "Empirical Estimation of the Computation Required to Discover Approximate Solutions to the Traveling Salesman Problem Using Evolutionary Programming." In *Proc. of the Second Ann. Conf.*

*on Evolutionary Programming*, edited by D. B. Fogel and W. Atmar. La Jolla, CA: Evolutionary Programming Society, pp. 56–61.

Fogel, D. B. (1993b). "Applying Evolutionary Programming to Selected Traveling Salesman Problems," *Cybernetics and Systems*, Vol. 24, pp. 27–36.

Fogel, D. B. (1993c). "Evolving Behaviors in the Iterated Prisoner's Dilemma," *Evolutionary Computation*, Vol. 1:1, pp. 77–97.

Fogel, D. B. (1993d). "On the Philosophical Differences between Evolutionary Algorithms and Genetic Algorithms." In *Proc. of the Second Ann. Conf. on Evolutionary Programming*, edited by D. B. Fogel and W. Atmar. La Jolla, CA: Evolutionary Programming Society, pp. 23–29.

Fogel, D. B. (1994). "Asymptotic Convergence Properties of Genetic Algorithms and Evolutionary Programming: Analysis and Experiments," *Cybernetics and Systems*, Vol. 25:3, pp. 389–407.

Fogel, D. B., and J. W. Atmar (1990). "Comparing Genetic Operators with Gaussian Mutations in Simulated Evolutionary Processes Using Linear Systems," *Biological Cybernetics*, Vol. 63, pp. 111–114.

Fogel, D. B., and W. Atmar, eds. (1992). *Proc. of the First Ann. Conf. on Evolutionary Programming*. La Jolla, CA: Evolutionary Programming Society.

Fogel, D. B., and W. Atmar, eds. (1993). *Proc. of the Second Ann. Conf. on Evolutionary Programming*. La Jolla, CA: Evolutionary Programming Society.

Fogel, D. B., and L. J. Fogel (1990). "Optimal Routing of Multiple Autonomous Underwater Vehicles through Evolutionary Programming." In *Proc. of the Symp. on Auton. Underwater Vehicle Tech.*, edited by C. E. Stuart. Piscataway, NJ: IEEE Press, pp. 44–47.

Fogel, D. B., and L. C. Stayton (1994). "On the Effectiveness of Crossover in Simulated Evolutionary Optimization," *BioSystems*, Vol. 32:3, pp. 171–182.

Fogel, D. B., L. J. Fogel, and J. W. Atmar (1991). "Meta-Evolutionary Programming." In *Proc. of the 24th Asilomar Conf. on Signals, Systems, and Computers*, edited by R. R. Chen. Pacific Grove, CA: IEEE Comp. Soc. Press, pp. 540–545.

Fogel, D. B., L. J. Fogel and V. W. Porto (1990). "Evolving Neural Networks," *Biological Cybernetics*, Vol. 63:6, pp. 487–493.

Fogel, D. B., L. J. Fogel, W. Atmar, and G.B. Fogel (1992). "Hierarchic Methods of Evolutionary Programming." In *Proc. of the First Ann. Conf. on Evolutionary Programming*, edited by D. B. Fogel and W. Atmar. La Jolla, CA: Evolutionary Programming Society, pp. 175–182.

Fogel, L. J. (1962a). "Autonomous Automata," *Industrial Research*, Vol. 4, pp. 14–19.

Fogel, L. J. (1962b). "Toward Inductive Inference Automata." In *Proc. of the Intern. Federation for Information Processing Congress*. Munich. pp. 395–400.

Fogel, L. J. (1962c). "Decision-Making by Automata." Technical Report GDA-ERR-AN-222, General Dynamics, San Diego.

Fogel, L. J. (1963). *Biotechnology: Concepts and Applications*. Englewood Cliffs, NJ: Prentice Hall.

Fogel, L. J. (1964). "On the Organization of Intellect." Ph.D. diss., UCLA.

Fogel, L. J. (1966). "On the Design of Conscious Automata." Final Report under Contract No. AF 49(638)-1651, AFOSR, Arlington, VA.

Fogel, L. J. (1968). "Extending Communication and Control through Simulated Evolution," Bioengineering—An Engineering View. In *Proc. Symp. Engineering Significance of the Biological Sciences*, edited by G. Bugliarello. San Francisco: San Francisco Press, pp. 286–304.

Fogel, L. J., and G. H. Burgin (1969). "Competitive Goal-Seeking through Evolutionary Programming." Final Report under Contract No. AF 19(628)-5927, Air Force Cambridge Research Labs.

Fogel, L. J., and M. J. Walsh (1964). "Research toward Automatic Pattern Recognition and Artificial Intelligence." Technical Report GDR-ERR-AN-568, General Dynamics, San Diego.

Fogel, L. J., A. J. Owens, and M. J. Walsh (1964). "On the Evolution of Artificial Intelligence." In *Proc. of the Fifth National Symp. on Human Factors in Electronics*. San Diego, CA: IEEE, pp. 63–76.

Fogel, L. J., A. J. Owens, and M. J. Walsh (1965a). "Artificial Intelligence through a Simulation of Evolution." In *Biophysics and Cybernetics Systems*, edited by A. Callahan, M. Maxfield, and L. J. Fogel. Washington DC: Spartan Books, pp. 131–156.

Fogel, L. J., A. J. Owens, and M. J. Walsh (1965b). "Intelligent Decision-Making through a Simulation of Evolution," *IEEE Trans. of the Professional Technical Group on Human Factors in Electronics*, Vol. 6:1.

Fogel, L. J., A. J. Owens, and M. J. Walsh (1966). *Artificial Intelligence through Simulated Evolution*. New York: John Wiley.

Forrest, S., ed. (1993). *Proc. of the Fifth Intern. Conf. on Genetic Algorithms*. San Mateo, CA: Morgan Kaufmann.

Forrest, S., and G. Mayer-Kress (1991). "Genetic Algorithms, Nonlinear Dynamical Systems, and Models of International Security." In *Handbook of Genetic Algorithms*, edited by L. Davis. New York: Van Nostrand Reinhold, pp. 166–185.

Forrest, S., and M. Mitchell (1993). "What Makes a Problem Hard for a Genetic Algorithm—Some Anomolous Results and Their Explanation," *Machine Learning*, Vol. 13:2–3, pp. 285–319.

Fraser, A. S. (1957a). "Simulation of Genetic Systems by Automatic Digital Computers. I. Introduction," *Australian J. of Biol. Sci.*, Vol. 10, pp. 484–491.

Fraser, A. S. (1957b). "Simulation of Genetic Systems by Automatic Digital Computers. II. Effects of Linkage on Rates of Advance Under Selection," *Australian J. of Biol. Sci.*, Vol. 10, pp. 492–499.

Fraser, A. S. (1960). "Simulation of Genetic Systems by Automatic Digital Computers. VI. Epistasis," *Australian J. of Biol. Sci.*, Vol. 13, pp. 150–162.

Fraser, A. S. (1962). "Simulation of Genetic Systems," *J. of Theoretical Biology*, Vol. 2, pp. 329–346.

Fraser, A. S. (1967). "Comments on Mathematical Challenges to the Neo-Darwinian Concept of Evolution." In *Mathematical Challenges to the Neo-Darwinian Interpretation of Evolution*, edited by P. S. Moorhead and M. M. Kaplan. Philadelphia: Wistar Institute Press, p. 107.

Fraser, A. S. (1968). "The Evolution of Purposive Behavior." In *Purposive Systems*, edited by H. von Foerster, J. D. White, L. J. Peterson, and J. K. Russell. Washington DC: Spartan Books, pp. 15–23.

Friedberg, R. M. (1958). "A Learning Machine: Part I," *IBM J. of Research and Development*, Vol. 2, pp. 2–13.

Friedberg, R. M., B. Dunham, and J. H. North (1959). "A Learning Machine: Part II," *IBM J. of Research and Development*, Vol. 3, pp. 282–287.

Friedman, G. J. (1959). "Digital Simulation of an Evolutionary Process," *General Systems Yearbook*, Vol. 4, pp. 171–184.

Galar, R. (1985). "Handicapped Individua in Evolutionary Processes," *Biological Cybernetics*, Vol. 53, pp. 1–9.

Galar, R. (1989). "Evolutionary Search with Soft Selection," *Biological Cybernetics*, Vol. 60, pp. 357–364.

Galar, R. (1991). "Simulation of Local Evolutionary Dynamics of Small Populations," *Biological Cybernetics*, Vol. 65, pp. 37–45.

Goldberg, D. E. (1983). "Computer-Aided Gas Pipeline Operation Using Genetic Algorithms and Rule Learning." Ph.D. diss., University of Michigan, Ann Arbor.

Goldberg, D. E. (1989). *Genetic Algorithms in Search, Optimization, and Machine Learning.* Reading, MA: Addison-Wesley.

Goldberg, D. E., K. Deb, and J. H. Clark (1992). "Genetic Algorithms: Noise, and the Sizing of Populations," *Complex Systems*, Vol. 6, pp. 333–362.

Grefenstette, J. J. (1986). "Optimization of Control Parameters for Genetic Algorithms," *IEEE Trans. Sys., Man, and Cybern.*, Vol. SMC-16:1, pp. 122–128.

Grefenstette, J. J., R. Gopal, B. Rosmaita, and D. Van Gucht (1985). "Genetic Algorithms for the Traveling Salesman Problem." In *Proc. of an Intern. Conf. on Genetic Algorithms and Their Applications*, edited by J. J. Grefenstette. Hillsdale, NJ: Lawrence Erlbaum, pp. 160–168.

Hart, W. E., and R. K. Belew (1991). "Optimizing an Arbitrary Function Is Hard for the Genetic Algorithm." In *Proc. of the Fourth Intern. Conf. on Genetic Algorithms*, edited by R. K. Belew and L. B. Booker. San Mateo, CA: Morgan Kaufmann, pp. 190–195.

Hoffmeister, F. (1991). "Scalable Parallelism by Evolutionary Algorithms." In *Parallel Comp. and Math. Opt.*, edited by D. B. Grauer. Berlin: Springer, pp. 177–198.

Holland, J. H. (1969). "Adaptive Plans Optimal for Payoff-Only Environments." In *Proc. of the Second Hawaii Intern. Conf. on System Sciences*, pp. 917–920.

Holland, J. H. (1975). *Adaptation in Natural and Artificial Systems.* Ann Arbor: University of Michigan Press.

Holland, J. H. (1992a). "Genetic Algorithms," *Scientific American*, July, pp. 66–72.

Holland, J. H. (1992b). *Adaptation in Natural and Artificial Systems*, 2nd ed. Cambridge, MA: MIT Press.

Hunter, J. S. (1958). "Some Statistical Principles Underlying EVOP," *Sec. Stevens Symp.*, pp. 63–75.

Hunter, J. S. (1960). "Optimize Your Process with EVOP," *Chem. Eng.*, Vol. 67, pp. 193–202.

Ingber, L., and B. Rosen (1992). "Genetic Algorithms and Very Fast Simulated Annealing—A Comparison," *Math. and Comp. Model.*, Vol. 16:11, pp. 87–100.

Jackson, P. C. (1974). *Introduction to Artificial Intelligence*. New York: Dover Publications (reprint).

Jefferson, D., R. Collins, C. Cooper, M. Dyer, M. Flowers, R. Korf, C. Taylor, and A. Wang (1991). "Evolution as a Theme in Artificial Life: The Genesys/Tracker System." In *Artificial Life II*, edited by C. G. Langton, C. Taylor, J. D. Farmer, and S. Rasmussen. Reading, MA: Addison-Wesley, pp. 549–578.

Kampfner, R. P., and M. Conrad (1983). "Computational Modeling of Evolutionary Learning Processes in the Brain," *Bull. Math. Biol.*, Vol. 45:6, pp. 931–968.

Kieras, D. E. (1976). "Automata and S-R Models," *J. of Mathematical Psychology*, Vol. 13, pp. 127–147.

Koehler, T. L. (1958a). "Evolutionary Operation: Some Actual Examples," *Sec. Stevens Symp.*, pp. 5–8.

Koehler, T. L. (1958b). "Evolutionary Operation: A Program for Optimizing Plant Operation," *Trans. All-Day Rutgers Qual. Contr. Conf.,* American Soc. Qual. Cont., pp. 25–45.

Koza, J. R. (1992). *Genetic Programming: On the Programming of Computers by Means of Natural Selection*, Cambridge, MA: MIT Press.

Kreinovich, V., C. Quintana, and O. Fuentes (1993). "Genetic Algorithms— What Fitness Scaling Is Optimal," *Cybernetics and Systems*, Vol. 24:1, pp. 9–26.

Krishnakumar, K., and D. E. Goldberg (1992). "Control System Optimization Using Genetic Algorithms," *J. Guidance, Control, and Dynamics*, Vol. 15:3, pp. 735–740.

Kristinsson, K., and G. A. Dumont (1992). "System Identification and Control Using Genetic Algorithms," *IEEE Trans. Sys., Man, and Cyber.*, Vol. 22:5, pp. 1033–1046.

Kuhn, W., and A. Visser (1992). "Identification of the System Parameter of a 6 Axis Robot with the Help of an Evolution Strategy," *Robotersysteme*, Vol. 8:3, pp. 123–133.

Langton, C. G., ed. (1989). *Artificial Life*. Reading, MA: Addison-Wesley.

Lenat, D. B. (1983). "The Role of Heuristic in Learning by Discovery: Three Case Studies." In *Machine Learning*, edited by R. S. Michalski, J. G. Carbonell, and T. M. Mitchell. Palo Alto, CA: Tioga Publishing, pp. 243–306.

Liepens, G. E., M. R. Hilliard, M. Palmer, and G. Rangarajan (1991). "Credit Assignment and Discovery in Classifier Systems," *Intern. J. of Intelligent Sys.*, Vol. 6:1, pp. 55–69.

Liepens, G. E., and M. D. Vose (1991). "Deceptiveness and Genetic Algorithm Dynamics." In *Foundations of Genetic Algorithms*, edited by G. J. E. Rawlins. San Mateo, CA: Morgan Kaufmann, pp. 36–52.

Lindsay, R. K. (1968). "Artificial Evolution of Intelligence," *Comtemp. Psychology*, Vol. 13:3, pp. 113–116.

Lohmann, R. (1992). "Structure Evolution and Incomplete Induction." In *Parallel Problem Solving from Nature 2*, edited by R. Männer and B. Manderick. Amsterdam: North-Holland, pp. 175–186.

Lutter, B. E., and R. C. Huntsinger (1969). "Engineering Applications of Finite Automata," *Simulation*, Vol. 13, pp. 5–11.

Mahfoud, S. W., and D. E. Goldberg (1992). "Parallel Recombinative Simulated Annealing: A Genetic Algorithm," IlliGAL Report No. 92002, University of Illinois, Urbana-Champaign.

Mallows, C. L. (1973). "Some Comments on $C_p$," *Technometrics*, Vol. 15, pp. 661–675.

Männer, R., and B. Manderick, eds. (1992). *Parallel Problem Solving from Nature 2*, Amsterdam: North-Holland.

Mayr, E. (1963). *Animal Species and Evolution*. Cambridge, MA: Belknap Press.

Mayr, E. (1988). *Toward a New Philosophy of Biology: Observations of an Evolutionist*. Cambridge, MA: Belknap Press.

McDonnell, J. R., and W. C. Page (1990). "Mobile Robot Path Planning Using Evolutionary Programming." In *Proc. of the 24th Asilomar Conf. on Signals, System, and Computers*, edited by R. R. Chen. Pacific Grove, CA: Maple Press, pp. 1025–1029.

McDonnell, J. R., and D. Waagen (1994). "Evolving Recurrent Perceptrons for Time-Series Prediction," *IEEE Trans. Neural Networks*, Vol. 5:1, pp. 24–38.

McDonnell, J. R., B. D. Andersen, W. C. Page, and F. Pin (1992). "Mobile Manipulator Configuration Optimization Using Evolutionary Programming." In *Proc. of the First Ann. Conf. on Evolutionary Programming*, edited by D. B. Fogel and W. Atmar. La Jolla, CA: Evolutionary Programming Society, pp. 52–62.

Michalewicz, Z. (1992). *Genetic Algorithms + Data Structures = Evolution Programs*. New York: Springer-Verlag.

Michie, D. (1970). "Future for Integrated Cognitive Systems," *Nature*, Vol. 228, pp. 717–722.

Minsky, M. L. (1961). "Steps toward Artificial Intelligence," *Proc. of the IRE*, Vol. 49:1, pp. 8–30.

Minsky, M. L., and O. G. Selfridge (1961). "Learning in Random Nets." In *Proc. of the Fourth Lond. Symp. on Information Theory*, edited by C. Cherry. London: Butterworths.

Montana, D. J. (1991). "Automated Parameter Tuning for Interpretation of Synthetic Images." In *Handbook of Genetic Algorithms*, edited by L. Davis. New York: Van Nostrand Reinhold, pp. 282–311.

Mühlenbein, H., M. Schomisch, and J. Born (1991). "The Parallel Genetic Algorithm as Function Optimizer," *Parallel Computing*, Vol. 17, pp. 619–632.

Nelson, K. (1994). "Function Optimization and Parallel Evolutionary Programming on the MasPar MP-1." In *Proc. of the Third Ann. Conf. on Evolutionary Programming*, edited by A. V. Sebald and L. J. Fogel. River Edge, NJ: World Scientific, pp. 324–334.

Ostermeier, A. (1992). "An Evolution Strategy with Momentum Adaptation of the Random Number Distribution." In *Parallel Problem Solving from Nature 2*, edited by R. Männer and B. Manderick. Amsterdam: North-Holland, pp. 197–206.

Qi, X., and F. Palmieri (1993). "Adaptive Mutation in the Genetic Algorithm." In *Proc. of the Second Ann. Conf. on Evolutionary Programming*, edited by D. B. Fogel and W. Atmar. La Jolla, CA: Evolutionary Programming Society, pp. 192–196.

Page, W. C., B. D. Andersen, and J. R. McDonnell (1992). "An Evolutionary Programming Approach to Multi-Dimensional Path Planning." In *Proc. of the First Ann. Conf. on Evolutionary Programming*, edited by D. B. Fogel and W. Atmar. La Jolla, CA: Evolutionary Programming Society, pp. 63–70.

Pitney, G., T. R. Smith, and D. Greenwood (1990). "Genetic Design of Processing Elements for Path Planning Networks." In *Proc. of the Intern.*

*Joint Conf. on Neural Networks 1990*, Vol. 3. Piscataway, NJ: IEEE, pp. 925–932.

Rada, R. (1981). "Evolution and Gradualness," *BioSystems*, Vol. 14, pp. 211–218.

Ray, T. S. (1991a). "An Approach to the Synthesis of Life." In *Artificial Life II*, edited by C. G. Langton, C. Taylor, J. D. Farmer, and S. Rasmussen. Reading, MA: Addison-Wesley, pp. 371–408.

Ray, T. S. (1991b). "Is It Alive or Is It GA?" In *Proc. of the Fourth Intern. Conf. on Genetic Algorithms*, edited by R. K. Belew and L. B. Booker. San Mateo, CA: Morgan Kaufmann, pp. 527–534.

Ray, T. S. (1994). Personal communication, ATR, Kyoto, Japan.

Rechenberg, I. (1965). "Cybernetic Solution Path of an Experimental Problem." Royal Aircraft Establishment, Library Translation No. 1122, August.

Rechenberg, I. (1973). *Evolutionsstrategie: Optimierung Technisher Systeme nach Prinzipien der Biologischen Evolution*. Stuttgart: Fromman-Holzboog Verlag.

Rechenberg, I. (1993). Personal communication, Technical University of Berlin, Germany.

Reed, J., R. Toombs, and N. A. Barricelli (1967). "Simulation of Biological Evolution and Machine Learning," *J. Theoretical Biology*, Vol. 17, pp. 319–342.

Riolo, R. (1991). "Modeling Simple Human Category Learning with a Classifier System." In *Proc. of the Fourth Intern. Conf. on Genetic Algorithms*, edited by R. K. Belew and L. B. Booker. San Mateo, CA: Morgan Kaufmann, pp. 324–333.

Rissanen, J. (1978). "Modeling by Shortest Data Description," *Automatica*, Vol. 14, pp. 465–471.

Rizki, M. M., and M. Conrad (1985). "Evolve III: A Discrete Events Model of an Evolutionary Ecosystem," *BioSystems*, Vol. 18, pp. 121–133.

Rudolph, G. (1994). "Convergence Properties of Canonical Genetic Algorithms," *IEEE Trans. on Neural Networks*, Vol. 5:1, pp. 96–101.

Saravanan, N., and D. B. Fogel (1994). "Learning of Strategy Parameters in Evolutionary Programming: An Empirical Study." In *Proc. of the Third Ann. Conf. on Evolutionary Programming*, edited by A. V. Sebald and L. J. Fogel. River Edge, NJ: World Scientific, pp. 269–280.

Schaffer, J. D., and L. J. Eshelman (1991). "On Crossover as an Evolutionarily Viable Strategy." In *Proc. of the Fourth Intern. Conf. on Genetic Algorithms*, edited by R. K. Belew and L. B. Booker. San Mateo, CA: Morgan Kaufmann, pp. 61–68.

Schraudolph, N. N. (1993). Personal communication, Salk Institute, La Jolla, CA.

Schraudolph, N. N., and R. K. Belew (1992). "Dynamic Parameter Encoding for Genetic Algorithms," *Machine Learning*, Vol. 9:1, pp. 9–21.

Schwefel, H.-P. (1965). "Kybernetische Evolution als Strategie der Experimentellen Forschung in der Strömungstechnik." Diploma Thesis, Technical University of Berlin.

Schwefel, H.-P. (1981). *Numerical Optimization of Computer Models*. Chichester: John Wiley.

Sebald, A. V., and L. J. Fogel, eds. (1994). *Proc. of the Third Ann. Conf. on Evolutionary Programming*. River Edge, NJ: World Scientific.

Sebald, A. V., and J. Schlenzig (1994). "Minimax Design of Neural Net Controllers for Highly Uncertain Plants," *IEEE Trans. Neural Networks*, Vol. 5:1, pp. 73–82.

Solis, F. J., and R. J.-B. Wets (1981). "Minimization by Random Search Techniques," *Math. Operations Research*, Vol. 6, pp. 19–30.

Solomonoff, R. J. (1966). "Some Recent Work in Artificial Intelligence," *Proc. of the IEEE*, Vol. 54:12, pp. 1687–1697.

Spears, W. M., and K. A. De Jong (1991). "On the Virtues of Parameterized Uniform Crossover." In *Proc. of the Fourth Intern. Conf. on Genetic Algorithms*, edited by R. K. Belew and L. B. Booker. San Mateo, CA: Morgan Kaufmann, pp. 230–236.

Spiessens, P., and B. Manderick (1991). "A Massively Parallel Genetic Algorithm: Implementation and First Analysis." In *Proc. of the Fourth Intern. Conf. on Genetic Algorithms*, edited by R. K. Belew and L. B. Booker. San Mateo, CA: Morgan Kaufmann, pp. 279–286.

Syswerda, G. (1989). "Uniform Crossover in Genetic Algorithms." In *Proc. of the Third Intern. Conf. on Genetic Algorithms*, edited by J. D. Schaffer. San Mateo, CA: Morgan Kaufmann, pp. 2–9.

Syswerda, G. (1991). "Schedule Optimization Using Genetic Algorithms." In *Handbook of Genetic Algorithms*, edited by L. Davis. New York: Van Nostrand Reinhold, pp. 332–349.

Takeuchi, A. (1980). "Evolutionary Automata—Comparison of Automaton Behavior and Restle's Learning Model," *Information Sciences*, Vol. 20, pp. 91–99.

Turing, A. M. (1950). "Computing Machinery and Intelligence," *Mind*, Vol. 59, pp. 433–460.

Vignaux, G. A., and Z. Michalewicz (1991). "A Genetic Algorithm for the Linear Transportation Problem," *IEEE Trans. on Sys., Man, and Cybern.*, Vol. 21:2, pp. 445–452.

Whitley, L. D. (1991). "Fundamental Principles of Deception in Genetic Search." In *Foundations of Genetic Algorithms*, edited by G. J. E. Rawlins. San Mateo, CA: Morgan Kaufmann, pp. 221–241.

Wilde, D. J. (1964). *Optimum Seeking Methods*. Englewood Cliffs, NJ: Prentice Hall.

Wilde, D. J., and C. S. Beightler (1967). *Foundations of Optimization*. Englewood Cliffs, NJ: Prentice Hall.

Wright, A. H. (1991). "Genetic Algorithms for Real Parameter Optimization." In *Foundations of Genetic Algorithms*, edited by G. J. E. Rawlins. San Mateo, CA: Morgan Kaufmann, pp. 205–218.

# 4

# Theoretical and Empirical Properties of Evolutionary Computation

## 4.1 THE DIFFICULTIES

Evolutionary methods of optimization, indeed all optimization algorithms, can be analyzed and evaluated. Inquiries into the efficiency of the procedures, including the rate of convergence, the quality of the evolved solution, the computational requirements, and other properties, can be focused along two lines of investigation: theoretical and empirical. The theoretical approach attempts to discover mathematical truths about the algorithm that will hold in a reasonably broad domain of application. The empirical approach attempts to assay the performance of the algorithm in specific domains through statistical means. Both procedures are inherently limited.

Mathematical proofs regarding the properties of algorithms are always more powerful than mere empirical evidence. But it may be very difficult or even impossible to formulate a purely theoretical analysis. Evolutionary computations generally incorporate complex nonlinear stochastic processes. To make analysis tractable, the actual procedure is often simplified, but then the true algorithm is not being studied. One may legitimately question the degree to which what may be proved for the simplified procedure will hold for the true procedure.

Similarly, through statistical analysis the algorithm can be tested over successive trials on a specific problem and a probabilistic description of the procedure's performance can be determined. This can be a useful method for comparing the efficiency of two or more algorithms applied to the same task. But again, the performance of an algorithm on one sample problem may not immediately convey information on how it will perform on any other problem.

In the extreme, it may be argued that if a theoretical analysis is conducted on a procedure that is even the slightest bit a simplification of the real process, then nothing is truly learned about the real process. Further, one may argue that empirical evidence is useless for assessing the general performance of an algorithm because it is strictly limited to the domain of experimentation and may not be more broadly applicable.

The position adopted here will be an intermediate one. It is possible to gain insight into the behavior of a complex algorithm by proving mathematical properties associated with simplifications of the algorithm. Furthermore, it is possible to generalize about the properties of a complex algorithm by assessing its performance across a variety of domains. Of course, such generalization may be in error. Yet it is only through this two-pronged investigation that real insight into the effectiveness and efficiency of evolutionary computation can be garnered. To forsake one approach in favor of the other would be foolish.

## 4.2 THEORETICAL ANALYSIS OF GENETIC ALGORITHMS

### 4.2.1 The Framework for Genetic Operators

As detailed in Chapter 3, the framework for the genetic algorithm was described in Holland (1975). Earlier investigation by Holland assessed the optimal allocation of trials in a hyperspace (Holland, 1969) but was not plainly set in a genetic system of crossover, inversion, and mutation. While Fraser (1957a, 1957b, 1960, 1962, 1967, 1968) proposed and examined an algorithm that consisted of these genetic operators, Holland (1975) provided a mathematical basis for employing these techniques.

Before analyzing the algorithm, it must be explained in detail. Goldberg (1989) and Davis (1991) describe the standard genetic algorithm. There are many variations of the standard procedure; although all are worthy of study, only the standard method with some limited extensions will be analyzed here. A top-level description following Davis (1991a, p. 5) is as follows.

1. Initialize a population of solutions.
2. Evaluate each solution in the population.
3. Create new solutions by mating current solutions; apply mutation and recombination as the parent solutions mate.
4. Delete members of the population to make room for the new solutions.
5. Evaluate the new solutions and insert them into the population.
6. If the available time has expired, halt and return the best solution; if not, go to step 3.

As suggested by Holland (1975), the coding for a solution, termed a *chromosome*, is described as a string of symbols from $\{0, 1\}$. These components of the chromosome are then labeled *genes*. The number of bits that must be used to describe each variable parameter is problem-dependent. Let each solution in the population of $m$ such solutions, $x_i$, $i = 1, \ldots, m$, be a string of symbols $\{0, 1\}$ of length $k$. Typically, the initial population of $m$ solutions is selected completely at random, with each bit of each solution having a 50 percent chance of taking the symbol 0.

Evaluation is made with respect to some extrinsically defined payoff (objective) function. This function can itself be a function of the evolving population, although this is not traditionally practiced. For the sake of discussion, consider the function to be a real-valued mapping (i.e., a functional) from the bit strings of length $k$ to $\Re$. For example, the payoff function, $f(y)$, might be

$$f(y) = y_1^2 + y_2^2,$$

where $y_1$ is determined from the first $j$ bits of solution $x_i$ and $y_2$ is determined from the remaining bits. There are no restrictions on which bits must be used for each parameter, but once chosen they should remain fixed for the duration of the simulation.

The creation of new solutions is accomplished as follows. First, "reproduction with emphasis" is applied to the existing parents. One common method to accomplish this is termed *roulette wheel parent selection* (see Chapter 3 and also Davis, 1991a, p. 13). This method proceeds by summing the fitnesses of all the population members. Call this value $S$. A uniformly distributed random number $u$ ranging over $[0, S]$ is selected. Reproduction is subsequently applied to the first population member whose fitness, summed with the fitnesses of the preceding population members, is greater than or equal to $u$. Therefore, the chance of a parent being selected for reproduction is directly proportional to its fitness (which is constrained to be positive). Reproduction is carried out until the population size of the next generation is filled.

The resulting population of strings is then modified according to "genetic" operators. The primary operators are bit mutations and one-point crossover. Other forms of crossover, such as two-point or uniform crossover, have been proposed but will not be analyzed from a theoretical perspective here. Experiments with these other operators are detailed later in this chapter. Also, inversion has been suggested as an important genetic operator (Holland, 1975), although "it has not in general been found to be useful in genetic algorithm practice" (Davis, 1991a, p. 21).

There has been some confusion about the specific application of inversion. Holland (1975, p. 107) proposed that inversion merely alters the specific index of the bits in a string, thus the evaluation of the string remains the same (Figure 4-1). But earlier analysis (Martin, 1973) indicated that inversion was proposed as a direct reordering of the bit string. Regardless, as current research in genetic algorithms generally does not employ inversion, it will not be considered here.

Before Inversion: Choose Two Positions, $i$ & $j$

$$x_1^{(1)}\ x_2^{(2)}\ \ldots\ x_i^{(i)}\ x_{i+1}^{(i+1)}\ \ldots\ x_{j-1}^{(j-1)}\ x_j^{(j)}\ \ldots\ x_{k-1}^{(k-1)}\ x_k^{(k)}$$

After Inversion:

$$x_1^{(1)}\ x_2^{(2)}\ \ldots\ x_i^{(j)}\ x_{i+1}^{(j-1)}\ \ldots\ x_{j-1}^{(i+1)}\ x_j^{i}\ \ldots\ x_{k-1}^{(k-1)}\ x_k^{(k)}$$

**Figure 4-1** The inversion operation is applied to a single string and reorders the index of selected positions along the chromosome. In this way, loci that are normally far removed and would have little chance of belonging to a building block can be brought together or *linked*. Crossover would then be applied based on the index values, not the specific location along the chromosome. The superscript in parentheses indicates the index.

Bit mutation is accomplished in one of two methods: by considering each bit of each solution in the population and with a certain probability either (1) flipping it to the complementary value (i.e., changing the bit) or (2) randomly choosing a value with a certain probability (e.g., a 50 percent chance of changing the bit). The probability of bit mutation is generally set at a very small number, say 0.008 (Davis, 1991a, p. 15). Both methods of implementation can be made equivalent by adjusting the mutation rate. Mutation is employed to ensure that all bits have some probability of entering the population.

One-point crossover creates two offspring from two parents. The parents are selected at random (typically in accordance with a uniform distribution[1]), a crossover point, $c_x$, is selected at random (also in accordance with a uniform distribution), and two offspring are made by both concatenating the bits that precede $c_x$ in the first parent with those that follow (and include) $c_x$ in the second parent and performing the obverse operation (Figure 4-2). "Crossover is an extremely important component of a genetic algorithm. Many genetic algorithm practitioners believe that if we delete the crossover operators from a genetic algorithm the result is no

Crossover Point

Parent #1:  1 1 0 1 | 0 1 1 1 1 0 1        Offspring #1:  1 0 1 0 0 1 1 1 1 0 1

→

Parent #2:  1 0 1 0 | 0 0 0 0 1 0 0        Offspring #2:  1 1 0 1 0 0 0 0 1 0 0

**Figure 4-2**  The one-point crossover operator is applied to two parents and creates two offspring. A crossover point is selected, and the sections of the parental strings that precede the crossover point are exchanged.

longer a genetic algorithm" (Davis, 1991a, p. 17). "Genetic algorithm researchers believe that the performance [of evolutionary algorithms not employing crossover] will not be as good, in general, as that of genetic algorithms" (Davis, 1991a, p. 18).

To make room for the new solutions generated through reproduction, mutation, and crossover, solutions are deleted from the population. This

---

[1]Rather than apply crossover after reproduction with emphasis has generated a completely new population, an essentially equivalent procedure could be implemented to create offspring immediately after reproducing each pair of parents.

process is then iterated until the known global optimum solution is discovered or until the available computer time is exhausted.

## 4.2.2 Convergence Properties of Genetic Algorithms

The efficacy of genetic algorithms can be assessed in a variety of ways. One obvious criterion relates to convergence. Holland (1975, pp. 16–17, p. 124) suggested that convergence was not a useful performance measure, noting that there are procedures for searching large finite spaces that converge to global optima but require an excessively long time (e.g., enumeration). Such procedures are generally useless in complex problems. But any optimization algorithm that avoids entrapment in local optima possesses an infinity-to-one speed advantage over a search algorithm that becomes easily entrapped (Atmar, 1990). Holland (1975, p. 104) and other students of genetic algorithms have offered that genetic algorithms do not get entrapped in local optima when further improvements are possible. If this is correct, then convergence should be a useful measure of performance. It should also be a reasonable measure for assessing the efficiency of genetic algorithm approaches in searching complex state spaces and for comparisons to other, more classic methods.

*4.2.2.1 Genetic Algorithms without Bit Mutation.* To provide an initial examination of the convergence properties of a genetic algorithm, consider a state space of possible solutions to be coded as strings of $k$ bits $\{0, 1\}$. Let there be a population of $m$ such bit strings, and let each possible configuration have a fitness $f_i$, $i = 1, \ldots, 2^k$. Let $f^*$ be the globally optimum value. Let a genetic algorithm with only crossover (no inversion or bit mutation) and selection (differential reproduction) operate on the bit strings.

The search can be formulated as a finite-dimension Markov chain (Fogel, 1992, 1994a; others, including Eiben et al., 1991, Davis and Principe, 1994, and Rudolph, 1994a, have also studied genetic algorithms within the framework of Markov chains) (see Goodman, 1988, for a discussion of Markov chains) characterized by a state vector $\pi$ and a transition matrix $P$. Given $\pi$, a row vector describing the probability of being in each state, $\pi P$ yields the probability of being in each state after one transition. Thus the probability of being in each state after $n$ transitions is $\pi P^n$.

For genetic algorithms, the states of the chain can be defined by every possible configuration of an entire population of bit strings. There are $2^{mk}$

such states. For example, if $k = 2$ and $m = 2$, then the following possibilities exist:

$$(00, 00), (00, 01), (00, 10), (00, 11),$$

$$(01, 00), (01, 01), (01, 10), (01, 11),$$

$$(10, 00), (10, 01), (10, 10), (10, 11),$$

$$(11, 00), (11, 01), (11, 10), (11, 11).$$

Each of these 16 collections of pairs of bit strings represents a possible state in the chain. For practical problems, often $m = 100$ and $k > 50$; thus there may be more than $2^{5000}$ possible states in the chain. Yet the chain is of finite dimension and possesses the *time homogeneous* and *no memory* properties required (Goodman, 1988, p. 127).

A Markov chain is said to be *irreducible* if every state communicates with every other state. Two states, $i$ and $j$, are said to *communicate* if there is at least one path from $i$ to $j$ and vice versa. Such a path may require multiple steps (i.e., there exists $P_{ij}^x > 0$, $P_{ji}^y > 0$, for some $0 \le x < M$, $0 \le y < M$, where there are $M$ states and where $P_{ij}$ is the probability of transitioning from state $i$ to state $j$ in one step).

The chain defined by the genetic algorithm with only crossover and selection is not irreducible because there are absorbing states (i.e., states that do not communicate with any other state). Let the only *ergodic* classes (i.e., sets of states from which every path leads to a state in the set) be single absorbing states; no oscillations between states will be considered.

A state in this chain will be absorbing if all the members of the population are identical. Under such conditions, crossing over bit strings in the population simply yields the original population. Otherwise, a state is transient. As time progresses, the behavior of the chain will be described by either (1) a transition to an absorbing state, (2) a transition to a state from which there may be a transition to an absorbing state with some nonzero probability, or (3) a transition to a state from which there is no probability of transitioning to an absorbing state in a single step. Thus the states can be indexed such that the state transition matrix, $P$, for the chain satisfies

$$P = \begin{bmatrix} I_a & 0 \\ R & Q \end{bmatrix} \tag{4-1}$$

where $P$ is the transition matrix, $I_a$ is an $a \times a$ identity matrix describing its absorbing states, $R$ is a $t \times a$ transition submatrix describing transitions to an absorbing state, $Q$ is a $t \times t$ transition submatrix describing transitions to transient states and not to an absorbing state, and $a$ and $t$ are positive integers.

The behavior of such a chain satisfies

$$P^n = \begin{bmatrix} I_a & 0 \\ N_n R & Q^n \end{bmatrix} \qquad (4\text{-}2)$$

where $P^n$ is the $n$-step transition matrix, $N_n = I_t + Q + Q^2 + Q^3 + \ldots + Q^{n-1}$, and $I_t$ is the $t \times t$ identity matrix. As $n$ tends to infinity,

$$\lim_{n \to \infty} P^n = \begin{bmatrix} I_a & 0 \\ (I_t - Q)^{-1} R & 0 \end{bmatrix} \qquad (4\text{-}3)$$

(Goodman, 1988, p. 158). The matrix $(I_t - Q)^{-1}$ is guaranteed to exist (Goodman, 1988, p. 160). Therefore, given infinite time, the chain will transition with probability one to an absorbing state. Note that there is a nonzero probability that the absorbing state may not be the global best state unless all the absorbing states are globally optimal.

The results may be summarized by the following theorem.

**THEOREM.** Let $\Gamma \equiv \{0, 1\}$, $m$ be the number of solutions in $\Gamma^k$ maintained at each iteration, the loss function $L : (\Gamma^k)^m \to \Re_d$, where $\Re_d$ describes the set of real numbers representable in a given digital machine, and $L(\gamma), \gamma \in (\Gamma^k)^m$, be single-valued. After $n$ iterations, the genetic algorithm without bit mutation (see above) arrives at a state $\gamma$:

$$\gamma \in (\Gamma^k)^m \ni Pr\,(\gamma \in A) = \sum_{i=1}^{a} (\pi^* P^n)_i \qquad (4\text{-}4)$$

$$= \sum_{i=1}^{a} \left( \pi^* \begin{bmatrix} I_a \\ N_n R \end{bmatrix} \right)_i \qquad (4\text{-}5)$$

where $(\pi^* P^n)_i$ denotes the $i$th element in the row vector $(\pi^* P^n)$, $A$ is the set of all absorbing states, $\pi^*$ is the row vector describing the initial probability of being in each state, $P$ is the transition matrix defining the Markov chain of the form

$$P = \begin{bmatrix} I_a & 0 \\ R & Q \end{bmatrix}, \tag{4-6}$$

$N_n = I_t + Q + Q^2 + Q^3 + \ldots + Q^{n-1}$, and $I_a$ is an $a \times a$ identity matrix. The limit of the probability of absorption is

$$\lim_{n \to \infty} \sum_{i=1}^{a} \left( \pi^* \begin{bmatrix} I_a \\ N_n R \end{bmatrix} \right)_i = \sum_{i=1}^{a} \left( \pi^* \begin{bmatrix} I_a \\ (I-Q)^{-1} R \end{bmatrix} \right)_i = 1. \tag{4-7}$$

∎

It is natural to examine the number of absorbing states in such a chain. Absorbing states are those in which each bit string in the population is identical. There are $2^k$ such absorbing states. The total number of states is $2^{mk}$, and this leads to two observations: The density of absorbing states decreases exponentially with the length of the bit string (i.e., $2^{k(1-m)}$), but the actual number of absorbing states increases exponentially with the length of the bit string (i.e., $2^k$). For codings other than bit strings, the base of 2 will change but the relationships will not.[2]

Because the chain must eventually transition to an absorbing state under the rules of the transition matrix described above (Eq. 4-3), if the transitions between states are of equal probability, the time required to find an absorbing state may increase exponentially with $k$. When such a state is found, the likelihood of it being a globally optimum state may decrease exponentially with $k$. Of course, for matrices in which the transition probabilities are not equal, as would be the case in practice, the specific entries in each matrix will determine the mean waiting time before absorption and the likelihood of discovering a global optimum versus becoming trapped at a suboptimum. Further, should any particular bit be fixed across the population to a value that is not associated with a global optimum solution, a global optimum will never be discovered.

### 4.2.2.2 Genetic Algorithms with Bit Mutation.
A bit mutation operation is incorporated in genetic algorithms to aid in forestalling the problems of premature convergence associated with the repeated use of crossover. "Mutation is a 'background' operator, assuring that the crossover

---

[2]The order of the elements in the population is generally irrelevant, and the procedure could be perhaps better characterized by describing the states in the chain as unordered multisets. The basic asymptotic convergence properties will remain unchanged under such a description, but the density of absorbing states will increase.

operator has a full range of alleles [i.e., bits] so that the adaptive plan is not trapped on local optima" (Holland, 1975, p. 111). The term *local optima* may be somewhat misleading in this context, however. Typically, a point is locally optimal if no improvement can be made by searching in a nonempty neighborhood around that point. This may not be the case for genetic algorithms relying solely on crossover. The sequence of trials may stagnate anywhere, at any homogeneous collection of points (all identical). Under such conditions, the point is locally optimal only because the search algorithm is incapable of proceeding further. Many researchers (e.g., De Jong, 1975; Baker, 1985; Grefenstette, 1987; Deb and Goldberg, 1989; Davis, 1991a, p. 26) have recognized this problem and some have proposed that to fine tune the search, hill-climbing and other heuristic procedures be employed after execution of a genetic algorithm.

If each bit is given a probability of mutation (i.e., flipping), $p_m \in (0, 1)$, then the absorbing states of the transition matrix defined by the genetic algorithm operating only with crossover that are not globally optimal will become transient. All globally optimal states can be collected and described as a single state. The mean time before entering this state if the chain starts in state $i$ can be calculated by

$$\sum_{j \in T} n_{ij} \qquad (4-8)$$

where $N = (I - Q)^{-1} = [n_{ij}]$, and $T$ is the set of all transient states (Goodman, 1988, p. 161). Thus the specific number of steps taken until reaching a globally optimal state is highly dependent on the characteristics of $P$.

Because the probability for bit mutation is generally very low (e.g., Davis, 1991a, p. 15, suggests a 0.008 probability per bit), this operation may indeed be viewed as a background operator, following Holland (1975, p. 111). It will be likely that the chain of states generated by crossover and bit mutation will generally follow the chain generated by crossover alone, with mutation serving to prevent complete stagnation (Holland, 1975, p. 111). Thus the path is likely to transition to a *metastable state* (an absorbing state of the chain defined by the genetic algorithm relying only on crossover), whereupon it will wait for mutation to affect the appropriate changes of bits of chromosomes in the population and then proceed to another such metastable state, and so forth.

Such transitions may require a very long waiting time, depending on the number of bits that must be flipped simultaneously. The probability of flipping $b$ specific bits in a single chromosome (i.e., a bit string) and not flipping any others is $p_m^b(1 - p_m)^{k-b}$, where $p_m$ is the probability of flipping a single bit. As the length of the codings, $k$, grows longer, the number of metastable states increases exponentially and very long waiting times become virtually certain.

Davis (1991a, p. 26) commented that "when the population has converged on a chromosome that would require mutation of a good many bits to cause any improvement, the run of the genetic algorithm is for all intents and purposes completed. Rather than continuing to run it to no avail, a better usage of computer cycles might be to run the algorithm again using a different random number seed and take the best result, or to use a hill-climbing heuristic to search methodically for improvements." Davis (1991a) edited a compilation of genetic algorithm applications and noted that premature convergence "frequently occurs in runs of the genetic algorithms discussed later in [the] text" (Davis, 1991a, p. 26).

Premature convergence may also be a somewhat misleading term in this context. Rudolph (1994a), using Markov chain analysis, showed that the canonical genetic algorithm (Holland, 1975) is not convergent at all, regardless of the initialization, crossover operator, and objective function: It does not generate a sequence of solutions that converges to any point in the sample space, including any global optima. But the search can easily be made to globally converge by adding *elitist selection*, that is, by incorporating a heuristic to always maintain the best solution in the population into successive generations. Premature convergence merely indicates that the search becomes stagnant for a long and random amount of time.

The specific waiting times in the metastable states are problem-dependent. There may well be problems for which such waiting times are relatively short or for which the paths to metastable states are unlikely. Because it is infeasible to analyze the behavior of individual components in transition matrices that may be larger than $2^{5000} \times 2^{5000}$, the degree to which immensely long waiting times is endemic to genetic algorithms can only be reasonably assessed through experimentation. But premature convergence has been widely observed in genetic algorithm research and should be expected.

### 4.2.3  Minimizing Expected Losses

The search for appropriate solutions may be viewed as a problem of allocating trials in a large state space. To optimally allocate trials, a loss function describing the worth of each trial must be formulated. Holland

(1975, pp. 75–83) examined a simplified sampling problem involving two random variables. This analysis was then extended to sampling from any number of random variables. The results were used to guide the formulation of the genetic algorithm, so it is important to review this analysis and its consequences.

### 4.2.3.1 The Two-Armed Bandit Problem.

For the sake of mathematical tractability, Holland (1975, pp. 75–83) examined the two-armed bandit problem. In this problem, there are two random variables, $RV_1$ and $RV_2$ (representing two slot machines), from which samples may be taken. The two random variables are assumed to be independent and possess some unknown means ($\mu_1$, $\mu_2$) and unknown variances ($\sigma_1^2$, $\sigma_2^2$). A trial is conducted by sampling from a chosen random variable; the result of the trial is the payoff. Suppose that some number of trials has been devoted to each random variable ($n_1$ and $n_2$, respectively) and that the average payoff (the sum of the individual payoffs divided by the number of trials) from one random variable is greater than for the other. Let $RV_{high}$ be the random variable for which the greater average payoff has been observed (not necessarily the random variable with the greater mean), and let $RV_{low}$ be the other random variable. The objective in this problem is to allocate trials to each random variable so as to minimize the expected loss function:

$$L(n_1, n_2) = [q(n_1, n_2)n_1 + (1 - q(n_1, n_2))n_2] \, |\mu_1 - \mu_2| \qquad (4\text{-}9)$$

where $L(n_1, n_2)$ describes the total expected loss from allocating $n_1$ samples to $RV_1$ and $n_2$ samples to $RV_2$ and

$$q(n_1, n_2) = \begin{cases} Pr(\bar{x}_1 > \bar{x}_2), & \text{if } \mu_1 < \mu_2; \\ Pr(\bar{x}_1 < \bar{x}_2), & \text{if } \mu_1 > \mu_2; \end{cases} \qquad (4\text{-}10)$$

where $\bar{x}_1$ and $\bar{x}_2$ designate the mean payoffs (sample means) for having allocated $n_1$ and $n_2$ samples to $RV_1$ and $RV_2$, respectively. Note that specific measurements and the number of samples yield explicit values for the sample means.

As summarized by Goldberg (1989, p. 37), Holland (1975, pp. 77–78) proved the following (notation consistent with Holland, 1975):

THEOREM. Given $N$ trials to be allocated to two random variables with means $\mu_1 > \mu_2$ and variances $\sigma_1^2$ and $\sigma_2^2$, respectively, and with the expected loss function described in Eq. 4-9, the minimum expected loss results when the number of trials allocated to the random variable with the lower observed average payoff is

$$n^* \cong b^2 \ln \left[ \frac{N^2}{8\pi b^4 \ln N^2} \right], \tag{4-11}$$

where $b = \sigma_1/(\mu_1 - \mu_2)$. The number of trials to be allocated to the random variable with the higher observed average payoff is $N - n^*$.    ∎

### 4.2.3.2 Extending the Analysis for Optimally Allocating Trials.

If the assumptions associated with the proof (Holland, 1975, pp. 75–83) hold true, the above analysis will apply equally well to a $k$-armed bandit as to a two-armed bandit. Holland related the preceding analysis to the previously described sampling problem in the following manner. Each bit-string coding is composed of many symbols. Subsets of the complete coding structure can be isolated and analyzed. Let any particular set of strings be identified using symbols from the set {0, 1, #}, where {0, 1} is the alphabet of bits and # is a "don't care" symbol that represents either a 0 or a 1. For example, the set of strings {1##0} includes 1000, 1010, 1100, and 1110. There are many such sets of strings (each being termed a *schema*), and each may be viewed as a distribution from which samples may be drawn. The worth of any particular schema may be described as the average of the worth of all complete strings contained in the schema. Holland (1975, p. 71) speculated that bit strings would provide the optimal representation for problems addressed by a genetic algorithm because the greatest number of schemata are created when a problem is coded as a string of bits {0, 1}.

Holland likened the problem of minimizing expected losses while sampling from $k$-armed bandits to the problem of minimizing expected losses while sampling from the various schemata. From the previous analysis, it was proposed that to allocate trials among the competing schemata in each solution optimally, an exponential amount of attention (in terms of reproductive emphasis) should be devoted to the observed best solutions so as to minimize the expected losses while sampling over all schemata.

It has been widely asserted (e.g., Holland, 1975, pp. 102–103; Davis, 1991a, pp. 19–20) that if the number of copies of a solution composed of independent schemata is made proportional to its fitness (reproduction with emphasis), then the relative increase or decrease of the frequency of any schema, $s$, in that solution follows the relationship

$$E(s) = \frac{m_s f_s}{f_m} - d, \qquad (4\text{-}12)$$

where $E(s)$ is the expected number of solutions in the population containing $s$, $m_s$ is the current number of solutions in the population containing $s$, $f_s$ is the mean fitness of all solutions in the population that contain $s$, $f_m$ is the average fitness of all solutions in the population, and $d$ is a residual effect of "disruption" caused by crossover and mutation. This result is known as the *schema theorem.* "In effect, the schema theorem says that a schema occurring in a chromosome with above-average evaluations will tend to occur more frequently in the next generation, and one occurring with below-average evaluations will tend to occur less frequently (ignoring the effects of mutation and crossover)" (Davis, 1991a, p. 20).

### 4.2.3.3 Limitations of the Analysis.
One important drawback to the analysis of the optimal allocation of trials is that it only describes how to allocate trials to minimize expected losses when independent samples are drawn from the random variables. Even if the schemata were in fact random variables (in many cases they are not), most genetic algorithms employ coding strings such that schemata are not sampled independently (see Davis, 1985). Moreover, there may be very few samples of any particular schema, lower than required for the central limit theorem arguments made to justify the analysis in Holland (1975). Strictly, it is difficult to prove that the optimal allocation of trials (Holland, 1975, pp. 75–83) applies to most genetic algorithm applications.

Moreover, the utility of minimizing expected losses in this sampling problem may be questioned. Such a criterion may preclude the discovery of a globally optimal solution. Consider two random variables with corresponding distributions of the worth of their various members of a given schema, as depicted in Figure 4-3. The first distribution has mean $\mu_1$ and variance $\sigma_1^2$ while the second distribution has mean $\mu_2 < \mu_1$ and variance $\sigma_2^2 \gg \sigma_1^2$. To minimize the expected loss (Eq. 4-9), all trials should be devoted to the first distribution because it has the larger mean. This in turn precludes the discovery of the best string, because it is a member of the second distribution. Identifying a schema with above-average performance does not, in general, provide information about which particular complete solution, which may be described by very many schemata, has the greatest fitness. The single solution with the greatest fitness (i.e., the globally optimal solution) may be described in schemata with below-average per-

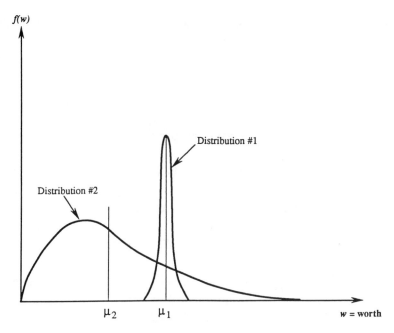

**Figure 4-3**  Minimizing expected losses does not always correspond to maximizing potential gains. The illustration depicts two distributions of the fitness of various strings contained within each schema (typically viewed as random variables). Although the mean of the first distribution is greater than the second, strings with greater fitness reside in the second. To minimize expected losses, trials should be devoted to the first distribution, which thereby precludes discovering the global best string.

formance. The criterion of minimizing expected losses is quite conservative and may prevent successful optimization.

## 4.3  THEORETICAL ANALYSIS OF EVOLUTIONARY ALGORITHMS

### 4.3.1  Detailing the Evolutionary Algorithm

To provide a suitable mathematical analysis of evolutionary algorithms, including evolution strategies and evolutionary programming, a very broad class of optimization problems should be studied. The problem studied here will be that of discovering a real-valued vector that is associated with the extremum of a functional, $F$:

$$F: \Re^n \to \Re.$$

The coding for this class of function optimization problems will naturally be taken as a vector in $\Re^n$. Unlike genetic algorithms, which generally operate on a bit-string coding of the parameter set rather than on the parameters themselves (Goldberg and Kuo, 1987) (although this restriction is being relaxed in genetic algorithm applications, Davis, 1991a), evolution strategies and evolutionary programming generally impose no restrictions on the coding that may be employed for a specific optimization task. Attention will first be given to the basic asymptotic convergence properties of evolutionary programming (Fogel, 1992, 1994a), although the results also extend to evolution strategies.

Fogel (1991, pp. 45–46) outlined an evolutionary programming procedure for real-valued function optimization. This is described here with only a minor difference in the competition rules as taken from Fogel (1991, p. 116). The task is function minimization. Evolutionary programming is conducted as a sequence of operations.

1. The initial population is determined by setting $s_i = S_i \sim U(a_k, b_k)^k$ $i = 1, \ldots, m$, where $S_i$ is a random vector, $s_i$ is the outcome of the random vector, $U(a_k, b_k)^k$ denotes a uniform distribution ranging over $[a_k, b_k]$ in each of $k$ dimensions, and $m$ is the number of parents.

2. Each $s_i$, $i = 1, \ldots, m$, is assigned a fitness score $\vartheta(s_i) = G(F(s_i), v_i)$, where $F$ maps $s_i \to \Re$ and denotes the true fitness of $s_i$, $v_i$ represents random alteration in the instantiation of $s_i$, random variation imposed on the evaluation of $F(s_i)$, or satisfies another relation with $s_i$, and $G(F(s_i), v_i)$ describes the fitness score to be assigned. In general, the functions $F$ and $G$ can be as complex as required. For example, $F$ may be a function not only of a particular $s_i$, but of other members of the population, conditioned on a particular $s_i$.

3. Each $s_i$, $i = 1, \ldots, m$, is altered and assigned to $s_{i+m}$ such that

$$s_{i+m,j} = s_{i,j} + N(0, \beta_j \vartheta(s_i) + z_j), \quad j = 1, \ldots, k,$$

where $s_{i,j}$ denotes the $j$th element of the $i$th individual, $N(\mu,\sigma^2)$ represents a Gaussian random variable with mean $\mu$ and variance $\sigma^2$, $\beta_j$ is a constant of proportionality to scale $\vartheta(s_i)$, and $z_j$ represents an offset to guarantee a minimum amount of variance.

4. Each $s_{i+m}$, $i = 1, \ldots , m$, is assigned a fitness score

$$\vartheta(s_{i+m}) = G(F(s_{i+m}), v_{i+m}).$$

5. For each $s_i$, $i = 1, \ldots , 2m$, a value $w_i$ is assigned according to

$$w_i = \sum_{t=1}^{c} w_t^*$$

$$w_t^* = \begin{cases} 1, & \text{if } \vartheta(s_i) \le \vartheta(s_\rho); \\ 0, & \text{otherwise}; \end{cases}$$

where $\rho = [2mu_1 + 1]$, $\rho \ne i$, $[x]$ denotes the greatest integer less than or equal to $x$, $c$ is the number of competitions, and $u_1 \sim U(0, 1)$.

6. The solutions $s_i$, $i = 1, \ldots , 2m$, are ranked in descending order of their corresponding value $w_i$ [with preference to their actual scores $\vartheta(s_i)$ if there are more than $m$ solutions attaining a value of $c$]. The first $m$ solutions are transcribed along with their corresponding values $\vartheta(s_i)$ to be the basis of the next generation.

7. The process proceeds to step 3 unless the available execution time is exhausted or an acceptable solution has been discovered.

Various modifications of this routine are considered later in this chapter.

### 4.3.2 Analyzing the Evolutionary Algorithm as a Markov Chain

The basic asymptotic convergence properties of the preceding evolutionary algorithm can be easily developed by imposing some simplifications. To begin, let $\beta_j = 1$ and $z_j = 0$, $j = 1, \ldots , k$. Let the algorithm use $G(F(s_i), v_i) = F(s_i) > 0$, that is, no random perturbation will be imposed on the response surface and the surface is positive. This latter restriction is only for convenience; the following analysis will hold for nonpositive response surfaces if alternative settings are made for $\beta_j$ and $z_j$. Let $1 \leq c < 2m$. Let each $[a_k, b_k]$ be a finite-length discretized interval in $\Re$, and let $m$ be finite. Further, as the algorithm must be implemented on a computer, let any continuous Gaussian random variable with mean $\mu$ and variance $\sigma^2$ be discretized such that all possible values in the range of the computer have nonzero probability. As before with the genetic algorithm, the evolutionary algorithm can now be viewed as a finite-dimensional Markov chain.

The states of the Markov chain again comprise the entire collection of vectors in the population. The components of the vectors are no longer bits $\{0, 1\}$ but rather discretized real numbers. For instance, if $a_1 = 0$, $a_2 = 0$, $b_1 = 1$, $b_2 = 1$, $k = 2$, and $m = 2$, then two possible instances of states in the chain are

$$(0, 0; 1, 1), (0.1, 0.523; 0.7, 0.003).$$

By the competition and selection rules in steps 5 and 6, the best vector in the population will always be retained during selection. Form an equivalence class of all states that contain a global best vector, and describe this class as a single state. For example, if the global optimum is uniquely $(0, 0)$, then all collections of vectors containing $(0, 0)$ are characterized as the same state. The Markov chain may then be written in the form

$$P_{EA} = \begin{bmatrix} 1 & 0 \\ R & Q \end{bmatrix} \tag{4-13}$$

where $P_{EA}$ is the transition matrix, 1 is a $1 \times 1$ identity matrix describing the absorbing state, $R$ is a strictly positive (all entries are greater than zero) $t \times 1$ transition submatrix, $Q$ is a $t \times t$ transition submatrix, and $t$ is a positive integer. The state containing global optima is the only absorbing state, and all other states are transient.

Asymptotic global convergence of the evolutionary algorithm is then transparent because every absorbing chain will reach an absorbing state, and in this case there is just one such state. Further, the matrix $P_{EA}$ is a special case of the matrix in Eq. 4-1:

$$P = \begin{bmatrix} I_a & 0 \\ R & Q \end{bmatrix} \tag{4-14}$$

It has already been shown (Eq. 4-2) that a Markov chain described by $P$ will proceed as

$$P^n = \begin{bmatrix} I_a & 0 \\ N_n R & Q^n \end{bmatrix} \qquad (4\text{-}15)$$

Thus (as in Eq. 4-3)

$$\lim_{n \to \infty} P^n_{EA} = \begin{bmatrix} 1 & 0 \\ (I_t - Q)^{-1} R & 0 \end{bmatrix} \qquad (4\text{-}16)$$

Therefore, the probability of absorption (that is, the probability of discovering a global optimum solution) for the chain with transition matrix $P_{EA}$ increases over $n$ steps as a geometric series $(N_n R)$ converging to 1.0. This result can be summarized in the following theorem.

THEOREM.    Let $\Gamma \equiv \mathfrak{R}_d$ the set of elements of $\mathfrak{R}$ representable in a given digital machine, $m$ be the number of maintained solutions, $L : (\Gamma^k)^m \to \Gamma$ be the loss function, and $L(\gamma)$, $\gamma \in (\Gamma^k)^m$, be single valued. Then, after $n$ iterations, the evolutionary algorithm arrives at a state:

$$\gamma \in (\Gamma^k)^m \ni Pr(\gamma \in A) = (\pi^* P^n_{EA})_1 = \pi^* \begin{bmatrix} 1 \\ N_n R \end{bmatrix} \qquad (4\text{-}17)$$

where the subscript 1 denotes the first entry in the row vector $(\pi^* P^n_{EA})$, $A$ is the singleton set containing the absorbing state, $\pi^*$ is the $1 \times (t + 1)$ row vector describing the initial probability of being in each state, $P_{EA}$ is the transition matrix defining the Markov chain, of the form

$$P_{EA} = \begin{bmatrix} 1 & 0 \\ R & Q \end{bmatrix}, \qquad (4\text{-}18)$$

and $N_n = I_t + Q + Q^2 + Q^3 + \ldots + Q^{n-1}$.

Furthermore, the limit of the probability of absorption is:

$$\lim_{n\to\infty} \pi^* \begin{bmatrix} 1 \\ N_n R \end{bmatrix} = \pi^* \begin{bmatrix} 1 \\ \cdot \\ \cdot \\ \cdot \\ 1 \end{bmatrix} = \sum_{i=1}^{t+1} \pi_i^* = 1. \tag{4-19}$$

■

This theorem directly indicates a convergence in probability, but can be extended to imply convergence with probability one. Convergence in probability sufficiently fast implies convergence with probability one (Serfling, 1980, p. 10). More specifically, given a sequence $x_n$, if

$$\sum_{n=1}^{\infty} Pr\left(|x_n - x| > \varepsilon\right) < \infty \quad \text{for every } \varepsilon > 0, \tag{4-20}$$

then $x_n$ converges with probability one to $x$ ($x_n \overset{wp1}{\to} x$).

This result can be applied to obtain the following theorem.

THEOREM. Given a $(t+1) \times (t+1)$ state transition matrix of the form $P_{EA}$ (Eq. 4-13), where there is a single absorbing state and $t$ transient states, and an initial $1 \times (t+1)$ state probability row vector $\pi^*$ describing a Markov chain, let $\pi_t^*$ be the $1 \times t$ row vector describing the probability of starting in each of the transient states. Form the sequence

$$x_n(\omega) = \begin{cases} 1, & \text{if the chain has reached the absorbing} \\ & \text{state by the } n\text{th iteration;} \\ 0, & \text{otherwise.} \end{cases}$$

The sequence $x_n(\omega) \overset{wp1}{\to} 1$.

*PROOF*

Consider the two cases (1) $n = 0$ or $n = 1$ and (2) $n \geq 2$.

1. The probability of arriving at the absorbing state by the zeroth or first iteration is simply $\pi^* \begin{bmatrix} 1 \\ R \end{bmatrix} = p_a$.

2.  To analyze the sequence for $n \geq 2$, it is useful to note the following. For $\mathbf{v}Q^m \neq 0$, where $Q$ is a $t \times t$ substochastic matrix (Eq. 4-13), $\mathbf{v}$ is a $1 \times t$ row vector, $\mathbf{v} \neq 0$, $v_i \geq 0 \ \forall \ i = 1, \ldots, t$, $\forall \ m = 0, 1, 2, \ldots$ ($\mathbf{v}Q^m = 0$ indicates $x_n(\omega) \overset{wp1}{\rightarrow} 1$, trivially), since $q_{ij} < 1$,

$$\left\| \frac{\mathbf{v}}{\|\mathbf{v}\|_1} \cdot Q \right\|_2 < \left\| \frac{\mathbf{v}}{\|\mathbf{v}\|_1} \cdot Q \right\|_1 \tag{4-21}$$

$$= \|\boldsymbol{\pi} Q\|_1, \quad \boldsymbol{\pi} = \frac{\mathbf{v}}{\|\mathbf{v}\|_1} \tag{4-22}$$

$$= \sum_{i=1}^{t} \pi_i \sum_{j=1}^{t} q_{ij} \tag{4-23}$$

$$\leq \sum_{i=1}^{t} \pi_i \max_i \sum_{j=1}^{t} q_{ij} \tag{4-24}$$

$$= \max_i \sum_{j=1}^{t} q_{ij} \tag{4-25}$$

$$= \gamma \tag{4-26}$$

$$< 1. \tag{4-27}$$

Hence, $\forall \ n \geq 2, \boldsymbol{\pi}_t^* \neq 0, \pi_{t_i}^* \geq 0 \ \forall \ i = 1, \ldots, t$, and $\varepsilon > 0$,

$$P(|\ x_n(\omega) - 1\ | > \varepsilon) = P(x_n(\omega) \neq 1) \tag{4-28}$$

$$= \boldsymbol{\pi}_t^* Q^n \begin{bmatrix} 1 \\ \cdot \\ \cdot \\ \cdot \\ 1 \end{bmatrix}. \tag{4-29}$$

Therefore,

$$\sum_{n=2}^{\infty} P(x_n(\omega) \neq 1) = \sum_{n=2}^{\infty} \pi_t^* Q^n \begin{bmatrix} 1 \\ \cdot \\ \cdot \\ \cdot \\ 1 \end{bmatrix}. \tag{4-30}$$

$$= \sum_{n=2}^{\infty} \left\| \pi_t^* Q^n \begin{bmatrix} 1 \\ \cdot \\ \cdot \\ \cdot \\ 1 \end{bmatrix} \right\|_2 \tag{4-31}$$

$$\leq \sum_{n=2}^{\infty} \| \pi_t^* Q^n \|_2 \sqrt{t} \quad \text{(Cauchy–Schwarz inequality)} \tag{4-32}$$

$$= \sum_{n=2}^{\infty} \| \pi_t^* Q^{n-1} Q \|_2 \sqrt{t} \tag{4-33}$$

$$= \sum_{n=2}^{\infty} \| \pi_t^* Q^{n-1} \|_1 \left\| \frac{\pi_t^* Q^{n-1}}{\| \pi_t^* Q^{n-1} \|_1} \cdot Q \right\|_2 \sqrt{t} \tag{4-34}$$

$$\leq \sum_{n=2}^{\infty} \| \pi_t^* Q^{n-1} \|_1 \cdot \gamma \cdot \sqrt{t}, \quad 0 \leq \gamma < 1 \tag{4-35}$$

$$= \sum_{n=2}^{\infty} \| \pi_t^* Q^{n-2} \|_1 \left\| \frac{\pi^* Q^{n-2}}{\| \pi_t^* Q^{n-2} \|_1} \cdot Q \right\|_1 \cdot \gamma \cdot \sqrt{t} \tag{4-36}$$

$$\leq \sum_{n=2}^{\infty} \| \pi_t^* Q^{n-2} \|_1 \cdot \gamma^2 \cdot \sqrt{t} \tag{4-37}$$

$$\leq \sum_{n=2}^{\infty} \| \pi_t^* \|_1 \cdot \gamma^n \cdot \sqrt{t} \tag{4-38}$$

$$\leq \sum_{n=2}^{\infty} K \gamma^n \tag{4-39}$$

$$< \infty. \qquad \blacksquare$$

This result also implies a stronger *complete convergence* (Hsu and Robbins, 1947; cf. *convergence everywhere*, Papoulis, 1984, p. 189).

### 4.3.3  Convergence Rates for Evolutionary Algorithms

Although the above analysis indicates asymptotic global convergence of evolutionary algorithms, it is far more important to assess the rate of convergence in specific problems. The most insightful theoretical analyses of evolutionary algorithms have been contributed by German researchers in evolution strategies (e.g., Rechenberg, 1973; Schwefel, 1981; Bäck et al., 1991; Bäck et al., 1993). Many of these results carry over to evolutionary programming and other stochastic optimization techniques; they have also provided a framework for improving these procedures (Rudolph, 1994b).

The most simple evolution strategy for real-valued continuous optimization problems, described as a (1+1)–ES, starts with a single parent, $x$, creates a single offspring, $x'$, from this parent by imposing a multivariate Gaussian perturbation with mean zero and standard deviation $\sigma$ to the parent, and then selects the better of the two trial solutions as the parent for the next iteration. This is essentially equivalent to the evolutionary algorithm described on pages 136–137 with $m = 1$ and without the inclusion of any stochastic competition (step five in the algorithm).

The same standard deviation $\sigma$ is applied to each component of the vector $x$ during mutation. For some problems, the variation of $\sigma$ (i.e., the step-size control parameter in each dimension) can be computed to yield an optimal rate of convergence. Let the convergence rate be defined as the ratio of the Euclidean distance covered toward the optimum solution to the number of trials required to achieve the improvement. Rechenberg (1973) calculated the convergence rates for two functions:

$$f_1(x) = F(x_1) = c_0 + c_1 x_1, \forall i \in \{2, \ldots, n\} : \frac{-b}{2} \le x_i \le \frac{b}{2} \qquad (4\text{-}40)$$

$$f_2(x) = \sum_{i=1}^{n} x_i^2 \qquad (4\text{-}41)$$

where $x = (x_1, \ldots, x_n)^T \in \Re^n$, and where to remain consistent with notation in Rechenberg (1973) $n$ is now the number of dimensions. Function $f_1$ is termed the *corridor model* and represents a linear function with inequality constraints. Improvement is accomplished by moving along the first axis of the search space inside a corridor of width $b$. Function $f_2$ is termed the *sphere model* and is a simple $n$-dimensional quadratic bowl.

The expected rates of convergence, $\varphi_1$ and $\varphi_2$, for $f_1$ and $f_2$ (Rechenberg, 1973) are

$$\varphi_1 = \sigma(2\pi)^{-0.5}[1 - (2/\pi)^{0.5}(\sigma/b)]^{n-1}, \quad n \gg 1 \tag{4-42}$$

$$\varphi_2 = \sigma(2\pi)^{-0.5} \exp\left[-\left(\frac{n\sigma}{r\sqrt{8}}\right)\right]^2$$

$$- \sigma(2\pi)^{-0.5}\left(\sqrt{\pi}\left[\frac{n\sigma}{r\sqrt{8}}\right]\left\{1 - \mathrm{erf}\left[\frac{n\sigma}{r\sqrt{8}}\right]\right\}\right), \quad n \gg 1 \tag{4-43}$$

where $\mathrm{erf}(x)$ refers to the error function and $r$ refers to the distance from the optimum solution. By taking the derivatives of $\varphi_1$ and $\varphi_2$ with respect to $\sigma$, setting them equal to zero, and solving for $\sigma$, the optimum settings for the standard deviation to use, and the optimum rates of convergence, can be calculated as

$$\sigma_1^{\mathrm{opt}} = \left(\frac{\pi}{2}\right)^{0.5}\left(\frac{b}{n}\right); \quad \varphi_1^{\mathrm{max}} = (2e)^{-1}\left(\frac{b}{n}\right) \tag{4-44}$$

$$\sigma_2^{\mathrm{opt}} = 1.224\left(\frac{r}{n}\right); \quad \varphi_2^{\mathrm{max}} = 0.2025\left(\frac{r}{n}\right) \tag{4-45}$$

The optimum convergence rate is obtained for both functions when the standard deviation for the multivariate Gaussian perturbation is inversely proportional to the dimension $n$. Further, the maximum rate of convergence is also inversely proportional to $n$.

Given the optimum standard deviations, the optimum probability of generating a successful mutation can be calculated as

$$p_1^{\mathrm{opt}} = (2e)^{-1} \approx 0.184 \tag{4-46}$$

$$p_2^{\mathrm{opt}} \approx 0.270. \tag{4-47}$$

Rechenberg (1973), noting the similarity of these two values, suggested the following rule.

*The ratio of successful mutations to all mutations should be 1/5. If this ratio is greater than 1/5, increase the variance; if it is less, decrease the variance.*

Schwefel (1981) suggested measuring the success probability on-line over $10n$ trials (where there are $n$ dimensions) and adjusting $\sigma$ at iteration $t$ by:

$$\sigma(t) = \begin{cases} \sigma(t-n) \cdot \delta, & \text{if } p_s < 0.2; \\ \sigma(t-n)/\delta, & \text{if } p_s > 0.2; \\ \sigma(t-n), & \text{if } p_s = 0.2; \end{cases} \qquad (4\text{-}48)$$

with $\delta = 0.85$ and $p_s$ equaling the number of successes in $10n$ trials divided by $10n$, which yields convergence rates of geometric order for both $f_1$ and $f_2$ (Bäck et al., 1993; see Bäck, 1994 for corrections to the update rule offered in Bäck et al., 1993).

Schwefel (1977, 1981) introduced the population-based evolution strategies, described by $(\mu+\lambda)$–ES and $(\mu, \lambda)$–ES. In the former, $\mu$ parents create $\lambda$ offspring, and the best $\mu$ solutions from among all $\mu + \lambda$ are selected to become parents of the next generation. In the latter, the best $\mu$ solutions are selected only from the $\lambda$ offspring. Each solution is characterized not only by an $n$-dimensional vector of object variables $\mathbf{x}$, but by potentially as many as $n(n + 1)/2$ additional mutation parameters, which may include up to $n$ different variances $c_{ii} = \sigma_i^2 (i \in \{1, \ldots, n\})$ as well as up to $n(n - 1)/2$ covariances $c_{ij}$ $(i \in \{1, \ldots, n - 1\}, j \in \{i + 1, \ldots, n\}$, $c_{ij} = c_{ji})$ describing an $n$-dimensional Gaussian random vector with probability density function

$$p(\mathbf{z}) = \frac{\exp(-0.5\mathbf{z}'C^{-1}\mathbf{z})}{\sqrt{(2\pi)^n |C|}}. \qquad (4\text{-}49)$$

For convenience in ensuring that $C^{-1}$ remains positive definite, the algorithm operates on equivalent rotation angles $\alpha_l$ $(0 \leq \alpha_l < 2\pi)$, $l \in \{1, \ldots, n(n-1)/2\}$, rather than directly on the coefficients $c_{ij}$. The algorithm is cumbersome to explicate in the form of pages 136–137, but in pseudocode becomes

$t = 0$;

*initialize* $P(0) = \{a_1(0), \ldots, a_\mu(0)\}$

    where $a_i(0) = (\mathbf{x}_i(0), \sigma_i(0), \alpha_i(0))$,

    $\mathbf{x}_i(0) \in \Re^n, \sigma_i(0) \in \Re^{+n}, \alpha_i(0) \in [0,2\pi)^{n(n-1)/2}, i = 1, \ldots, \mu$;

*evaluate* $P(0)$;

**while** *termination criterion not fulfilled* **do**

       *recombine*: $a_i'(t) = r(P(t)), i = 1, \ldots, \lambda$;

       *mutate*: $a_i''(t) = m(a_i'(t)), i = 1, \ldots, \lambda$;

       *evaluate*: $P'(t) = \{a_1''(t), \ldots, a_\lambda''(t)\}$;

       /* yields $\{f(\mathbf{x}_1''(t), \ldots, f(\mathbf{x}_\lambda''(t))\}$ */

       *select* $P(t + 1) =$

          $s_{(\mu,\lambda)}(P'(t))$ if $(\mu,\lambda)$–ES

          $s_{(\mu+\lambda)}(P'(t) \cup P(t))$ if $(\mu+\lambda)$–ES;

       $t = t + 1$;

**od**

The mutation operator is extended (without referring to the time counter $t$) as

$$m(a_k) = a_k' = (\mathbf{x}', \sigma', \alpha') \tag{4-50}$$

with each operation as follows:

$$\sigma_i' = \sigma_i \cdot \exp(\tau_0 \cdot \Delta\sigma_0) \cdot \exp(\tau \cdot \Delta\sigma_i) \tag{4-51}$$

$$\alpha_j' = \alpha_j + \beta \cdot \Delta\alpha_j \tag{4-52}$$

$$x_i' = x_i + z_i(\sigma', \alpha'). \tag{4-53}$$

with $i = 1, \ldots, n, j = 1, \ldots, n(n-1)/2$.

The mutations of the object variables, $\mathbf{x}$, are correlated according to the pairwise rotation vector $\alpha'$ and scaling vector $\sigma'$. Alterations $\Delta\sigma_0$, $\Delta\sigma_i$, and $\Delta\alpha_j$ are again standard Gaussian random variables, and the constants $\tau \propto 1/\sqrt{2\sqrt{n}}$, $\tau_0 \propto 1/\sqrt{2n}$, and $\beta \approx 0.0873$ (5°) as suggested by Bäck et al. (1993) are robust to diverse response surfaces. A global scaling that affects all $\sigma_i, i \in \{1, \ldots, n\}$, is $\Delta\sigma_0$ scaled by $\tau_0$, while $\Delta\sigma_i$ is recalculated for each $i \in \{1, \ldots, n\}$, allowing for individual changes to the mean step sizes $\sigma_i$.

Recombination can be implemented in many ways. Bäck et al. (1993) suggest the following methods, which are described for object variables, but they can also be applied to mutation strategy variables:

$$x'_i = \begin{cases} x_{S,i} & (1) \\ x_{S,i} \quad \text{or} \quad x_{T,i} & (2) \\ x_{S,i} + u(x_{T,i} - x_{S,i}) & (3) \\ x_{S_i,i} \quad \text{or} \quad x_{T_i,i} & (4) \\ x_{S_i,i} + u_i(x_{T_i,i} - x_{S_i,i}) & (5), \end{cases} \qquad (4\text{-}54)$$

where $S$ and $T$ denote two arbitrary parents, $u$ is a uniform random variable over the interval $[0, 1]$ and the different variations are (1) no recombination; (2) discrete recombination; (3) intermediate recombination; and the global versions (4) and (5) of (2) and (3), respectively, in which any two parents can contribute to each $x'_i$. The utility of these operations is highly problem-dependent. The discrete or intermediate recombination of object (pheno-typic) variables, as opposed to the mutation (genotypic) parameters, is not appropriate from an evolutionary perspective because it implicitly assumes a one-gene/one-trait relationship between the genotype and phenotype, or a blending system, and neither of these characteristics adequately describes natural evolved systems. But such considerations are irrelevant from a purely engineering perspective.

ES-type algorithms can be shown to have geometric convergence rates on certain response surfaces (Bäck et al., 1993). The actual rate varies by problem and appropriate analysis requires restricting attention to specific surfaces (e.g., strongly convex surfaces). Consider the following definitions with notation from Bäck et al. (1993):

**DEFINITION 1.**   A random vector $\mathbf{z}$ of dimension $n$ is said to possess an *elliptical distribution* iff it has stochastic representation $\mathbf{z} = rA'\mathbf{u}$, where the random vector $\mathbf{u}$ is uniformly distributed on a hypersphere surface of dimension $n$, stochastically independent to a nonnegative random variable $r$, and where the matrix $A : k \times n$ with rank $(A'A) = k$. If $A : n \times n$ and $A = I$, then $\mathbf{z}$ is said to possess a *spherical (symmetric) distribution*. If $\mathbf{z}$ is used to describe the mutation probability density function and is chosen to be a multivariate normal random variable with zero mean and covariance $C = \sigma^2 I$, then the step size $r$ has a central $\chi_n(\sigma)$-distribution (Fang et al., 1990; Bäck et al., 1993). If the matrix $A$ and the distribution of $r$ are fixed during the optimization, the evolution strategy may be said to have a *stationary* step-size distribution; otherwise the distribution is described as being *adaptive*.

**DEFINITION 2.**    The value $\delta_t \equiv E[f(X_t) - f^*]$, where $X_t$ is the stochastic process defining the sequence of trial solutions and $f^*$ is the minimum value of the function $f$, is said to be the *expected error* at step $t$. An algorithm has a *sublinear convergence* rate iff $\delta_t = O(t^{-b})$ with $b > 0$ and a *geometric convergence rate* iff $\delta_t = O(r^t)$ with $r \in (0, 1)$.

**DEFINITION 3.**    A function $f : \Re^n \to \Re$ is said to be $(l, Q)$-*strongly convex* iff it is continuously differentiable and with some constants $l > 0$, $Q \geq 1$ there holds

$$l \cdot \|x - y\|^2 \leq (\nabla f(x) - \nabla f(y))'(x - y) \leq Ql \cdot \|x - y\|^2$$

for all $x, y \in M_F$, where $\nabla f$ denotes the gradient of $f$ and $M_F$ denotes the feasible region for $x$ and $y$.

The following theorem can now be stated by applying the above definitions.

**THEOREM.**    Let $f$ be a $(l, Q)$-strongly convex function and $z \equiv r\mathbf{u}$, where $r$ has nonvoid support $(0, a) \subseteq \Re$. Then the expected error of a $(1+1)$–ES decreases for any starting point $x_0 \in M_F$ with the following rates:

$$E[f(X_t) - f^*] \leq \begin{cases} O(t^{-2/n}), & \text{stationary step-size distribution;} \\ O(\beta^t), & \text{adapted step-size distribution;} \end{cases}$$

with $\beta \in (0, 1)$.    ∎

To ensure geometric convergence, the step sizes $R$ can be adjusted by choosing $R(t + 1) = \zeta \|\nabla f(x(t))\| \cdot R(t)$, $\zeta > 0$. Alternatively, the procedure offered by Rappl (1984), in which the step size is decreased by a factor $\gamma_1 \in (0, 1)$ if the trial solution is worse than the parent and increased by a factor $\gamma_2 > 1$ if the trial solution is better than the parent, can be guaranteed to yield geometrical convergence for $\gamma_1 \cdot \gamma_2 > 1$ (Bäck et al., 1993).

Bäck et al. (1993) provided a simple example. Let $f(x) = \|x\|^2$ with $M_F = \Re^n$. It is clear then that $f$ is $(2, 1)$-strongly convex:

$$(\nabla f(x) - \nabla f(y))'(x - y) = 2\|x - y\|^2. \tag{4-55}$$

If $z$, the mutation vector, is Gaussian with zero mean and covariance $C = \sigma^2 I$, the distribution of objective values follows:

$$f(\mathbf{x}(t) + \mathbf{z}(t)) \sim \sigma^2 \chi_n^2(\kappa), \tag{4-56}$$

where $\chi_n^2(\kappa)$ is a noncentral $\chi^2$-distribution with $n$ degrees of freedom and noncentrality parameter $\kappa = \|\mathbf{x}(t)\|^2/\sigma^2$. By Johnson and Kotz (1970, p. 135):

$$\frac{\chi_n^2(\kappa) - (n + \kappa)}{(2(n + 2\kappa))^{0.5}} \to N \sim N(0, 1) \tag{4-57}$$

for $n \to \infty$. The relative variation of the objective function, $V$, can therefore be approximated as:

$$V \equiv \frac{f(\mathbf{x}(t)) - f(\mathbf{x}(t + 1))}{f(\mathbf{x}(t))} \tag{4-58}$$

$$\sim 1 - \frac{\sigma^2}{\|\mathbf{x}(t)\|^2} \chi_n^2(\kappa) \tag{4-59}$$

$$\to 1 - \frac{\sigma^2}{\|\mathbf{x}(t)\|^2} (n + \kappa + (2n + 4\kappa)^{0.5}N) \tag{4-60}$$

$$= -\frac{s^2}{n} - \frac{s^2}{n} \left( \frac{2}{n} + \frac{4}{s^2} \right)^{0.5} N \tag{4-61}$$

$$\approx -\frac{s^2}{n} - \frac{2s}{n} N \tag{4-62}$$

where $\sigma = s\|\mathbf{x}(t)\|/n$. As the $(1+1)$–ES only accepts improvements, attention can be restricted to the expectation of the random variable $V^+ = \max \{0, V\}$:

$$E[V^+] = \int_0^\infty \frac{nu}{2s\sqrt{2\pi}} \cdot \exp\left[ -0.5\left( \frac{nu+s^2}{2s} \right)^2 \right] du \tag{4-63}$$

$$= (1/n)\left( s(2/\pi)^{0.5}\exp\left( \frac{-s^2}{8} \right) - s^2\left[ 1 - \Phi\left( \frac{s}{2} \right) \right] \right) \tag{4-64}$$

where $u$ is a variable of integration and $\Phi(.)$ denotes the cumulative distribution function (c.d.f.) of a standard normal random variable. The expectation is maximized for $s^* = 1.224$ (see Figure 4-4) such that $E[V^+] = 0.405/n$ and $\sigma^* = (1.224/n)\sqrt{f(\mathbf{x})} = (0.612/n)\|\nabla f(\mathbf{x})\|$. The latter description

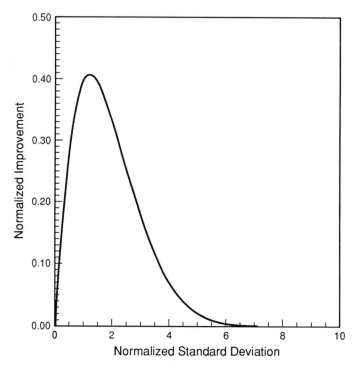

**Figure 4-4**  The normalized expected improvement $nE[V^+]$ plotted as a function of the normalized standard deviation $s = n\sigma/f(x_i)^{0.5}$. The expected improvement is maximized for $s^* = 1.224$. (After Bäck et al., 1993.)

is more general and will hold for any $f(\mathbf{x}) = \|\mathbf{x} + \mathbf{c}_1\|^2 + c_2$, where $\mathbf{c}_1 \in \mathfrak{R}^n$, $c_2 \in \mathfrak{R}$.

This convergence rate can be improved by generating multiple solutions from each parent. Schwefel (1977, 1981) considered the convergence properties of the $(1+\lambda)$–ES. First, $\lambda$ independent trials are generated from the best solution of the previous generation, and then the best of those trials is taken to be the new parent if it outperforms the previous parent. The relative variation of the objective function value for a single trial is

$$V \approx \frac{-s^2}{n} - \frac{2s}{n} N \equiv \frac{-s^2}{n} + \frac{2s}{n} N \qquad (4\text{-}65)$$

from above. The c.d.f. of $V$ is $\Phi[(x - \theta)/\eta])$, with $\theta = -s^2/n$ and $\eta = 2s/n$. The distribution of the maximal relative variation of $\lambda$ trials, $V_\lambda$, is given by

$$F_{V_\lambda}(x) \equiv \Phi^\lambda \left[ \frac{x - \theta}{\eta} \right], \tag{4-66}$$

because the $\lambda$ trials are i.i.d. The expectation of $V_\lambda$ is

$$E[V_\lambda] = 1/\eta \int_{-\infty}^{\infty} u \cdot g\left( \frac{u - \theta}{\eta}, \lambda \right) du, \tag{4-67}$$

where

$$g(x, \lambda) \equiv \frac{d\Phi^\lambda(x)}{dx} = \frac{\lambda}{\sqrt{2\pi}} \cdot \exp\left( \frac{-x^2}{2} \right) \Phi^{\lambda-1}(x). \tag{4-68}$$

Let the random variable $V_\lambda^+ \equiv \max\{0, V_\lambda\}$ describe the relative improvement after $\lambda$ trials. The expectation

$$E[V_\lambda^+] = \frac{1}{\eta} \int_0^\infty u \cdot g\left[ \frac{u - \theta}{\eta}, \lambda \right] du. \tag{4-69}$$

Substituting $v = (u - \theta)/\eta$ yields:

$$E[V_\lambda^+] = \int_{-\theta/\eta}^\infty (v\eta + \theta) \cdot g(v, \lambda)\, dv \tag{4-70}$$

$$= 2s/n \int_{s/2}^\infty v \cdot g(v, \lambda)\, dv - \frac{s^2}{n} \left[ 1 - \Phi^\lambda(s/2) \right]. \tag{4-71}$$

Unfortunately, no closed-form expression for this integral appears available. But the optimal normalized standard deviations and improvements can be computed numerically (Figure 4-5). As seen in Figure 4-5b, the normalized improvement increases at what appears to be a logarithmic rate (Bäck et al., 1993).

Schwefel (1977, 1981) and Scheel (1985) have examined the rates of convergence for $(1,\lambda)$–ES on the same class of functions and have also identified the expected increase in convergence based on $\lambda$. The expected relative improvement of $\lambda$ trials is the maximal relative variation $V_\lambda$. Substituting $v = (u - \theta)/\eta$ into Eq. 4-67 yields:

$$E[V_\lambda] = \int_{-\infty}^\infty (v\eta + \theta) \cdot g(v, \lambda)\, dv \tag{4-72}$$

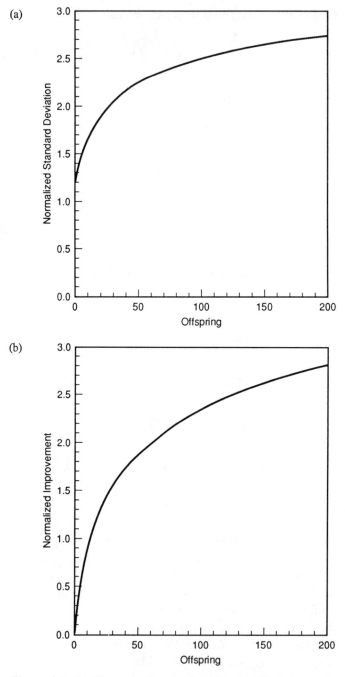

**Figure 4-5** (a) The optimal normalized standard deviation plotted as a function of the number of offspring. (b) The optimal normalized improvement $nE[V^+]$ plotted as a function of the number of offspring. As only the outcome of the best trial is of relevance here, when more trials are conducted within each generation they may be performed with more risk, corresponding to a larger step size. Both plots are from Bäck et al., 1993.

$$= \frac{2s}{n} \int_{-\infty}^{\infty} v \cdot g(v, \lambda) \, dv - \frac{s^2}{n} \qquad (4\text{-}73)$$

$$= \frac{2s \cdot c_{1,\lambda} - s^2}{n}, \qquad (4\text{-}74)$$

where

$$c_{1,\lambda} \equiv \int_{-\infty}^{\infty} v \cdot g(v, \lambda) \, dv \qquad (4\text{-}75)$$

denotes the expectation of the maximum of $\lambda$ i.i.d. standard Gaussian random variables.

Differentiating Eq. 4-74 with respect to $s$ yields the optimum normalized standard deviation $s^* = c_{1,\lambda}$ so that the optimal standard deviation is

$$\sigma^* = \left( \frac{c_{1,\lambda}}{2n} \right) \| \nabla f(\mathbf{x}) \| \qquad (4\text{-}76)$$

for large $n$. The expected improvement is then $E[V] = c_{1,\lambda}^2/n$, which can be described asymptotically.

Let $X_i \sim N(0,1)$ for $i = 1, \dots, \lambda$. Then $M_\lambda \equiv \max\{X_1, \dots, X_\lambda\}$ is a random variable with c.d.f. $P(M_\lambda \leq x) = \Phi^\lambda(x)$. Consequently, $c_{1,\lambda} = E[M_\lambda]$. The normalized random variable $(M_\lambda - b_\lambda)/a_\lambda$ converges weakly to the random variable $Y$, which has Gumbel distribution $G(y) = \exp(-e^{-y})$. The normalizing constants are

$$a_\lambda = (2 \log \lambda)^{-0.5} \qquad (4\text{-}77)$$

$$b_\lambda = (2 \log \lambda)^{-0.5} - \frac{\log \log \lambda + \log (4\pi)}{2\sqrt{2 \log \lambda}}. \qquad (4\text{-}78)$$

Thus

$$E\left[ \frac{(M_\lambda - b_\lambda)}{a_\lambda} \right] \rightarrow E[Y] = \gamma \approx 0.577 \dots, \qquad (4\text{-}79)$$

where $\gamma$ denotes Euler's constant. Continuing,

$$E[M_\lambda] \rightarrow b_\lambda + \gamma \cdot a_\lambda \tag{4-80}$$

$$= \sqrt{2 \log \lambda} + \frac{2\gamma - \log \log \lambda - \log(4\pi)}{2\sqrt{2 \log \lambda}} \tag{4-81}$$

$$\approx \sqrt{2 \log \lambda}, \tag{4-82}$$

and the expected optimal relative improvement becomes

$$E^*[V_\lambda] \approx \frac{2 \log \lambda}{n} \tag{4-83}$$

for large $n$ and large $\lambda$. This asymptotic expression also holds for the $(1+\lambda)$–ES and lends support to the apparent logarithmic increase exhibited in Figure 4-5b.

This result enables the computation of the relative speedup of processing $\lambda$ trials in parallel [the $(1,\lambda)$–ES] over processing a single new trial [the $(1+1)$–ES]. Let

$$\beta \equiv E\left[\frac{f(\mathbf{x}(t)) - f(\mathbf{x}(t+1))}{f(\mathbf{x}(t))}\right] \tag{4-84}$$

$$= \begin{cases} 0.405/n, & \text{if } (1+1)\text{–ES}; \\ (2 \log \lambda)/n, & \text{if } (1,\lambda)\text{–ES}. \end{cases} \tag{4-85}$$

The expected error at step $t$ is then

$$E[f(\mathbf{x}(t)) - f^*] = (1 - \beta)[f(\mathbf{x}(t-1)) - f^*] \tag{4-86}$$

$$= (1 - \beta)^t[f(\mathbf{x}(0)) - f^*] \tag{4-87}$$

$$= (1 - \beta)^t \delta_0. \tag{4-88}$$

Let $E[t_1]$ and $E[t_\lambda]$ denote the expected number of steps required to achieve an error of $\varepsilon$ for a $(1+1)$–ES and a $(1,\lambda)$–ES, respectively. Then the relative increase in speed, $S_\lambda$, satisfies

$$S_\lambda \equiv \frac{E[t_1]}{E[t_\lambda]} \tag{4-89}$$

$$= \frac{\log(\varepsilon/\delta_0)}{\log(1 - 0.405/n)} \cdot \frac{\log\left(1 - \frac{c_{1,\lambda}^2}{n}\right)}{\log(\varepsilon/\delta_0)} \tag{4-90}$$

$$= \frac{\log(1 - 2\log(\lambda)/n)}{\log(1 - 0.405/n)} \tag{4-91}$$

$$\approx \frac{2\log(\lambda)/n}{0.405/n} \tag{4-92}$$

$$= O(\log \lambda). \tag{4-93}$$

Thus the relative increase in speed for using $\lambda$ offspring is logarithmic.

## 4.4 EMPIRICAL ANALYSIS

### 4.4.1 Variations of Crossover

Theoretical results regarding the rate of convergence under genetic algorithms have been difficult to obtain. Consequently, there have been many efforts to quantify the performance of various procedures empirically (Grefenstette, 1986; Schaffer et al., 1989; and others). Syswerda (1989) examined the utility of various crossover operators, concentrating on one-point, two-point, and uniform crossover. One-point crossover is as defined on page 125. Two-point crossover operates on two parents, but as the name suggests, two points rather than a single point are selected at random and the sequence of components between the points are exchanged (Figure 4-6a). Uniform crossover generates two offspring from two parents by selecting each component from either parent with a given probability (which was set at 0.5 in Syswerda, 1989) (Figure 4-6b).

Several binary function optimization problems were studied. Of these, three specific functions were

$$(1) \ f(\mathbf{x}) = \sum_{i=1}^{30} x_i, \ n = 30 \tag{4-94}$$

(a)
Two-Point Crossover:

Parent #1: $x_{1,1} \ x_{1,2} \ldots x_{1,c_1} \ x_{1,c_1+1} \ldots x_{1,c_2} \ x_{1,c_2+1} \ldots x_{1,k}$

Parent #2: $x_{2,1} \ x_{2,2} \ldots x_{2,c_1} \ x_{2,c_1+1} \ldots x_{2,c_2} \ x_{2,c_2+1} \ldots x_{2,k}$

Offspring #1: $x_{1,1} \ x_{1,2} \ldots x_{2,c_1} \ x_{2,c_1+1} \ldots x_{2,c_2} \ x_{1,c_2+1} \ldots x_{1,k}$

Offspring #2: $x_{2,1} \ x_{2,2} \ldots x_{1,c_1} \ x_{1,c_1+1} \ldots x_{1,c_2} \ x_{2,c_2+1} \ldots x_{2,k}$

(b)
Uniform Crossover:

Parent #1: $x_{1,1} \ x_{1,2} \ldots x_{1,k-1} \ x_{1,k}$

Parent #2: $x_{2,1} \ x_{2,2} \ldots x_{2,k-1} \ x_{2,k}$

Offspring #1: $x_{1,1} \ x_{2,2} \ldots x_{1,k-1} \ x_{2,k}$

Offspring #2: $x_{2,1} \ x_{1,2} \ldots x_{2,k-1} \ x_{1,k}$

**Figure 4-6** (a) Two-point crossover operates in a similar manner as one-point crossover. Two points are selected along the coding string ($c_1$ and $c_2$), and the segments in-between these points are exchanged. (b) Uniform crossover creates two offspring by choosing each component from either parent with a specific probability. The figure depicts one such possible crossover.

(2) $f(\mathbf{x}) = \sum\limits_{i=1}^{30} x_i, \ n = 300 \quad$ (bits 31–300 are irrelevant) $\hspace{2cm}$ (4-95)

(3) $f(\mathbf{x}) = (K^{-1} + \sum\limits_{j=1}^{25} f_j(\mathbf{x})^{-1})^{-1},$ $\hspace{3cm}$ (4-96)

$f_j(\mathbf{x}) = c_j + \sum\limits_{i=1}^{2} (x_i - a_{ij})^6,$

$[a_{ij}] = \begin{bmatrix} -32, -16, & 0, & 16, & 32, -32, -16, \ldots, & 0, 16, 32 \\ -32, -32, -32, -32, -32, -16, -16, \ldots, & 32, 32, 32 \end{bmatrix}$

$c_j = j,$

$K = 500.$

The third function is known as Shekel's foxholes and the specific constants are taken from De Jong (1975) (also see page 96). A fourth function involved a 16-city traveling salesman problem where the cities were uniformly spaced around a circle of radius 45 units. The objective function was chosen as the length of the tour subtracted from 1600, with the goal, therefore, of maximizing the objective value. The representation assigned a group of six bits to each city, with each group treated as a binary number. These values were sorted into increasing order, and this implied the order of the cities to visit. Fifty trials were conducted on each function and the population size was set at 50, except in the traveling salesman problem, for which it was set at 100.

The results for the first two functions are shown in Figures 4-7 and 4-8. Uniform crossover is seen to outperform both two-point and one-point crossover on average, and considerably so in the second problem. Figure 4-9a indicates the mean results for Shekel's foxholes. Two-point crossover performs best, followed by one-point and uniform crossover. Syswerda tried a second set of 50 trials in which the bit positions were randomly shuffled. Figure 4-9b indicates the results for the revised problem. Uniform crossover achieves similar performance as before, but the performance of both one-point and two-point crossover are considerably poorer. Finally, Figure 4-10 indicates the results for the traveling salesman problem. Again, uniform crossover is seen to outperform two-point and one-point crossover. The results for the other problems studied in Syswerda (1989) are similar. Generally, uniform crossover yielded better performance than two-point crossover, which in turn yielded better performance than one-point crossover.

These results were somewhat surprising (Spears and De Jong, 1991a). The traditional view in genetic algorithms was that one-point and two-point crossover would be better at assembling and maintaining building blocks (subsections of schema) with above-average performance because these operators are less disruptive than uniform crossover. But Spears and De Jong (1991b) indicated that disruptiveness need not always be viewed negatively. For example, if a population is prematurely converged at a suboptimum point (with a nearly homogeneous population), disrupting the coding strings is the only mechanism for advancing the search.

Uniform crossover is capable of generating more diverse new offspring than is one-point or two-point crossover. Consider the two 10-bit parent strings:

**Figure 4-7**   Results of one-point, two-point, and uniform crossover on the one max function. (After Syswerda, 1989.) Uniform crossover provides the best performance.

**Figure 4-8**   Results of one-point, two-point, and uniform crossover on the sparse one max function. (After Syswerda, 1989.) Uniform crossover provides substantially improved performance.

(a)

(b)

**Figure 4-9**   (a) Results of one-point, two-point, and uniform crossover on Shekel's foxholes. Two-point crossover is observed to give the best performance. (b) Results comparing the same operators on Shekel's foxholes when the components of the coding strings are randomly shuffled. Uniform crossover achieves similar performance as observed in (a), but two-point and one-point crossover are less effective. (After Syswerda, 1989.)

**Figure 4-10**  Results of one-point, two-point, and uniform crossover on a 16-city traveling salesman problem. The initial rate of optimization is slower under uniform crossover, but it eventually provides superior performance. (After Syswerda, 1989.)

$P_1$: 1 1 1 1 1 1 1 1 1 1

$P_2$: 0 0 0 0 0 0 0 0 0 0.

Uniform crossover can generate any point in the entire sample space from these two parents, while operators relying on a fixed number of crossover points cannot. But generating diverse samples does not ensure an efficient search. Drawing new strings completely at random guarantees the potential for diversity but results in an inefficient, essentially enumerative procedure. There is a crucial balance to be maintained between *exploration*, generating diverse new trials, and *exploitation*, making use of gains that have already been achieved.

There is no single optimum operator for searching all possible response surfaces. Uniform crossover may outperform *n*-point crossover in some cases, or perhaps the majority of cases, but other factors (e.g., population size) can affect the outcome of such comparisons (Spears and De Jong, 1991a). The experiments of Syswerda (1989) and others do indicate the potential for taking a positive view of disrupting schemata when implementing a genetic algorithm. The usefulness of such disruptions will be highly problem-dependent, and mechanisms that allow for the self-adaptation of search operators (Schwefel, 1981; Fogel et al., 1992) should provide for increased efficiency and robustness (Schaffer and Morishima, 1987; Davis, 1989; Spears and De Jong, 1991a, 1991b; Bäck, 1992).

### 4.4.2  Dynamic Parameter Encoding

Schraudolph and Belew (1992) recognized a potential limitation to using traditional genetic algorithms for continuous function optimization. The typical procedure codes real-valued parameters as a series of bits (say, of length $k$), and the choice for the number of bits determines the precision of the search as well as the size of the sample space. "Unfortunately, the [genetic algorithm] searches long place-value codes rather inefficiently" (Schraudolph and Belew, 1992) because much of the early computational effort is directed at the least significant digits of each parameter. The search may prematurely converge on these digits, fixating the population at these values. This leaves a constrained search for the best settings of the most significant digits and is exactly the obverse of what would be desired.

To overcome this difficulty, Schraudolph and Belew (1992) introduced a method for continuously rescaling the precision of each $k$-bit coded parameter, termed *dynamic parameter encoding* (DPE). Essentially, each parameter of a continuous fitness function, $f$, is presumed to vary over an interval $[a_i, b_i)$, where $i$ refers to the $i$th parameter. The binary coding for each parameter then corresponds to some point (or region) within this interval. The interval is divided into subintervals (Figure 4-11). At each

**Figure 4-11**  Under dynamic parameter encoding, a current search interval (as depicted ranging from $a$ to $b$) is divided up into possible target intervals. Whenever the histogram of the population appears converged in a particular target interval, the search is rescaled to continue within that interval. (After Schraudolph and Belew, 1992.)

generation, a histogram of the population is constructed over the quarters of the current search interval formed by the two most significant bits of the coding for each parameter. The population count for each of three overlapping target intervals is then obtained from the histogram. If the largest count exceeds a preselected threshold (e.g., 90 percent of the population), the algorithm is considered converged and the search is rescaled (*zoomed*) to continue within that subinterval.

Schraudolph and Belew (1992) tested this procedure on the response surfaces examined by De Jong (1975). Table 4-1 indicates the number of

| Function | Dimension | Bit Length |
|----------|-----------|------------|
| f1 | 3 | 10 |
| f2 | 2 | 12 |
| f3 | 5 | 10 |
| f4 | 30 | 8 |
| f5 | 2 | 17 |

| Function | Parameter Range |
|----------|-----------------|
| f1: $F(x) = \sum_{i=1}^{3} x_i^2$ | $[-5.12, 5.12]$ |
| f2: $F(x) = 100(x_1^2 - x_2)^2 + (1 - x_1)^2$ | $[-2.048, 2.048]$ |
| f3: $F(x) = \sum_{i=1}^{5} [x_i],$ | $[-5.12, 5.12]$ |
| f4: $F(x) = \sum_{i=1}^{30} ix_i^4 + N(0,1)$ | $[-1.28, 1.28]$ |
| f5: $F(x)^{-1} = 1/K + \sum_{j=1}^{25} f_j(x)^{-1},$ | $[-65.536, 65.536]$ |

$$f_j(x) = c_j + \sum_{i=1}^{2} (x_i - a_{ij})^6,$$

where $K = 500$, $c_j = j$, and

$$[a_{ij}] = \begin{bmatrix} -32, -16, & 0, & 16, & 32, -32, -16, & \ldots, & 0, 16, 32 \\ -32, -32, -32, -32, -32, -16, -16, & \ldots, & 32, 32, 32 \end{bmatrix}$$

**Table 4-1**  The number of parameters, the binary coding length and the functions studied in Schraudolph and Belew (1992). These follow previous efforts by De Jong (1975). The operation $[x_i]$ in f3 returns the greatest integer less than or equal to $x_i$. The $N(0, 1)$ in f4 represents a standard Gaussian random variable.

parameters, the binary coding length for each parameter and the functions studied. Schaffer et al. (1989) offered optimal control settings for this test suite. Schraudolph and Belew used these settings (population size of 30, cross-over rate = 0.95, mutation rate = 0.005) to execute the GAucsd/GENESIS software package with and without DPE. The search resolution for DPE was held constant at $k = 3$ to facilitate comparisons across the test suite.

Figure 4-12 shows the mean results of 10 trials conducted to 10,080 offspring on each function, both with and without DPE (Schraudolph and Belew, 1992). The curves are exponentially smoothed with a window of 10 generations. Improved performance under DPE is most evident on functions

**Figure 4-12** The mean results of 10 trials conducted to 10,080 offspring on each function, both with and without dynamic parameter encoding. The solid lines indicate the performance of the standard genetic algorithm, while the dotted lines indicate the performance of dynamic parameter encoding. The curves are exponentially smoothed. Dynamic parameter encoding offers the greatest advantages on functions f1 and f3, but results on f5 are actually worse than simply using a standard genetic algorithm. (After Schraudolph and Belew, 1992.)

f1 and f3: The average function values achieved with DPE are $6 \times 10^{-10}$ and $4 \times 10^{-7}$ (off the chart), respectively, whereas the standard genetic algorithm stalls out around $10^0$ in both cases. Substantial improvements are also evidenced on functions f2 and f4, but results on f5 are actually worse using DPE. Schraudolph and Belew (1992) speculate that this performance was due to the limited number of bits per parameter (i.e., three) and noted improved performance on f5 when the number of bits per parameter was doubled to six.

DPE is a promising heuristic for improving optimization using genetic algorithms. It is essentially "best characterized as a succession of [genetic algorithms] over search spaces iteratively refined through bisection" (Schraudolph and Belew, 1992). The zoom operation can only reduce the interval for each parameter as the population converges; no mechanism is offered for expanding the search interval should the global optimum not be contained within the initial specified range in each parameter. Schraudolph and Belew (1992) discuss some of the problems associated with determining the appropriate conditions for expanding these intervals and conclude that establishing a well-founded criterion for employing an "inverse zoom" is impossible. Yet it would appear necessary to provide some mechanism for extending the search beyond a priori limits. Even randomly perturbing the interval width at each generation might be useful in this regard.

### 4.4.3 Comparing Crossover to Mutation

Considerable attention has been devoted to assessing the relative importance of crossover and mutation in evolutionary optimization. Holland (1975, p. 110) offered that mutation and selection is "little more than an enumerative plan retaining the best structure encountered to each point in time." He suggested that mutation's primary role in adaptation is not one of generating new structures ("a role very efficiently filled by crossing-over," Holland, 1975, p. 110), but rather that it assures that recombination operators have a full range of possible allelic values to explore. Similar comments relating the importance of crossover as opposed to random mutation have been offered in Grefenstette (1986), Goldberg (1989, p. 106), Davis (1991a, pp. 17–18), Holland (1992), and many others. Koza (1992, p. 27) went so far as to claim, "Holland's view of the crucial importance of recombination and the relative unimportance of mutation contrasts sharply with the popular misconception of the role of mutation in evolution in nature and with the recurrent efforts to solve adaptive systems problems by merely 'mutating and saving the best.' "

Fogel and Atmar (1990) attempted to quantify the benefits, if any, of using genetic operators such as crossover and inversion as opposed to simple random mutation in a series of experiments aimed at solving linear systems of equations. Consider a system of linear equations of $n$ dimensions,

$$b_i = \sum_{j=1}^{n} a_{ij} x_j, \quad i = 1, \ldots, n, \tag{4-97}$$

where the vector $\mathbf{x}$ represents the coding structure of $n$ "gene" products, the vector $\mathbf{b}$ represents $n$ phenotypic behavioral responses, and the coefficients $a_{ij}$ of an $n \times n$ matrix $A$ represent the respective contribution of each component of $\mathbf{x}$ to each component of the response vector $\mathbf{b}$. Any such system will be pleiotropic (single genes expressing themselves through multiple effects) unless $a_{ij} = 0$ for all $i \neq j$.

The fitness function used to evaluate the quality of the evolved behavioral responses to the required response vector was

$$E = \sum_{i=1}^{n} |E_i|, \tag{4-98}$$

where

$$E_i = \sum_{j=1}^{n} a_{ij} x_j - b_i, \quad i = 1, \ldots, n. \tag{4-99}$$

Unless the matrix $A = [a_{ij}]$ is singular, there exists an ideal behavioral response $(A\mathbf{x}^*)$. The total amount of behavioral error, $E$, will equal zero when $x_j = x_j^*$, for $j = 1, \ldots n$.

Experiments were conducted with an arbitrary coefficient matrix $A$ of rank 10 and a randomly chosen desired response vector $\mathbf{b}$. The population was initialized with 150 vectors (genotypes) taken at random; components were distributed normally with zero mean and a standard deviation of 30. These vectors were randomly assigned to be one of three types. The first was altered only by mutation: A standard normally distributed random variable was added to each of its components. The second was altered by one-point crossover (80% chance per offspring) and inversion (50 percent chance per offspring). The third was altered by crossover and inversion and was also given a 1 percent chance per offspring of random mutation by altering components by a standard Gaussian (as in type 1).

Vectors were scored with respect to the above criterion and were probabilistically selected to survive into the subsequent generation based on a stochastic tournament. Each vector competed against 10 other vectors, with the probability of attaining a "win" equal to the opponent's error score divided by the sum of both vectors' error scores. Once this competition had occurred for all vectors, those with the most wins became the basis set of the next generation.

Linear systems of equations provided a convenient mechanism for examining the effects of these operators in domains of varying interactivity. Five sets of trials were conducted. Each set varied the degree of interactivity of the $A$ matrix by setting the probability of an off-diagonal entry being nonzero to 0.0, 0.25, 0.5, 0.75, and 1.0, respectively. When the probability was zero, the domain was minimally pleiotropic; each independent gene product contributed only to the fitness of its respective component. When the probability was 1.0, the domain was fully pleiotropic, with each gene product contributing to the total behavioral error summed over all behavioral responses. Each experiment consisted of 100 randomly chosen systems. In each system, evolution was halted after 5,000 offspring had been evaluated. The results appear in Table 4-2.

Advantage quickly accrued to those genotypes that were altered by random mutation alone. The observed number of trials in which simple random mutation dominated the population is significantly greater than would be expected under a null hypothesis of the behavior of the evolutionary process being independent of the utilized mutation or genetic operation ($P < 0.0001$, nonparametric chi-square test). Further, insufficient evidence exists to suggest that the degree of interactivity of the linear system of equations is associated with the degree to which those genotypes undergoing random mutation alone will overtake the population ($P > 0.12$). In light of these results, further experiments conducted on independent trials using different rates for crossover and mutation (inversion was omitted) showed no statistically significant advantage for crossover.

Fogel and Atmar (1990) concluded that "while specific circumstances (other than linear equations) may well exist for which crossover and inversion operations are especially appropriate, those conditions cannot be the hallmark of a broadly useful algorithm. . . . Rather than being fundamentally different from random mutation . . . crossover and inversion are merely

| Degree of interactivity | | Percentage of trials when more than 50% of the population consisted of the given type |
|---|---|---|
| 0 | Random Mutation Alone | 78% (70%)[a] |
| | Crossover/Inversion | 9% (5%) |
| | Crossover/Inversion/Mutation | 13% (4%) |
| 25 | Random Mutation Alone | 75% (72%) |
| | Crossover/Inversion | 10% (3%) |
| | Crossover/Inversion/Mutation | 15% (3%) |
| 50 | Random Mutation Alone | 83% (83%) |
| | Crossover/Inversion | 9% (7%) |
| | Crossover/Inversion/Mutation | 8% (4%) |
| 75 | Random Mutation Alone | 88% (86%) |
| | Crossover/Inversion | 2% (0%) |
| | Crossover/Inversion/Mutation | 10% (6%) |
| 100 | Random Mutation Alone | 76% (73%) |
| | Crossover/Inversion | 10% (6%) |
| | Crossover/Inversion/Mutation | 14% (6%) |

[a] The values in parentheses indicate the percentage of trials in which the given type had completly taken over 100% of the population.

**Table 4-2**    The percentage of trials when more than 50 percent of the population consisted of the given type (mutation alone, crossover, and inversion, or crossover, inversion, and mutation). The values in parentheses indicate the percentage of trials in which the given types had completely taken over 100 percent of the population. (After Fogel and Atmar, 1990.)

a subset of all random mutations. As in all subsets, their applicability will be strongly problem dependent, if advantageous at all."

Schaffer and Eshelman (1991) conducted a series of similar experiments comparing crossover with mutation on binary function optimization problems. The simulations started with a randomized population of 500 binary strings. In every problem, each string possessed 100 bits that encoded the trial solution to the task at hand, along with an additional bit that determined whether or not the string would be subject to crossover. Ten percent of the population was randomly chosen to have the crossover bit turned on. Evolution proceeded as follows:

1. Randomly mate the appropriate crossing individuals among themselves; replace them by their offspring.

2. If the selected mutation rate (see below) is positive, perform mutation on the entire gene pool (including the crossover bit).

3. Score all new solutions.

4. Select the best solutions for inclusion in the subsequent population.

5. Halt if two generations have transpired without any new off-spring or when 50,000 offspring have been evaluated.

Twenty trials were conducted with each of five functions. The first function was termed *onemax*: The fitness of a solution was simply the number of 1's in the string. The second function was termed *plateau*: A value of five was given for each five-bit segment of "00000." The overall evaluation was calculated as 100 minus the sum of the segment scores, so that the optimum score was zero and the worst possible was 100. The third function was termed *trap*: A value of five was again given for the sequence "00000," but for other patterns a value of 0.5 times the number of 1's was awarded. Thus the problem is "deceptive" (Goldberg, 1987) in that the average fitness of short-length building blocks (schemata) lead away from the global optimum. The fourth and fifth problems were simply variants of plateau and trap in which the segments were uniformly spaced throughout the 100 bits. That is, the bits of segment 1 were in positions 1, 21, 41, 61, and 81; the bits of segment 2 were in positions 2, 22, 42, 62, and 82; and so forth.

Mutation was evaluated in two forms: zero mutation and a rate of 0.0005. The latter rate was chosen empirically to balance the number of solutions that improve from both the mutation only and crossover sub-populations in the initial generation (Schaffer and Eshelman, 1991).

To provide a baseline for comparison, the experiments were first executed 20 times each with mutation alone, two-point crossover alone, and uniform crossover alone (i.e., no mutation). The population size was set at 500 in all cases. Subsequent experiments examined the tendency for solutions undergoing either two-point or uniform crossover to invade the population, with or without mutation.

The results were mixed. Four separate characteristics were observed: (1) The solutions created by crossover dominated the population and achieved a level of performance not attained by mutation alone, (2) the solutions created by crossover dominated the population and achieved a level of performance that was about the same as mutation alone but was achieved more quickly, (3) the solutions created by crossover dominated the population but the performance was ultimately worse than achieved by mutation alone, and (4) the solutions by crossover failed to dominate the population and performance was worse than achieved by mutation alone. When combined with mutation, both methods of crossover always came to dominate the population. Results that were superior to mutation alone were achieved by two-point crossover on the trap function, with and without mutation. But results that were inferior to mutation alone were achieved by uniform crossover on the plateau function, with and without mutation, and other combinations of two-point and uniform crossover on the various versions of plateau and trap also generated inferior results.

Broadly, the results again indicated that the utility of specific crossover and mutation operations is problem-dependent. Schaffer and Eshelman (1991) offered:

> We believe Fogel and Atmar are correct to point out the power of selection and mutation for search. This power is often underestimated in the [genetic algorithm] community. We believe it is not correct to infer from their results that crossover provides no added value. We believe that our experimental results begin to shed more light on the circumstances under which crossover will deliver the search power first described by Holland. However, these results also suggest circumstances in which crossover has a detrimental impact on search. It must be used with care.

Schaffer and Eshelman (1991) speculated that the results favoring mutation reported in Fogel and Atmar (1990) may have been due to: (1) the coupling of crossover with an inversion operator that actually reordered the coding string, rather than simply reindexing its components; and (2) applying crossover to real-valued instead of binary coding, preventing the possibility for crossover to perform any within-parameter search.

In light of these criticisms, Fogel and Stayton (1994) compared a simple version of evolutionary programming relying solely on real-valued coding and Gaussian mutation with the results offered in Schraudolph and Belew (1992), both with and without dynamic parameter encoding. Schraudolph (pers. comm.) kindly provided the raw data from those experiments, which as described above relied on binary coding and achieved some of the best optimization results on the test suite offered in De Jong (1975).

The evolutionary programming procedure was conducted as follows:

1. Thirty real-valued vectors, $x_i$, $i = 1, \ldots, 30$, $(P = 30)$ were initialized by sampling from a uniform distribution across the preselected range of each parameter (De Jong, 1975).

2. All vectors, $x_i$, $i = 1, \ldots, 30$, were scored with respect to the chosen function, $F(x)$.

3. From each vector, $x_i$, $i = 1, \ldots, 30$, one offspring was created, denoted by $x_{i+P}$, by adding a Gaussian random variable with

zero mean and variance equal to $F(\mathbf{x}_i)/n^2$ to each component, where $F(\mathbf{x}_i)$ represents the parent's error score and where there are $n$ dimensions in the optimization problem.

4. Each offspring, $\mathbf{x}_i$, $i = P+1, \ldots, 2P$, was scored with respect to $F(\mathbf{x})$.

5. For each $\mathbf{x}_i$, $i = 1, \ldots, 2P$, 10 competitors were selected at random from the population. Pairwise comparisons were made between $\mathbf{x}_i$ and each of the competitors. If the error score of $\mathbf{x}_i$ was less than or equal to that of its opponent, it was assigned a win.

6. The 30 vectors with the greatest number of wins were selected to be parents for the next generation.

7. The process repeated to step 3 until 10,080 vectors (336 generations) were evaluated.

Although the population was initialized randomly over the parameter ranges noted in Table 4-1, solutions were allowed to vary outside these ranges in subsequent generations. Unlike the experiments with dynamic parameter encoding, there was no requirement for the global minimum to be bounded by the initial search limits. One exception to this was required for the step function (f3), which continues stepping to successively lower values as the parameters tend toward negative infinity. For this problem, if any parameter of a new trial solution exceeded its initial limits, it was set equal to the limit it exceeded. For the noisy quartic function (f4), all trial solutions were reevaluated every generation. In the event that a solution's score was negative, the standard deviation for generating new trials from this solution was set equal to the small positive constant $10^{-3}$.

Of the five test functions from De Jong (1975), only the fifth possesses multiple local optima. This function is somewhat pathologic. To provide additional tests with more reasonable surfaces that possess local optima, three two-dimensional functions (Figure 4-13) were taken from Bohachevsky et al. (1986):

f6: $F(x, y) = x^2 + 2y^2 - 0.3\cos(3\pi x) - 0.4\cos(4\pi y) + 0.7$,

f7: $F(x, y) = x^2 + 2y^2 - 0.3[\cos(3\pi x)\cos(4\pi y)] + 0.3$,

f8: $F(x, y) = x^2 + 2y^2 - 0.3[\cos(3\pi x) + \cos(4\pi y)] + 0.3$.

(a)                                              (b)

(c)

**Figure 4-13**   Inverted and contour plots of the three Bohachevsky functions studied in Fogel and Stayton (1994).  (a) $F(x, y) = x^2 + 2y^2 - 0.3\cos(3\pi x) - 0.4\cos(4\pi y) + 0.7$.  (b) $F(x,y) = x^2 + 2y^2 - 0.3[\cos(3\pi x)\cos(4\pi y)] + 0.3$.  (c) $F(x, y) = x^2 + 2y^2 - 0.3[\cos(3\pi x) + \cos(4\pi y)] + 0.3$.

Schraudolph (pers. comm.) provided the GAucsd/GENESIS software and results were obtained on f6–f8 with and without dynamic parameter encoding using the same settings as offered in Schraudolph and Belew (1992). Ten trials were conducted with each genetic method on each function. For standard genetic algorithm experiments, the available range for each parameter was [–50, 50] with a coding length of 14 bits. Experiments with dynamic parameter encoding used three bits following Schraudolph and Belew (1992). Five hundred trials were conducted with evolutionary programming on each function f1–f8.

Table 4-3 indicates the best score in the population and the mean of all parents' scores after 10,080 function evaluations. Evolutionary programming outperforms both genetic algorithm methods on functions f1, f2, and f6–f8, and generates comparable performance on f3–f5. While the statistical significance of the data was often great (e.g., $P < 10^{-6}$ when comparing the mean best discovered solution using evolutionary programming with the standard genetic algorithm on f1), in many cases the data did not provide statistically significant evidence for a difference in the expected outcome between evolutionary programming and the genetic algorithm using dynamic parameter encoding despite a difference in performance of many orders of magnitude. This was due mainly to the small sample size provided in Schraudolph and Belew (1992) and the relatively large variance associated with their results.

The evidence consistently suggests that there is no requirement for incorporating recombination in evolutionary algorithms, nor does its inclusion always generate improvements over searches relying solely on mutation (cf. Davis, 1991a, p. 18). The representation used for describing alternative solutions in part determines the shape of the response surface being searched; thus the utility of various transformation operations will be representation-dependent as well. But no consistent advantage accrues from representing real-valued parameters as binary strings and allowing crossover to do within-parameter search (cf. Schaffer and Eshelman, 1991). Evolutionary algorithms relying solely on mutation can, in many cases, be used to greater advantage on function optimization problems.

### 4.4.4 Self-Adaptation in Evolutionary Algorithms

Rechenberg (pers. comm) introduced the possibility for allowing an evolution strategy to adapt the distribution of new trials in light of informa-

|        |     | Avg. Best:                                          | Avg. Mean:                                          |
|--------|-----|-----------------------------------------------------|-----------------------------------------------------|
| f1:    | EP  | $3.149 \times 10^{-66}$ ($2.344 \times 10^{-129}$)  | $1.087 \times 10^{-65}$ ($1.794 \times 10^{-128}$)  |
|        | DPE | $1.056 \times 10^{11}$ ($1.072 \times 10^{21}$)     | $3.618 \times 10^{-10}$ ($1.060 \times 10^{-18}$)   |
|        | GA  | $2.836 \times 10^{-4}$ ($4.587 \times 10^{-8}$)     | $6.135 \times 10^{-1}$ ($1.627 \times 10^{-1}$)     |
| f2:    | EP  | $1.215 \times 10^{-14}$ ($3.357 \times 10^{-26}$)   | $8.880 \times 10^{-14}$ ($2.399 \times 10^{-24}$)   |
|        | DPE | $2.035 \times 10^{-2}$ ($3.315 \times 10^{-3}$)     | $8.785 \times 10^{-2}$ ($8.090 \times 10^{-3}$)     |
|        | GA  | $2.914 \times 10^{-2}$ ($6.280 \times 10^{-4}$)     | $1.722 \times 10^{0}$ ($2.576 \times 10^{0}$)       |
| f3:    | EP  | $0.0$ ($0.0$)                                        | $0.0$ ($0.0$)                                        |
|        | DPE | $0.0$ ($0.0$)                                        | $0.0$ ($0.0$)                                        |
|        | GA  | $0.0$ ($0.0$)                                        | $1.307 \times 10^{0}$ ($1.172 \times 10^{-1}$)      |
| f4:    | EP  | $-2.575 \times 10^{0}$ ($7.880 \times 10^{-1}$)     | $-4.274 \times 10^{-1}$ ($3.206 \times 10^{-2}$)    |
|        | DPE | $-2.980 \times 10^{0}$ ($1.009 \times 10^{-1}$)     | $4.704 \times 10^{-1}$ ($1.283 \times 10^{-1}$)     |
|        | GA  | $-4.599 \times 10^{-1}$ ($4.265 \times 10^{-1}$)    | $1.312 \times 10^{1}$ ($2.941 \times 10^{0}$)       |
| f5:    | EP  | $4.168 \times 10^{0}$ ($9.928 \times 10^{0}$)       | $4.194 \times 10^{0}$ ($1.022 \times 10^{1}$)       |
|        | DPE | $3.502 \times 10^{0}$ ($1.265 \times 10^{1}$)       | $1.642 \times 10^{1}$ ($7.101 \times 10^{2}$)       |
|        | GA  | $9.980 \times 10^{-1}$ ($3.553 \times 10^{-15}$)    | $1.021 \times 10^{1}$ ($7.165 \times 10^{1}$)       |
| f6:    | EP  | $5.193 \times 10^{-96}$ ($1.348 \times 10^{-188}$)  | $9.392 \times 10^{-94}$ ($4.410 \times 10^{-184}$)  |
|        | DPE | $1.479 \times 10^{-9}$ ($1.460 \times 10^{-18}$)    | $8.340 \times 10^{-7}$ ($4.649 \times 10^{-14}$)    |
|        | GA  | $2.629 \times 10^{-3}$ ($1.013 \times 10^{-5}$)     | $4.022 \times 10^{1}$ ($6.467 \times 10^{3}$)       |
| f7:    | EP  | $8.332 \times 10^{-101}$ ($3.449 \times 10^{-198}$) | $2.495 \times 10^{-99}$ ($3.095 \times 10^{-195}$)  |
|        | DPE | $2.084 \times 10^{-9}$ ($6.831 \times 10^{-18}$)    | $6.520 \times 10^{-7}$ ($7.868 \times 10^{-14}$)    |
|        | GA  | $4.781 \times 10^{-3}$ ($2.146 \times 10^{-5}$)     | $3.541 \times 10^{1}$ ($2.922 \times 10^{3}$)       |
| f8:    | EP  | $1.366 \times 10^{-105}$ ($4.479 \times 10^{-208}$) | $3.031 \times 10^{-103}$ ($2.122 \times 10^{-203}$) |
|        | DPE | $1.215 \times 10^{5}$ ($5.176 \times 10^{-10}$)     | $3.764 \times 10^{1}$ ($9.145 \times 10^{-1}$)      |
|        | GA  | $2.444 \times 10^{-3}$ ($4.511 \times 10^{-5}$)     | $2.788 \times 10^{1}$ ($1.368 \times 10^{3}$)       |

**Table 4-3**  Results for the best score in the population and the mean of all parents' scores after 10,080 function evaluations, averaged over 10 trials with the genetic algorithm techniques (both with and without dynamic parameter encoding) and 500 trials with evolutionary programming. (After Fogel and Stayton, 1994.) Evolutionary programming outperforms both genetic methods on functions f1, f2, and f6–f8, and yields comparable performance on f3–f5. The values in parentheses indicate the standard deviations.

tion gained during the search in 1967. As detailed in Schwefel (1981), the application of independent identically distributed (i.i.d.) Gaussian random perturbations to each component of every solution distributes new trials in alignment with the coordinate axes (Figure 4-14). But the optimum search direction (e.g., the gradient) is rarely so oriented. In general, the search is retarded as the population zigzags across the gradient. Incorporating correlated mutations across the components of each parent vector provides a mechanism for significantly accelerating the rate of optimization.

As noted above, Schwefel (1981) described a procedure wherein each solution contains an $n$-dimensional vector of object variables x, and as many as $n(n + 1)/2$ additional mutation parameters, including standard deviations and correlations, describing an $n$-dimensional Gaussian random vector. These values are modified during the search as

$$\sigma_i' = \sigma_i \cdot \exp(\tau_0 \cdot \Delta\sigma_0) \cdot \exp(\tau \cdot \Delta\sigma_i) \tag{4-100}$$

$$\alpha_j' = \alpha_j + \beta \cdot \Delta\alpha_j \tag{4-101}$$

$$x_i' = x_i + z_i(\sigma', \alpha') \tag{4-102}$$

where $\sigma$ is the vector of standard deviations, $\alpha$ is the vector of rotation angles equivalent to the correlations between parameters, and x is the vector of object values to be manipulated in optimizing the objective function (see page 146 for particular recommended settings of specific parameters). The

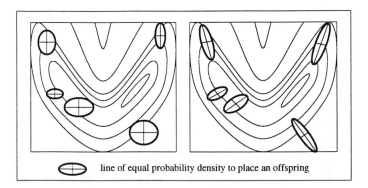

Figure 4-14   Self-adapting the mutation distributions on each solution allows for new trials to be generated in light of the contours of the response surface. Independent adjustment of the standard deviation in each dimension provides a mechanism for varying the width of the probability contour in alignment with each axis (left picture). Correlated standard deviations provide a mechanism for generating trials such that the probability contours are not aligned with the coordinate axes (right picture). (After Bäck et al., 1991.)

mutation parameters self-adapt in that both the standard deviations and rotation angles undergo perturbations (log-normal and Gaussian, respectively) based on their own current values. The resulting search can adapt to arbitrary contours on the response surface (Figure 4-14).

Fogel et al. (1991) independently offered a similar procedure for self-adapting uncorrelated standard deviations of Gaussian perturbations described as *meta-EP*. Each solution was coded as the vector of object variables, $x$, and the associated vector of standard deviations, $\sigma$, and offspring were generated according to

$$x_i' = x_i + \sigma_i \cdot z_i \qquad (4\text{-}103)$$

$$\sigma_i' = \sigma_i + \zeta\sigma_i \cdot z_i \qquad (4\text{-}104)$$

where $x_i$ and $\sigma_i$ are the $i$th components of $x$ and $\sigma$, respectively, $z_i$ follows a standard normal distribution, and $\zeta$ is a scaling constant chosen to assure that each $\sigma_i$ tends to remain positive. Whenever a mutated standard deviation becomes nonpositive, it is set to a small value, $\varepsilon > 0$.

Fogel et al. (1992), at the suggestion of Sebald (pers. comm.), provided a method for altering correlation coefficients between components. In addition to the self-adaptation of the standard deviations, a correlation coefficient matrix, $p = [\rho_{ij}]$, $i \neq j$, $\rho_{ij} = \rho_{ji}$, is incorporated. The components of $p$ are initialized uniformly over $[-1, 1]$, and mutation of this matrix is conducted by perturbing each component by adding i.i.d. normal random variables with zero mean and preselected standard deviation (e.g., 0.1). If the upper or lower bounds on any entry of $\rho$ exceed the range $[-1, 1]$, it is reset to the limit it exceeds.

Although both the methods of Schwefel (1981) and Fogel et al. (1991, 1992) are conceptually quite similar, they generate significant differences in performance. Initial comparisons between the two approaches have been restricted to uncorrelated self-adaptation. Bäck et al. (1993) evaluated a (30,200)–ES and a (200+200)–meta-EP on several functions including the sphere model, a scaled version of the sphere model, and the 30-dimensional multimodal function offered in Ackley (1987, pp. 13–14). The results indicated a general advantage to the methods of Schwefel (1981), although in subsequent discussion with Bäck (pers. comm.), it was agreed that these results may in some cases reflect the difference in parent population size as well as the choice of scaling factor for meta-EP. Saravanan and Fogel (1994) compared a (200+200)–ES with a (200+200)–meta-EP on five different functions including the sphere model, the Rosenbrock function, a Bohachevsky function, and other functions of 20 dimensions possessing local optima (e.g., generalized Ackley's function). The results more clearly indicate a general advantage to the log-normal perturbation scheme offered by Schwefel (1981).

There are three likely reasons for the observed advantage of the log-normal perturbation of the standard deviations over the Gaussian perturbation. First, the log-normal perturbation is guaranteed to yield strictly positive values, alleviating the necessity for selecting a value of $\varepsilon$ as is required in meta-EP. Second, it is easier for the standard deviations to vary from small values to large values under log-normal perturbations. Under Gaussian perturbations, once the standard deviations become small (e.g., $\varepsilon$), it may take a very low probability mutation to make a jump to a larger value. The search is essentially overconstrained. Third, the perturbation method of Schwefel (1981) incorporates both a global factor allowing for the overall change of the mutability of all components as well as local factors for adjusting the individual step sizes. This generates the potential for greater diversity than is allowed in the methods of Fogel et al. (1991, 1992).

## 4.5 DISCUSSION

The genetic algorithm has been widely studied as a function optimization technique (De Jong, 1975; Brindle, 1980; Bethke, 1981; and many others), and commercial software optimization packages that rely on these algorithms are currently available. But De Jong (1992, 1993) remarked that optimization per se (i.e., discovering the extremum of a functional) was not the motivation behind the original design of the genetic algorithm. Rather, the procedure was proposed as a robust method for allocating trials in a noisy, time-varying, sequential decision process with the goal of minimizing cumulative error. The quality of solutions to optimization problems has ranged widely (De Jong, 1993). Many useful heuristics have been advocated for accelerating the optimization properties of the procedures (e.g., scaling the fitness function to maintain selective pressure between competing individuals, rank-based selection, elitist selection, alternative representations, domain-specific operators, and so forth). But De Jong (1992, 1993) suggested that there should be no surprise when the canonical genetic algorithm fails to provide globally optimal solutions to function optimization problems because it was not created for that purpose.

Analysis in Holland (1975, pp. 75–83) addressing the optimal allocation of trials in a $k$-armed bandit problem is interesting but unfortunately is not broadly insightful for accelerating evolutionary optimization. The criterion of minimizing expected losses is very conservative; it may preclude an optimization algorithm from discovering the global best solution in a finite number of trials. Also, the analysis provided in Holland (1975, pp. 75–83) is only strictly valid for independent measurements from random variables. This is rarely the case in real-world optimization problems; the coding structures for such problems are almost always highly interdependent (Holland, 1975, pp. 5, 35, 136, 138–139, 160; Davis, 1985; and others).

The premature convergence common to genetic algorithms results from the primary reliance on crossover. Stagnation is promoted as selection purges diversity from the population. Further, the number of metastable states increases exponentially with the number of bits. Therefore, for real-world optimization problems requiring great precision and a long binary coding, it may be expected (although there will be counterexamples) that a genetic algorithm that does not employ a heuristic method for preventing or postponing premature convergence (e.g., dynamic parameter encoding) will not tend to discover nearly globally optimal solutions in a reasonable number of generations. Instead, the population will settle at a point (or points) on the response surface, after which further optimization will result only if there is an unlikely flipping of the correct bits. There may be specific problems, even complex ones, for which the repeated crossing over of a population of bit strings will quickly arrive at the global optimum solution. How common such problems might be in the real world remains an open question (Eshelman and Schaffer, 1993).

Theoretical analysis demonstrates that evolutionary algorithms that rely solely on mutation possess asymptotic global convergence properties. In general, these results are only of mathematical interest because the sample space being searched under the evolutionary simulation is necessarily finite and could therefore be enumerated in finite time. Analysis of the rate of convergence of evolutionary algorithms indicates a geometric reduction in error for strongly convex functions. Further, there is a logarithmic speed up for generating many trials from a single parent at each generation. Recent results in Zabinsky and Smith (1992) suggest the potential for generating an evolutionary algorithm with geometric convergence properties on some classes of nonconvex functions (noted in Bäck et al., 1993; Rudolph, 1994b).

The difficulties in obtaining theoretical results for genetic and evolutionary optimization algorithms have generated increased interest in empirical comparisons. But the problem of empirically assessing the utility of various optimization methods should not be underestimated. Whitley (1993) remarked, "Even if one is interested in optimization the results of any empirical test designed to demonstrate a 'more effective optimizer' may say as much about the nature of the functions being optimized as it does about any two algorithms which might be compared," indicating the "danger in the popular practice of declaring one algorithm 'superior' to another based on a few empirical tests." The response surfaces that have been examined in the literature certainly do not span all possible surfaces, nor can they. Empirical evidence can be useful for assessing the believability of null hypotheses in well-constructed statistical experiments, but caution must be used when generalizing specific results to a broader range of application.

The empirical evidence suggests that the effectiveness of specific genetic operators is problem-dependent and, moreover, condition-dependent. Syswerda (1989) found greater rates of optimization using uniform crossover as opposed to one-point and two-point crossover across a broad range of problems. But Spears and De Jong (1991a) indicated that two-point crossover could outperform uniform crossover on a 30-bit function optimization task simply by increasing the population size from 20 to 1,000.

These results focus attention on the building block hypothesis: the belief that genetic algorithms work by combining subsections from independent coding strings that are associated with above-average performance, thereby generating even further improvements (Forrest, 1993). Uniform crossover is more likely to disrupt these building blocks than, say, one-point crossover, and this effect is increased as the defining length of the building block is reduced (Spears, 1993). Increased schema disruption has been believed to lead to a suboptimal allocation of trials in light of the schema theorem (Holland, 1975, pp. 102–103). That uniform crossover could outperform one-point and two-point crossover brings into question the general relevance of the building block hypothesis in explaining the behavior of genetic algorithms.

Empirical comparisons between genetic and evolutionary algorithms on well-studied, real-valued optimization problems (Schraudolph and Belew, 1992; Fogel and Stayton, 1994) have indicated a statistically significant advantage for using Gaussian mutation in the absence of crossover. Further, these comparisons did not indicate circumstances that would statistically significantly favor the use of crossover. Other experimental comparisons have generated similar results (Fogel and Atmar, 1990; Fogel, 1991, 1992, 1994b; Rizki et al., 1993; Fukunaga et al., 1994; Bäck, 1994; Nettleton and Garigliano, 1994; and others).

Empirical comparisons between methods relying on primarily crossover or mutation on binary optimization problems have generated varied results (Schaffer and Eshelman, 1991). But the results favoring crossover may reflect the specific implementation of mutation. The typical method for assessing the effectiveness of crossover as opposed to mutation in the genetic algorithm literature is to execute the genetic algorithm with the standard parameter settings, execute the procedure without any crossover, and then compare the results (e.g., Axelrod, 1987; Schaffer and Eshelman, 1991). But this only tests one version of mutation, one of obviously limited efficacy.

The standard mutation operation in genetic algorithms is essentially constrained to provide only a local search as the probability of generating simultaneous independent mutations falls geometrically. Crossover provides for a larger effective step size during the initial phase of the search (before the population converges). Most completely randomly selected solutions are likely to be poor, and large steps away from such points typically offer a greater chance of discovering improved solutions than would concentrating the search around each poor solution's local neighborhood. Rather than indicate the superiority of crossover over mutation, such results, when observed, may simply indicate the general utility of taking big steps away from poor solutions instead of small steps.

The genetic algorithm literature has reflected a growing recognition of the importance of mutation (Caruana and Schaffer, 1988; Schaffer et al., 1989) in contrast with viewing it solely as a background operator. Forrest and Mitchell (1993) compared genetic algorithms with random-mutation hill climbing (mutate a solution at a single position and if its performance is at least as good as its parent, then it becomes a new parent) and observed that the latter method outperformed the genetic algorithm on functions constructed with explicit building blocks to be exploited by crossover. Davis (1991b) compared a similar simple random hill-climbing technique with genetic algorithms on the De Jong (1975) test suite: "[Random bit climbing] is an algorithm that manipulates one bit at a time and finds solutions from 3 to 23 times faster than the genetic algorithm, on the very problems that we have used to tune and compare genetic algorithms."

Ultimately, there is no inherent benefit from using any single method of generating new trials (any specific crossover, mutation, or any other operator) in all optimization problems. Rather, there is inherent benefit in allowing the evolutionary process to adapt its own transformations. Crossover operators are generally limited to transitions along the coordinate axes defined by the components in the coding structure. The procedures prematurely stagnate when grooves on the response surface that lead to regions of higher performance (lower error) are oriented across rather than along coordinate axes. Methods that can self-adapt the distribution of new trials to these contours in light of information gained during the search have the potential to accelerate optimization greatly. These methods are now commonly included in evolution strategies (Schwefel, 1981; Bäck et al., 1993) and evolutionary programming (Fogel et al., 1991, 1992), with the procedures of Schwefel generating better relative performance in empirical studies (Saravanan and Fogel, 1994). Similar speculations and procedures have recently been introduced in genetic algorithm research (Schaffer and Morishima, 1987; Spears and De Jong, 1991a; Bäck, 1992; Eshelman and Schaffer, 1993). The theoretical and empirical analysis of these techniques remains an open area of investigation.

## REFERENCES

Ackley, D. H. (1987). *A Connectionist Machine for Genetic Hill-Climbing*. Boston: Kluwer Academic Publishers.

Axelrod, R. (1987). "The Evolution of Strategies in the Iterated Prisoner's Dilemma." In *Genetic Algorithms and Simulated Annealing*, edited by L. Davis. London: Pitman, pp. 32–41.

Atmar, W. (1990). "Natural Processes Which Accelerate the Evolutionary Search." In *Proc. of the 24th Asilomar Conf. on Signals, Systems, and Computers*, edited by R. R. Chen. Pacific Grove, CA: Maple Press, pp. 1030–1035.

Bäck, T. (1992). "The Interaction of Mutation Rate, Selection, and Self-Adaptation within a Genetic Algorithm." In *Parallel Problem Solving from Nature 2*, edited by R. Männer and B. Manderick. Amsterdam: North-Holland, pp. 85–94.

Bäck, T. (1993). Personal communication, University of Dortmund, Germany.

Bäck, T. (1994). *Evolutionary Algorithms in Theory and Practice.* Philadelphia, PA: IOP Press, in press.

Bäck, T., F. Hoffmeister, and H.-P. Schwefel (1991). "A Survey of Evolution Strategies." In *Proc. of the Fourth Intern. Conf. on Genetic Algorithms,* edited by R. K. Belew and L. B. Booker. San Mateo, CA: Morgan Kaufman, pp. 2–9.

Bäck, T., G. Rudolph, and H.-P. Schwefel (1993). "Evolutionary Programming and Evolution Strategies: Similarities and Differences." In *Proc. of the Second Ann. Conf. on Evolutionary Programming,* edited by D. B. Fogel and W. Atmar. La Jolla, CA: Evolutionary Programming Society, pp. 11–22.

Baker, J. E. (1985). "Adaptive Selection Methods for Genetic Algorithms." In *Proc. of an Intern. Conf. on Genetic Algorithms and Their Applications,* edited by J. J. Grefenstette. San Mateo, CA: Morgan Kaufman, pp. 101–111.

Bethke, A. D. (1981). "Genetic Algorithms as Function Optimizers." Ph.D. diss., University of Michigan, Ann Arbor.

Bohachevsky, I. O., M. E. Johnson, and M. L. Stein (1986). "Generalized Simulated Annealing for Function Optimization," *Technometrics,* Vol. 28:3, pp. 209–218.

Brindle, A. (1980). "Genetic Algorithms for Function Optimization." Ph.D. diss. University of Alberta, Canada.

Caruana, R. A., and J. D. Schaffer (1988). "Representation and Hidden Bias: Gray vs. Binary Coding for Genetic Algorithms." In *Proc. of the Fifth Intern. Conf. on Machine Learning.* Los Altos, CA: Morgan Kaufmann, pp. 153–161.

Davis, L. (1985). "Applying Adaptive Algorithms to Epistatic Domains." In *Proc. of the Intern. Joint Conf. on Artificial Intelligence,* edited by A. Joshi. Los Altos, CA: Morgan Kaufmann, pp. 162–164.

Davis, L. (1989). "Adding Operator Probabilities in Genetic Algorithms." In *Proc. of the Third Intern. Conf. on Genetic Algorithms,* edited by J. D. Schaffer. San Mateo, CA: Morgan Kaufmann, pp. 61–69.

Davis, L., ed. (1991a). *Handbook of Genetic Algorithms.* New York: Van Nostrand Reinhold.

Davis, L. (1991b). "Bit-Climbing, Representational Bias, and Test Suite Design." In *Proc. of the Fourth Intern. Conf. on Genetic Algorithms,* edited by R. K. Belew and L. B. Booker. San Mateo, CA: Morgan Kaufmann, pp. 18–23.

Davis, T. E., and J. C. Principe (1993). "A Markov Chain Framework for the Simple Genetic Algorithm," *Evolutionary Computation*, Vol. 1:3, pp. 269–288.

Deb, K., and D. E. Goldberg (1989). "An Investigation of Niche and Species Formation in Genetic Function Optimization." In *Proc. of the Third Inter. Conf. on Genetic Algorithms*, edited by J. D. Schaffer. San Mateo, CA: Morgan Kaufmann, pp. 42–50.

De Jong, K. A. (1975). "The Analysis of the Behavior of a Class of Genetic Adaptive Systems." Ph.D. diss. University of Michigan, Ann Arbor.

De Jong, K. A. (1992). "Are Genetic Algorithms Function Optimizers?" In *Parallel Problem Solving from Nature 2*, edited by R. Männer and B. Manderick. Amsterdam: North-Holland, pp. 3–13.

De Jong, K. A. (1993). "Genetic Algorithms are NOT Function Optimizers." In *Foundations of Genetic Algorithms 2*, edited by L. D. Whitley. San Mateo, CA: Morgan Kaufmann, pp. 5–17.

Eiben, A. E., E. H. L. Aarts, and K. M. Van Hee (1991). "Global Convergence of Genetic Algorithms: A Markov Chain Analysis." In *Parallel Problem Solving from Nature*, edited by H.-P. Schwefel and R. Männer. Berlin: Springer, pp. 4–12.

Eshelman, L. J., and J. D. Schaffer (1993). "Crossover's Niche." In *Proc. of the Fifth Intern. Conf. on Genetic Algorithms*, edited by S. Forrest. San Mateo, CA: Morgan Kaufmann, pp. 9-14.

Fang, K.-T., S. Kotz, and K.-W. Ng (1990). *Symmetric Multivariate and Related Distributions*. Vol. 36 of Monographs on Statistics and Applied Probability. London: Chapman and Hall.

Fogel, D. B. (1991). *System Identification through Simulated Evolution: A Machine Learning Approach to Modeling*. Needham, MA: Ginn Press.

Fogel, D. B. (1992). "Evolving Artificial Intelligence," Ph.D. diss., UCSD.

Fogel, D. B. (1994a). "Asymptotic Convergence Properties of Genetic Algorithms and Evolutionary Programming: Analysis and Experiments," *Cybernetics and Systems*, Vol. 25:3, pp. 389–407.

Fogel, D. B. (1994b). "Applying Evolutionary Programming to Selected Control Problems," *Comp. Math. Appl.*, Vol. 27:11, pp. 89–104.

Fogel, D. B., and J. W. Atmar (1990). "Comparing Genetic Operators with Gaussian Mutations in Simulated Evolutionary Processes Using Linear Systems," *Biological Cybernetics*, Vol. 63, pp. 111–114.

Fogel, D. B., and L. C. Stayton (1994). "On the Effectiveness of Crossover in Simulated Evolutionary Optimization," *BioSystems*, Vol. 32:3, pp. 171–182.

Fogel, D. B., L. J. Fogel, and J. W. Atmar (1991). "Meta-Evolutionary Programming." In *Proc. of the 25th Asilomar Conf. on Signals, Systems, and Computers*, edited by R. R. Chen. Pacific Grove, CA: Maple Press, pp. 540–545.

Fogel, D. B., L. J. Fogel, W. Atmar, and G. B. Fogel (1992). "Hierarchic Methods of Evolutionary Programming." In *Proc. of the First Ann. Conf. on Evolutionary Programming*, edited by D. B. Fogel and W. Atmar. La Jolla, CA: Evolutionary Programming Society, pp. 175–182.

Forrest, S. (1993). "Genetic Algorithms: Principles of Natural Selection Applied to Computation," *Science*, Vol. 261, pp. 872–878.

Forrest, S., and M. Mitchell (1993). "Relative Building-Block Fitness and the Building-Block Hypothesis." In *Foundations of Genetic Algorithms 2*, edited by L. D. Whitley. San Mateo, CA: Morgan Kaufmann, pp. 109-126.

Fraser, A. S. (1957a). "Simulation of Genetic Systems by Automatic Digital Computers. I. Introduction," *Australian J. of Biol. Sci.*, Vol. 10, pp. 484–491.

Fraser, A. S. (1957b). "Simulation of Genetic Systems by Automatic Digital Computers. II. Effects of Linkage on Rates of Advance Under Selection," *Australian J. of Biol. Sci.*, Vol. 10, pp. 492–499.

Fraser, A. S. (1960). "Simulation of Genetic Systems by Automatic Digital Computers. VI. Epistasis," *Australian J. of Biol. Sci.*, Vol. 13, pp. 150–162.

Fraser, A. S. (1962). "Simulation of Genetic Systems," *J. Theo. Biol.*, Vol. 2, pp. 329-346.

Fraser, A. S. (1967). "Comments on Mathematical Challenges to the Neo-Darwinian Concept of Evolution." In *Mathematical Challenges to the Neo-Darwinian Interpretation of Evolution*, edited by P. S. Moorhead and M. M. Kaplan. Philadelphia: Wistar Institute Press, p. 107.

Fraser, A. S. (1968). "The Evolution of Purposive Behavior." In *Purposive Systems*, edited by H. von Foerster, J. D. White, L. J. Peterson, and J. K. Russell. Washington DC: Spartan Books, pp. 15–23.

Fukunaga, A., J. Marks, and J. T. Tgo (1994). "Automatic Control of Physically Realistic Animated Figures Using Evolutionary Programming." In *Proc. of the Third Ann. Conf. on Evolutionary Programming*, edited by A. V. Sebald and L. J. Fogel. River Edge, NJ: World Scientific, pp. 76–83.

Goldberg, D. E. (1987). "Simple Genetic Algorithms and the Minimal, Deceptive Problem." In *Genetic Algorithms and Simulated Annealing*, edited by L. Davis. San Mateo, CA: Morgan Kaufmann, pp. 74–88.

Goldberg, D. E. (1989). *Genetic Algorithms in Search, Optimization, and Machine Learning*. Reading, MA: Addison-Wesley.

Goldberg, D. E., and C. H. Kuo (1987). "Genetic Algorithms in Pipeline Optimization," *J. Comp. Civil Eng.*, Vol. 1:2, pp. 128–141.

Goodman, R. (1988). *Introduction to Stochastic Models.* Reading, MA: Benjamin/Cummings.

Grefenstette, J. J. (1986). "Optimization of Control Parameters for Genetic Algorithms," *IEEE Trans. on Systems, Man, and Cybernetics,* Vol. SMC-16, No. 1, pp. 122–128.

Grefenstette, J. J. (1987). "Incorporating Problem Specific Knowledge into Genetic Algorithms." In *Genetic Algorithms and Simulated Annealing*, edited by L. Davis. Los Altos, CA: Morgan Kaufmann, pp. 42–60.

Holland, J. H. (1969). "Adaptive Plans Optimal for Payoff-Only Environments." In *Proc. of the 2nd Hawaii Intern. Conf. on System Sciences*, pp. 917–920.

Holland, J. H. (1975). *Adaptation in Natural and Artificial Systems*. Ann Arbor: University of Michigan Press.

Holland, J. H. (1992). "Genetic Algorithms," *Scientific American*, July, pp. 66–72.

Hsu, P. L., and H. Robbins (1947). "Complete Convergence and the Law of Large Numbers," *Proc. Nat. Acad. Sci.*, Vol. 33:2, pp. 25–31.

Johnson, N. L., and S. Kotz (1970). *Distributions in Statistics: Continuous Distributions, 2*. Boston: Houghton Mifflin.

Koza, J. R. (1992). *Genetic Programming*. Cambridge, MA: MIT Press.

Martin, N. (1973). "Convergence Properties of a Class of Probabilistic Adaptive Schemes Called Sequential Reproductive Plans." Technical Report No. 210, Institute for Mathematical Studies in the Social Sciences, Stanford University, Stanford, CA.

Nettleton, D. J., and R. Garigliano (1994). "Evolutionary Algorithms and a Fractal Inverse Problem," *BioSystems*, in press.

Papoulis, A. (1984). *Probability, Random Variables, and Stochastic Processes.*, 2nd ed. New York: McGraw Hill.

Rappl, G. (1984). "Konvergenzraten von Random Search Verfahren zur globalen Optimierung," Dissertation, HSBw München, Germany.

Rechenberg, I. (1973). *Evolutionsstrategie: Optimierung technischer Systeme nach Prinzipien der biologischen Evolution.* Stuttgart: Frommann-Holzboog Verlag.

Rechenberg, I. (1994). Personal communication, Technical University of Berlin, Germany.

Rizki, M. M., L. A. Tamburino, and M. A. Zmuda (1993). "Evolving Multi-Resolution Feature Detectors." In *Proc. of the Second Ann. Conf. on Evolutionary Programming*, edited by D. B. Fogel and W. Atmar. La Jolla, CA: Evolutionary Programming Society, pp. 108–118.

Rudolph, G. (1994a). "Convergence Analysis of Canonical Genetic Algorithms," *IEEE Trans. on Neural Networks*, Vol. 5:1, pp. 96–101.

Rudolph, G. (1994b). "Massively Parallel Simulated Annealing and Its Relation to Evolutionary Algorithms," *Evolutionary Computation*, in press.

Saravanan, N., and D. B. Fogel (1994). "Learning of Strategy Parameters in Evolutionary Programming: An Empirical Study." In *Proc. of the Third Ann. Conf. on Evolutionary Programming*, edited by A. V. Sebald and L. J. Fogel. River Edge, NJ: World Scientific, pp. 269–280.

Schaffer, J. D., and L. J. Eshelman (1991). "On Crossover as an Evolutionarily Viable Strategy." In *Proc. of the Fourth Intern. Conf. on Genetic Algorithms*, edited by R. K. Belew and L. B. Booker. San Mateo, CA: Morgan Kaufmann, pp. 61–68.

Schaffer, J. D., and A. Morishima (1987). "An Adaptive Crossover Distribution Mechanism for Genetic Algorithms." In *Proc. of the Second Intern. Conf. on Genetic Algorithms*, edited by J. J. Grefenstette. Hillsdale, NJ: Lawrence Erlbaum, pp. 36–40.

Schaffer, J. D., R. A. Caruana, L. J. Eshelman, and R. Das (1989). "A Study of Control Parameters Affecting Online Performance of Genetic Algorithms for Function Optimization." In *Proc. of the Third Intern. Conf. on Genetic Algorithms*, edited by J. D. Schaffer. San Mateo, CA: Morgan Kaufmann, pp. 51–59.

Scheel, A. (1985). "Beitrag zur Theorie der Evolutionsstrategie." Dissertation, Technical University of Berlin, Berlin.

Schraudolph, N. N. (1992). Personal communication, Salk Institute, La Jolla, CA.

Schraudolph, N. N., and R. K. Belew (1992). "Dynamic Parameter Encoding for Genetic Algorithms," *Machine Learning*, Vol. 9, pp. 9–21.

Schwefel, H.-P. (1977). *Numerische Optimierung von Computer-Modellen mittels der Evolutionsstrategie*, Interdisciplinary Systems Research, Vol. 26. Basel: Birkhäuser.

Schwefel, H.-P. (1981). *Numerical Optimization of Computer Models*. Chichester, UK: John Wiley.

Sebald, A. V. (1991). Personal communication, UCSD.

Serfling, R. J. (1980). *Approximation Theorems of Mathematical Statistics*, New York: John Wiley.

Spears, W. M. (1993). "Crossover or Mutation?" In *Foundations of Genetic Algorithms 2*, edited by L. D. Whitley. San Mateo, CA: Morgan Kaufmann, pp. 221–237.

Spears, W. M., and K. A. De Jong (1991a). "On the Virtues of Parameterized Uniform Crossover." In *Proc. of the Fourth Intern. Conf. on Genetic Algorithms*, edited by R. K. Belew and L. B. Booker. San Mateo, CA: Morgan Kaufmann, pp. 230–236.

Spears, W. M., and K. A. De Jong (1991b). "An Analysis of Multi-Point Crossover." In *Foundations of Genetic Algorithms*, edited by G. J. E. Rawlins. San Mateo, CA: Morgan Kaufmann, pp. 301–315.

Syswerda, G. (1989). "Uniform Crossover in Genetic Algorithms." In *Proc. of the Third Intern. Conf. on Genetic Algorithms*, edited by J. D. Schaffer. San Mateo, CA: Morgan Kaufmann, pp. 2–9.

Whitley, L. D. (1993). "Introduction." In *Foundations of Genetic Algorithms 2*, edited by L. D. Whitley. San Mateo, CA: Morgan Kaufmann, pp. 1–4.

Zabinsky, Z. B., and R. L. Smith (1992). "Pure Adaptive Search in Global Optimization," *Mathematical Programming*, Vol. 53, pp. 323–328.

# 5

# Intelligent Behavior

## 5.1 INTELLIGENCE REQUIRES ITERATIVE PREDICTION AND CONTROL

The process of adaptation is one of minimizing surprise to the adaptive organism. It requires three basic elements: prediction, control, and feedback. Prediction operates as a mechanistic mapping from a set of observed environmental symbols to another set of symbols that represents the expected new circumstance. The mapping is essentially a model that relates previous experiences to future outcomes. Prediction is an essential ingredient of intelligence, for if a system cannot predict future events, every environmental occurrence comes as a surprise and adaptation is impossible. But an intelligent system must not simply predict its environment; rather, it must use its predictions to affect its decision making and thereby control its behavior. Any system that allocates its resources (i.e., controls its behavior) without regard to the anticipated consequences of those actions relegates its future to nothing but pure luck. Furthermore, the adaptive organism must act on the error in prediction and the associated cost of inappropriate behaviors to improve the quality of its forecasting. Every intelligent system adapts to its environment by predicting future events, controlling its actions in light of those predictions, and revising its bases for making predictions in light of feedback on the degree to which it is achieving its goals.

The examples offered in this chapter illustrate this fundamental concept. The instances focus primarily on the use of evolutionary algorithms, but similar demonstrations can be achieved with genetic techniques. The chosen examples highlight the ability of evolutionary computation (1) to induce predictive models of systems and to use such models for control in light of a purpose, (2) to adapt behavior while interacting with other purposive agents, and (3) to achieve success in general problem solving without relying on credit assignment algorithms. The experimental designs for these examples follow Fogel (1992, 1993a, 1993b, 1994), and the extended results are previously unpublished. These cases are not offered as exhaustive evidence of the range of possible demonstrations, but instead are meant to serve as a foundation for the thesis that machine intelligence can be achieved by simulating evolution and that such intelligence can be used for good engineering purpose. In each case, the evolutionary simulation iteratively improves algorithms that operate on experienced data and generate increasingly appropriate behaviors in the light of environmental demands.

## 5.2 EVOLUTIONARY IDENTIFICATION AND CONTROL OF A NONLINEAR, UNSTABLE PLANT: THE CART-POLE SYSTEM

The classic cart-pole system has received considerable attention (e.g., Barto et al., 1983; Wieland, 1991; Koza, 1992, pp. 289–307; Fogel, 1992, 1994; and many others). Figure 5-1 indicates the configuration of the system, governed by the following equations:

$$\ddot{\theta}_t = \frac{g \sin \theta_t + \cos \theta_t \left[ \dfrac{-F_t - m_p l \dot{\theta}_t^2 \sin \theta_t + \mu_c \, \mathrm{sgn}(\dot{x}_t)}{m_c + m_p} \right] - \dfrac{\mu_p \dot{\theta}_t}{m_p l}}{l \left[ \dfrac{4}{3} - \dfrac{m_p \cos^2 \theta_t}{m_c + m_p} \right]} \qquad (5\text{-}1)$$

$$\ddot{x}_t = \frac{F_t + m_p l [\dot{\theta}_t^2 \sin \theta_t - \ddot{\theta}_t \cos \theta_t] - \mu_c \, \mathrm{sgn}(\dot{x}_t)}{m_c + m_p},$$

where, following Barto et al. (1983),

$g = -9.8$ m/s², acceleration due to gravity,

$m_c = 1.0$ kg, mass of the cart,

$m_p = 0.1$ kg, mass of the pole,

$l = 0.5$ m, half-pole length,

$\mu_c = 0.0005$, coefficient of friction of the cart on the track,

$\mu_p = 0.000002$, coefficient of friction of the pole on the cart, and

$F_t =$ the force applied to the cart's center of mass at time $t$.

The dynamics of the cart-pole system are simple to encode, yet its behavior involves trigonometric functions, sign (sgn) functions, friction terms, and a coupling between the cart's state vector and the pole's state vector. It is a fairly complicated nonlinear unstable system.

The primary control goal is to maintain the system in balance (i.e., do not let the cart hit either end of the track nor allow the pole to exceed a specified deflection angle) by pushing or pulling on the cart, and ultimately to move the cart and pole to a position of 0.0 meters and 0.0 radians, given any initial conditions. Barto et al. (1983), and others later, chose limits of ±12 degrees for the pole and ±2.4 meters for the cart, while employing a bang-bang application of ±10 newtons (i.e., either push or pull with +10

**Figure 5-1**    The cart-pole system. A single pole is mounted on the center of a cart. The cart moves along a track. The system is nonlinear and unstable. The system is considered to have "failed" if the pole exceeds a specified angle of deflection or the cart hits either end of the track.

newtons of force). The current experiments decreased these allowable ranges to ±0.2 radians (±11.5 degrees) and ±1 meter for the pole and cart, respectively, while only allowing the application of ±1 newton of force. This provided more stringent conditions yet still incorporated nonlinearities associated with the trigonometric functions.

An evolutionary procedure was implemented (1) to estimate a model of the system given the observed stimulus-response sequence and (2) to generate a control input to the system simultaneously. For ease of coding, only linear models were considered, despite the actual system being non-linear. More specifically, the linear systems were of the general form

$$y(t) = a_1y(t-1) + \ldots + a_ky(t-k) + b_1u(t-1) + \ldots + \\ b_ju(t-j) + e(t) + c_1e(t-1) + \ldots + c_me(t-m), \tag{5-2}$$

where the sequence $\{y(t)\}$ is the output of the system, the sequence $\{u(t)\}$ is the control input, and $\{e(t)\}$ represents unknown disturbances. Thus the previous $k$ values of the output along with the previous $j$ controls, as well as the current and previous $m$ disturbances, determine the response of the system, $y(t)$. For notational simplicity, such systems are often described as

$$A(q)y(t) = B(q)u(t) + C(q)e(t), \tag{5-3}$$

where the terms in $y$ are collected on the left-hand side of the equation and where $A(q)$, $B(q)$, and $C(q)$ are polynomials in a shift operator $q^{-1}$ that define the coefficients modifying each term in the equation.

As the cart-pole system involves coupled equations, the class of approximate linear models to be searched also included such coupling. The hypothesized multidimensional equations provided to the evolutionary program took the form

$$A_1(q)y_1(t) = B_1(q)u(t) + C_1(q)e_1(t) + D_1(q)y_2(t)$$
$$A_2(q)y_2(t) = B_2(q)u(t) + C_2(q)e_2(t) + D_2(q)y_1(t), \tag{5-4}$$

where $A_1(q)$, $A_2(q)$, $B_1(q)$, $B_2(q)$, $C_1(q)$, $C_2(q)$, $D_1(q)$, and $D_2(q)$ are polynomials in $q^{-1}$, $y_1(t)$ represents the pole position, $y_2(t)$ represents the cart position, $u(t)$ represents the single-force input to the system (i.e., the force applied to the cart in newtons), and $e_1(t)$ and $e_2(t)$ represent random perturbations and discrepancies between the true system and the hypothesized models. The number of lag terms for polynomials $A_1(q)$, $A_2(q)$, $B_1(q)$, $B_2(q)$,

$D_1(q)$, and $D_2(q)$ were allowed to vary from one to four. The number of lag terms for polynomials $C_1(q)$ and $C_2(q)$ were allowed to vary from zero to three.

Following Barto et al. (1983), the cart-pole system was simulated using Euler's method and time step of 0.02 seconds. The cart and pole were initialized at positions in accordance with Gaussian random variables having zero mean and standard deviation of 0.01. This constituted the first observation (i.e., a single observation included both the position of the cart and pole), and the time step $t$ was set equal to 1. The system was then allowed to operate in the absence of any control input, and a second observation was made.

A population of 50 random models was constructed. The number of lag terms in each polynomial varied uniformly over the appropriate range (see above), and the coefficients for each term were initialized uniformly over $[-0.5, 0.5]$. Each model was evaluated with respect to how well it fit the observed stimulus-response sequence; at first, just two observations. That is, the first observation was offered to each model, and the sums of the squared error between the actual and predicted cart and pole positions for the second observation were compared. Any terms that referred to data before time $t = 1$ were ignored. Each model was evaluated not only with respect to its predictive error on the second observation, but also with respect to the number of degrees of freedom that the model employed. Overly complex models can provide for less error on observed sequences simply because they overfit random perturbations or components that are uncorrelated with the system's output. But the consequence of such over-specification is that such models are typically less capable of generalizing about the system's future behavior.

The problem of optimally trading off a model's goodness-of-fit for its degrees of freedom has been well studied, and several criteria have been proposed (Wallace and Boulton, 1968; Mallows, 1973; Akaike, 1974; Schwarz, 1977; Rissanen, 1978; Barron, 1982; and others). The method chosen here was Akaike's information criterion (AIC) (Akaike, 1974). Explanation of the principles underlying this criterion is beyond the scope of this book; see Akaike (1974). Operationally, under an assumption of Gaussian residuals, the criterion simplifies to

$$\text{AIC}(\theta) = t \ln (SSE/t) + 2p,$$

where $\theta$ is the vector of parameters being estimated, $SSE$ is the sum of the squared errors, $t$ is the number of observations since the start of the simulation or the last failure, and $p$ is the number of degrees of freedom in $\theta$. As the goodness-of-fit increases, the AIC decreases. But as the number of degrees of freedom increases, so does the AIC. The appropriateness of adding any additional degrees of freedom can be quantitatively measured by how much each reduces the overall error of the model. The best model is that which minimizes the AIC.

Offspring models were created from these parents and were also evaluated over the observed data sequence in light of the AIC. Each parent was copied to provide one offspring, and mutation then acted on each offspring. First, each polynomial term was given a 50 percent chance of varying its order. If it did vary, it was again given a 50 percent chance of increasing or decreasing, up to the maximum and down to the minimum number of lags. The actual number of lags to increase or decrease was chosen in accordance with a Poisson random variable with mean $\lambda = 0.1$. New terms in the polynomials were initialized uniformly over $[-0.5, 0.5]$. Finally, each existing coefficient was altered by adding a Gaussian random variable with zero mean and standard deviation 0.01.

Selection acted to stochastically cull the 50 worst models. A round-robin competition was conducted in which each model competed for wins against 10 other models randomly selected from the population. In each competition, the chosen model received a win if it had an AIC score equal to or lower than its opponent. The 50 models with the most wins were retained as parents for the next generation.

Before continuing on with another round of mutation and selection, the best model (in terms of lowest AIC) was used to determine the force to apply to the cart: If a positive control input was indicated the force was set equal to +1 newton, otherwise it was set equal to –1 newton. Thus only a single iteration of mutation and selection was allowed at any time step. Control was performed on-line. A weighted function of the distance between the pole's position and its maximum allowable range, and the cart's position and its maximum allowable range, was utilized to calculate the best control at each time step.

Specifically, the control goal was to minimize

$$J_w = w_1[y_1(t) - T_1(t)]^2 + w_2[y_2(t) - T_2(t)]^2, \tag{5-5}$$

where $w_1$ and $w_2$ are the weights associated with each error and $T_1(t)$ and $T_2(t)$ are the target values for the pole and cart, respectively. To determine the appropriate control, given the best solution (a pair of models describing the dynamics of the pole and cart) at each time step, the expected output of $y_1(t)$ and $y_2(t)$ could be estimated for any particular input $u(t-1)$. That is,

$$y_1(t) = K_1 + B_1 u(t-1)$$
$$y_2(t) = K_2 + B_2 u(t-1)$$
(5-6)

where $K_1$ and $K_2$ are values equal to the sum of the known quantities in each equation, respectively, and $B_1$ and $B_2$ refer to the first coefficients in the polynomials $B_1(q)$ and $B_2(q)$, respectively.

If the weights $w_1$ and $w_2$ are constrained to be positive and equal (equal emphasis), then the task is to minimize

$$T_1^2 - 2T_1 K_1 - 2T_1 B_1 u + K_1^2 + 2K_1 B_1 u + B_1^2 u^2$$
$$+ T_2^2 - 2T_2 K_2 - 2T_2 B_2 u + K_2^2 + 2K_2 B_2 u + B_2^2 u^2.$$
(5-7)

Taking the derivative with respect to the control input and setting it equal to zero yields

$$\frac{d}{du} = u(2B_1^2 + 2B_2^2) - 2T_1 B_1 + 2K_1 B_1 - 2T_2 B_2 + 2K_2 B_2 = 0.$$
(5-8)

Solving for $u$,

$$u = \frac{T_1 B_1 + T_2 B_2 - K_1 B_1 - K_2 B_2}{B_1^2 + B_2^2}.$$
(5-9)

To verify that this is a minimum, the second derivative,

$$\frac{d^2}{du^2} = 2B_1^2 + 2B_2^2,$$
(5-10)

is always positive.

If the weights $w_1$ and $w_2$ are positive and $w_1 \neq w_2$, then, following the same procedure, taking the derivative of the weighted function and setting it equal to zero yields

$$\frac{d}{du} = -2T_1 B_1 w_1 + 2K_1 B_1 w_1 + 2w_1 B_1^2 u - 2T_2 B_2 w_2 + 2K_2 B_2 w_2 + 2w_2 B_2^2 u = 0.$$
(5-11)

Solving for $u$,

$$u = \frac{T_1 B_1 w_1 + T_2 B_2 w_2 - K_1 B_1 w_1 - K_2 B_2 w_2}{w_1 B_1^2 + w_2 B_2^2}. \qquad (5\text{-}12)$$

To verify that this is a minimum, the second derivative,

$$\frac{d^2}{du^2} = 2w_1 B_1^2 + 2w_2 B_2^2, \qquad (5\text{-}13)$$

is always positive for $w_1, w_2 \geq 0$.

For the current experiments, the weights were chosen such that they were equal to the percentage of the distance traversed to the maximum allowable range. For example, if the pole position were 0.1 radians and the cart position were 0.8 meters, then the weighting would be $w_1 = 0.5$, $w_2 = 0.8$, because the pole would be positioned halfway between the target and the maximum allowable angle of deflection, and because the cart would be positioned 80 percent of the way between the target and the end of the track. The chosen weighting appeared reasonable but perhaps was not optimal.

If the cart or pole exceeded its allowable thresholds, the system was restarted at random in accordance with a multivariate Gaussian distribution with mean (0, 0) and standard deviation (0.01, 0.01). The parent population carried over as the initial basis for generating offspring, and the observed data length was reset to $t = 1$. If the cart-pole system was maintained within the tolerable range of performance for 40 seconds (2,000 time steps), the current trial was halted and a new trial was begun. It was recognized that the arbitrary threshold of 40 seconds of control did not indicate indefinite success. Figure 5-2 provides a flowchart of the procedure.

A series of 50 trials was conducted using this procedure. A histogram of the total number of failures incurred before attaining 40 seconds of balance appears in Figure 5-3. The minimum number of failures was five, while the maximum was 174. For the best performance, Figures 5-4 and 5-5 indicate the actual position of the pole and cart during the simulation. The control input as a function of time is indicated in Figure 5-6. The applied force had a periodic characteristic. Figure 5-7 depicts both the pole and cart positions during the 40 seconds of balance. As would be expected, the pole and cart tended to oscillate in opposition while being centered around the target of zero radians of deflection and zero meters from center. Figures 5-8 and 5-9 indicate the actual and predicted pole and cart positions during the

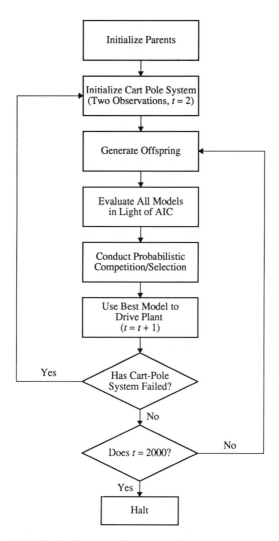

**Figure 5-2** A flowchart of the evolutionary algorithm for controlling the cart-pole system. The cart and pole are initialized, and two observations are made. A random collection of linear models are evaluated with respect to how well they fit these data in light of Akaike's information criterion, which also penalizes models for their number of degrees of freedom. Selection probabilistically removes the 50 poorest models. The best-surviving model (in terms of AIC) is used to offer a control to the system, pushing or pulling on the cart with 1 newton of force. If neither the cart nor pole exceed their specified thresholds, the new observation is added to the environmental sequence and the process of evaluating all the surviving parents and their new offspring in light of the extended sequence of observations is continued. If either the cart or pole exceed their limits, the system is restarted and the evolutionary algorithm proceeds with the current population. The process is halted after the system has been balanced for 2,000 continuous time steps, each corresponding to 0.02 seconds.

**Figure 5-3** A histogram of the number of failures incurred before attaining 40 seconds of balance when the length of the pole is 0.5 meters across all 50 trials. The best performance incurred only five failures, while the worst performance incurred 174 failures.

**Figure 5-4** The position of the pole (radians) during the trial with the fewest number of failures (five). All five failures were due to the pole exceeding its limit of ±0.2 radians.

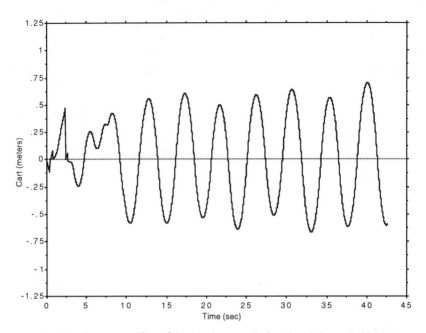

**Figure 5-5** The position of the cart (meters) during the trial with the fewest number of failures (five). None of the failures was due to the cart exceeding its limit of ±1 meter.

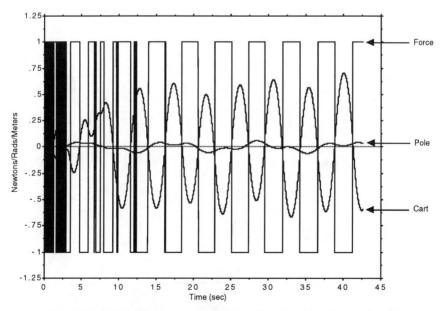

**Figure 5-6** The force (newtons) applied to the cart-pole system in the trial with best performance. The graph overlays the force with the position of the pole (radians) and cart (meters). The force is seen to take on a characteristic periodicity in which the cart is pushed when it crosses to the negative side of the track and is pulled when it crosses back to the positive side. The pole swings in opposition to the force.

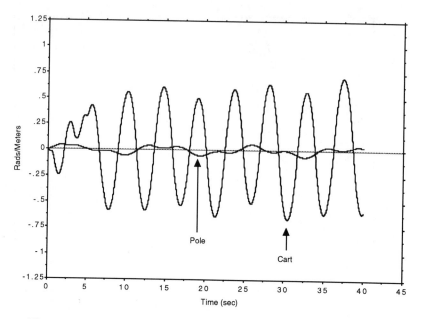

**Figure 5-7** An overlay of the position of the pole (radians) and the cart (meters) during the balanced 40 seconds. After a brief period of wobble, the cart and pole oscillate in opposition to each other.

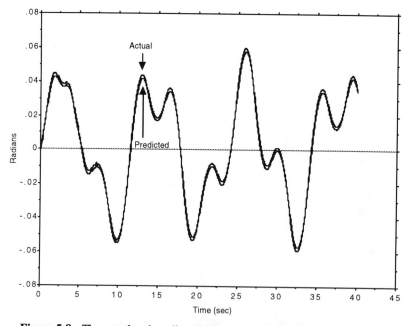

**Figure 5-8** The actual and predicted pole position (radians) using the final best-evolved model from the trial with five failures (see Table 5-1). The predictive error is always considerably smaller than 0.01 radians.

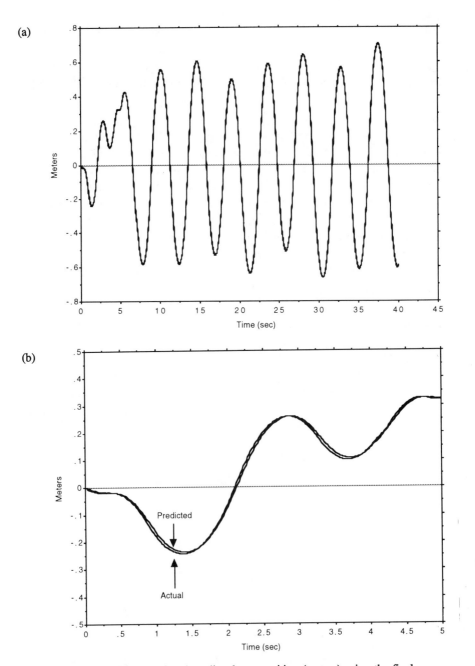

**Figure 5-9** The actual and predicted cart position (meters) using the final best-evolved model from the trial with five failures (see Table 5-1). (a) The predictive error is too small to be seen when the scaling reflects the range of motion of the cart. (b) The slight predictive error can be observed in this section depicting the behavior of the first five seconds of balance.

balanced period, respectively, using the final best-evolved model. Note that this model was not necessarily the one used to generate a control at any time before the final time step. The final best-evolved model (Table 5-1) generated good predictions of the system's behavior.

Table 5-2 shows the final evolved model after balancing the cart-pole system in the worst trial (174 failures). Figures 5-10 and 5-11 indicate the actual and predicted pole and cart positions during the balanced period from this trial. Although there is little resemblance between the models evolved in the best and worst case, their predictive capabilities are notably similar. This illustrates the effect of selection acting only on the exhibited behavior of a system and not on its specific form. Independently evolved behaviors often converge despite significant differences in structure.

Two sets of 50 additional trials were conducted with exactly the same procedure in which the half-length of the pole was increased to 0.75 meters and subsequently decreased to 0.25 meters. Figure 5-12 indicates the histograms of the number of failures incurred before obtaining 40 seconds of balance in each of these experiments.

These results demonstrate evolved intelligent behavior: The evolutionary program adapted its behavior to meet a specified goal in a range of environments. The goal was to apply $\pm 1$ newton of force to the cart so as to bring the pole closer to 0.0 radians of deflection and the cart closer to 0.0

Model Form:

$$A_1(q)\, y_1(t) = B_1(q)\, u(t) + C_1(q)\, e_1(t) + D_1(q)\, y_2(t)$$

$$A_2(q)\, y_2(t) = B_2(q)\, u(t) + C_2(q)\, e_2(t) + D_2(q)\, y_1(t)$$

$$
\begin{aligned}
A_1(1) &= -0.889584 \\
A_1(2) &= -0.108392 \\
B_1(1) &= -0.000912 \\
C_1(1) &= -0.302475 \\
C_1(2) &= 0.154752 \\
D_1(1) &= 0.000110 \\
A_2(1) &= -1.001456 \\
B_2(1) &= 0.001768 \\
C_2(1) &= -0.352155 \\
D_2(1) &= -0.055473
\end{aligned}
$$

**Table 5-1**   The final best-evolved model for the trial with five failures on the cart with a pole length of 0.5 m. The pole is represented by $y_1$, and the cart is represented by $y_2$. The coefficients for the polynomials are indicated, and the value in parentheses indicates the order of the lag term for the respective polynomial.

Model Form:

$$A_1(q)\, y_1(t) = B_1(q)\, u(t) + C_1(q)\, e_1(t) + D_1(q)\, y_2(t)$$

$$A_2(q)\, y_2(t) = B_2(q)\, u(t) + C_2(q)\, e_2(t) + D_2(q)\, y_1(t)$$

$$A_1(1) = -1.005333$$
$$B_1(1) = 0.001449$$
$$C_1(1) = 0.653425$$
$$D_1(1) = 0.001631$$
$$A_2(1) = -0.482032$$
$$A_2(2) = 1.496446$$
$$B_2(1) = 0.002918$$
$$C_2(1) = 0.836396$$
$$D_2(1) = 0.045087$$

**Table 5-2**    The final best-evolved model for the trial with 174 failures on the cart with a pole length of 0.5 m. The pole is represented by $y_1$, and the cart is represented by $y_2$. The coefficients for the polynomials are indicated, and the value in parentheses indicates the order of the lag term for the respective polynomial.

meters of displacement in accordance with the weighting offered in Eq. 5-5. The environments spanned poles with half-lengths of 0.25, 0.5, and 0.75 meters. The same evolutionary program was able to balance each of these systems in each of 50 trials. The algorithm generated increasingly appropriate predictive models of the nonlinear unstable plant and required no more than 222 failures (in the case of a pole half-length of 0.75 m) to maintain the tested cart-pole systems in balance for 40 seconds.

The evolutionary program was handicapped in several regards. Only a single iteration of mutation and selection was allowed at each time step. Generating an appropriate control input was therefore difficult, especially during the initial stages. The control procedure depended on the best-evolved model of the system, yet the identification of the system was performed in closed-loop, and it began with just a pair of observations as the basis for predicting the system's future behavior. Improved performance would be expected if additional iterations of mutation and selection could be executed before having to offer a control. Further, mutation was applied with fixed distributions, in terms of the probability of varying the number of lags, the actual number of lags to vary, and the perturbation of existing coefficients. Moreover, the defining parameters of these distributions were chosen somewhat arbitrarily. Faster convergence to suitable models could

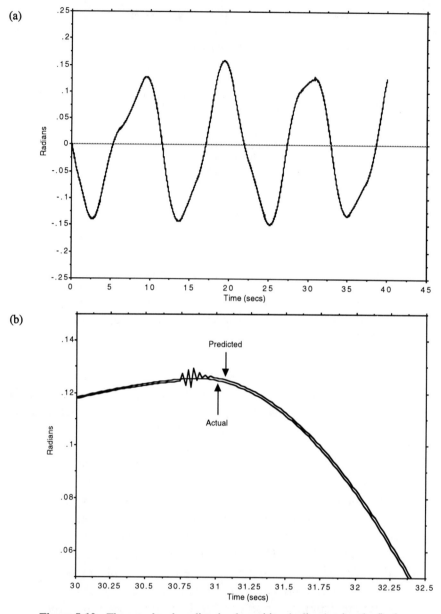

**Figure 5-10** The actual and predicted pole position (radians) using the final best-evolved model (see Table 5-2) from the trial with the worst performance (174 failures). (a) The predictive error is too small to be seen when the scaling reflects the range of motion of the pole, although a slight disturbance can be seen at about the 31st second. (b) The predicted and actual position of the pole over a 2.5-second interval starting at 30 seconds into the balanced period indicates a deviation by the model followed by a slight increase in predictive error.

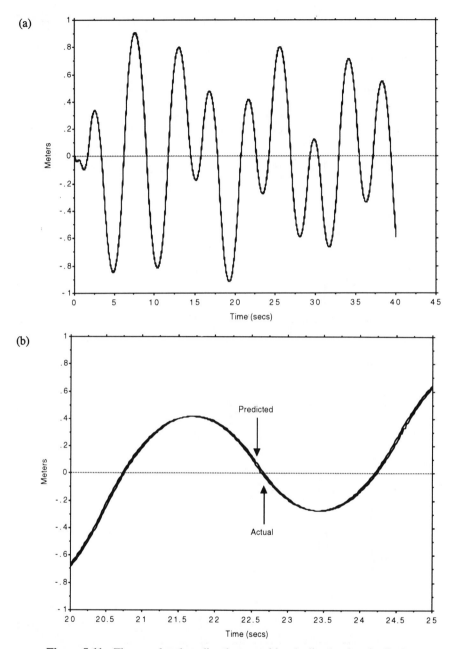

**Figure 5-11** The actual and predicted cart position (radians) using the final best-evolved model (see Table 5-2) from the trial with the worst performance (174 failures). (a) The predictive error is too small to be seen when the scaling reflects the range of motion of the cart. (b) Even when attention is focused on a five-second interval starting at 20 seconds into the balanced period, the predictive error with respect to the cart is quite small.

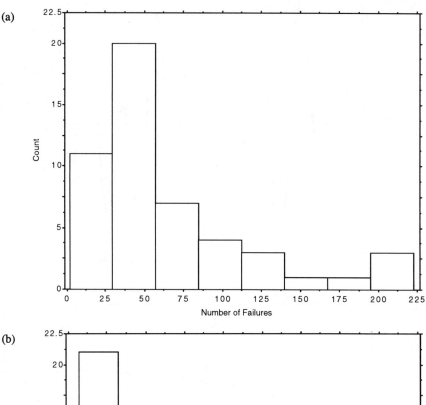

**Figure 5-12** Histograms of the number of failures incurred before achieving 40 seconds of balance. (a) The case where the pole length is 0.75 meters. The maximum number of failures was 222. (b) The case where the pole length is 0.25 meters. The maximum number of failures was 192.

have been achieved if mutation were made a function of error, or self-adaptive.

Although the evolutionary program did generate intelligent behavior, these experiments should not be viewed as evidence of general problem solving. Significant information was offered to the evolutionary program to facilitate its performance. The class of linear models to be searched provided an adequate representation of the system and specifically included the coupling between the pole and the cart. Further, the AIC was employed to prevent overfitting the observed stimulus-response sequence. Perhaps most importantly, a minimum variance weighted control scheme was designed specifically to make the control input sensitive to the pole and cart's positions relative to their respective prescribed tolerance limits. These a priori hints indicate the domain specificity of this investigation.

## 5.3  THE PRISONER'S DILEMMA: COEVOLUTIONARY ADAPTATION

The conditions that foster the evolution of cooperative behaviors among individuals of a species (or among species) are not generally well understood. In intellectually advanced social animals, cooperation between individuals, when it exists, is often ephemeral and quickly reverts to selfishness, with little or no clear indication of the specific circumstances that prompt the change. Simulation games such as the prisoner's dilemma have been used to gain insight into the precise conditions that promote the evolution of either decisively cooperative or selfish behavior in a community of individuals. Even simple games often generate very complex and dynamic optimization surfaces. The computational problem is to determine reliably any ultimately stable strategy (or strategies) for a specific game situation.

The prisoner's dilemma is an easily defined nonzero-sum, noncooperative game. The term *nonzero-sum* indicates that whatever benefits accrue to one player do not necessarily imply similar penalties imposed on the other player. The term *noncooperative* indicates that no preplay communication is permitted between the players. Typically, two players are involved in the game, each having two alternative actions: cooperate or defect. Cooperation implies increasing the total gain of both players; defecting implies increasing one's own reward at the expense of the other player.

The optimal policy for a player depends on the policy of the opponent (Hofstadter, 1985, p. 717). Against a player who always defects, defection is the only rational play. But it is also the only rational play against a player who always cooperates, for such a player is a fool. Only when there is some mutual trust between the players does cooperation become a reasonable policy.

The general form of the game is represented in Table 5-3 (after Scodel et al., 1959). The game is conducted on a trial-by-trial basis (a series of moves). Each player must choose to cooperate or defect on each trial. The payoff matrix defining the game is subject to the following constraints (Rapoport, 1966):

$$2\gamma_1 > \gamma_2 + \gamma_3 \tag{5-14}$$

$$\gamma_3 > \gamma_1 > \gamma_4 > \gamma_2. \tag{5-15}$$

The first rule prevents any obvious desire for mutual cooperation. The second rule motivates each player to play noncooperatively.

Defection dominates cooperation in a game theoretic sense (Rapoport, 1966). But joint defection results in a payoff, $\gamma_4$, to each player that is smaller than the payoff, $\gamma_1$, that could be gained through mutual cooperation. If the game is played for only a single trial, the clearly compelling behavior is

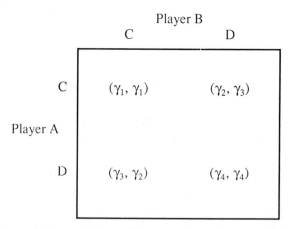

**Table 5-3**  The general form of the payoff function in the prisoner's dilemma, where $\gamma_1$ is the payoff to each player for mutual cooperation, $\gamma_2$ is the payoff for cooperating when the other player defects, $\gamma_3$ is the payoff for defecting when the other player cooperates, and $\gamma_4$ is the payoff for mutual defection. An entry ($\alpha$, $\beta$) indicates the payoffs to players A and B, respectively.

defection. If the game is iterated over many trials, the correct behavior becomes less clear. If there is no possibility for communication with the other player, then the iterated game degenerates into a sequence of independent trials, with defection again yielding the maximum expected benefit. But if the outcome of earlier trials can affect the decision-making policy of the players in subsequent trials, learning can take place and both players may seek to cooperate.

### 5.3.1  Background

In 1979, Axelrod organized a prisoner's dilemma tournament and solicited strategies from game theorists who had published in the field (Axelrod, 1980a). The 14 entries were competed, along with a 15th entry: on each move, cooperate or defect with equal probability. Each strategy was played against all others and itself over a sequence of 200 moves. The specific payoff function used is shown in Table 5-4. The winner of the tournament, submitted by Anatol Rapoport, was "Tit-for-Tat":

1.  Cooperate on the first move.
2.  Otherwise, mimic whatever the other player did on the previous move.

Subsequent analysis by Axelrod (1984), Hofstadter (1985, pp. 721–723), and others indicates that this Tit-for-Tat strategy is robust because it never defects first and is never taken advantage of for more than one iteration at a time. Boyd and Lorberbaum (1987) indicated that Tit-for-Tat is not evolutionarily stable (*sensu* Maynard Smith, 1982). Nevertheless, in a second tournament, Axelrod (1980b) collected 62 contending entries, and again the winner was Tit-for-Tat.

Axelrod (1984) noted that eight of the 62 entries in the second tournament can be used to reasonably account for how well a given strategy did with the entire set. Axelrod (1987) used these eight strategies as opponents for a simulated evolving population of policies based on a genetic algorithm approach. Consideration was given to the set of strategies that is deterministic and uses outcomes of the three previous moves to determine a current move. Because there were four possible outcomes for each move, there were $4^3$ or 64 possible sets of three possible moves. The coding for a

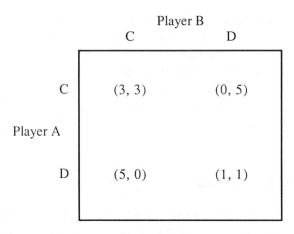

**Table 5-4** The specific payoff function used in Axelrod (1980a).

policy was therefore determined by a string of 64 bits, where each bit corresponded with a possible instance of the preceding three interactions, and six additional bits that defined the player's move for the initial combinations of under three interactions. Thus there were $2^{70}$ (about $10^{21}$) possible strategies.

The simulation was conducted as a series of steps: (1) Randomly select an initial population of 20 strategies; (2) execute each strategy against the eight representatives and record a weighted-average payoff; (3) determine the number of offspring from each parent strategy in proportion to their effectiveness; (4) generate offspring by crossing over two parent strategies and, with a small probability, affect a mutation by randomly changing components of the strategy; and (5) continue to iterate this process. Crossover and mutation probabilities averaged one crossover and one-half a mutation per generation. Each game consisted of 151 moves (the average of the previous tournaments). A run consisted of 50 generations. Forty trials were conducted. From a random start, the technique created populations whose median performance was just as successful as Tit-for-Tat. The behavior of many of the strategies actually resembled Tit-for-Tat (Axelrod, 1987).

Another experiment (Axelrod, 1987) required the evolving policies to play against each other, rather than against the eight representatives. This was a much more complex environment: The opponents that each individual faced were concurrently evolving. As more effective strategies propagated throughout the population, each individual had to keep pace or face elimination through selection. Ten trials were conducted with this format. Typically, the population evolved away from cooperation initially, but then tended toward reciprocating whatever cooperation could be found. The average score of the population increased over time as "an evolved ability to discriminate between those who will reciprocate cooperation and those who won't" was attained (Axelrod, 1987).

### 5.3.2 Evolving Finite State Representations

Fogel (1993a), following earlier investigation (Fogel, 1991), implemented a population of 100 coevolving finite state machines (FSMs) (50 parents), each possessing a maximum of eight states. This limit was chosen to provide a reasonable chance for explaining the behavior of any machine through examination of its structure. Eight-state FSMs do not subsume all the behaviors that could be generated under the coding of Axelrod (1987), but do allow for a dependence on sequences of greater than third-order. The input alphabet consisted of {(C, C), (C, D), (D, C), (D, D)}, where the first symbol indicated the FSM's previous move and the second symbol indicated the opponent's previous move. The output alphabet consisted of {C, D}. Each FSM represented a predictive algorithm that operated on a sequence of stimulus pairs and generated a behavior in light of the expected next response of the opponent and the payoff for alternative interactions. Mutation was conducted as in Fogel et al. (1966)—that is, change an output symbol, state-transition, or start state, add a state, or delete a state—with an additional mutation operation being defined on the start symbol associated with each machine (i.e., will the machine cooperate or defect on the first move?). The initial machines possessed one to five states, with all responses and connections randomly determined. Each member of the population faced every other member in competition (round-robin). Scoring was made with respect to the payoff function in Axelrod (1987); refer to Table 5-4. Each game consisted of 151 moves, with the maximum number of generations per evolutionary trial being set to 200. Twenty trials were conducted.

The results of two representative trials are indicated in Figure 5-13. The results were fairly consistent across all 20 trials. In each evolution, there was an initial tendency for mutual defection—that is, selfish behavior—but after a few generations (e.g., five to 10), machines evolved that would cooperate if they "recognized" other cooperative machines. These machines received an average of nearly three points for each encounter with similar machines yet still retained their initial ability to defect against mutual defectors. As offspring were created from these new versatile machines, they tended to propagate and dominate the population until it became nearly impossible for even a small number of defectors to persist. The mean population fitness approached but never quite reached 3.0 as each machine tested its potential adversary, apparently checking if it could be exploited by defecting. These results are similar to those reported in Axelrod (1987) and Fogel (1991).

A second set of experiments was designed to examine the rate at which cooperative behavior is achieved in populations of various sizes. Trials were conducted with populations of 50, 100, 250, 500, and 1,000 parents. The execution time increased as the square of the population size due to the round-robin competitions. Although other mechanisms of competition could be formulated (Fogel et al., 1992), all the parameters were held constant except for the population size to provide a measure of comparison to the previous experiment. Each trial was halted at the 25th generation. This decision precluded assessing the stability of evolved cooperation but was necessary in light of the available computing facilities. Thirty trials were conducted with populations of 50 and 100 parents. Five trials were conducted with a population of 250 parents. Multiple trials could not be reasonably completed with populations of 500 and 1,000 parents on the available computing machinery (Sun 4/260).

The mean and median scores of the parents at each generation for all population sizes are shown in Figure 5-14. It would be inappropriate to formulate statistical conclusions in light of the small sample size, but it can be stated that the time to evolve cooperation does not necessarily decrease as the population size is decreased. On the average, cooperative behavior is evidenced before the tenth generation. Thirty additional trials were conducted with populations of 50 and 100 parents to test whether there was any difference in the mean performance of all parents after 25 generations. The two-sided Smith-Satterthwaite $t$-test indicated that there was insufficient evidence to suggest any difference in average performance ($t = 1.17$, $P > 0.2$). There appears to be very little qualitative difference between the evolved behavior for populations ranging from 50 to 1,000 parents.

An examination of the best FSM in each trial supports this view. Figure 5-15 indicates a best FSM after 25 generations with the number of parents varying over 50, 100, 250, 500, and 1,000. To simplify notation, $FSM_x$ will refer to the best-evolved FSM when using a population of $x$ parents. $FSM_{50}$ and $FSM_{100}$ are typical (in terms of behavior) of other FSMs generated across the 30 trials with 50 and 100 parents. $FSM_{250}$ is typical of those generated in the five trials with 250 parents. All the best-evolved FSMs are initially cooperative. Each exhibits many states in which mutual cooperation (C, C) elicits further cooperation (C). Continued defection in light of previous mutual defection is also a repeated pattern across all depicted FSMs.

It is of interest to compare the behavior that occurs when FSMs from independent trials play each other to that observed when FSMs play copies of themselves. Table 5-5 indicates the results of playing games between the following pairs of FSMs:

$(FSM_{50}, FSM_{100})$

$(FSM_{100}, FSM_{250})$

$(FSM_{250}, FSM_{500})$

$(FSM_{500}, FSM_{1000})$

$(FSM_{50}, FSM_{50})$

$(FSM_{100}, FSM_{100})$

$(FSM_{250}, FSM_{250})$

$(FSM_{500}, FSM_{500})$

$(FSM_{1000}, FSM_{1000})$.

Mutual cooperation is rapidly generated when the best FSMs play themselves. This may approximate the actual conditions in each trial, because the final populations of FSMs in any trial may only vary by a relatively small number of mutations. But mutual cooperation is not always the result of encounters between separately evolved FSMs. The games involving $(FSM_{50}, FSM_{100})$ and $(FSM_{100}, FSM_{250})$ lead to alternating cooperation and defection [(C, D), (D, C)].

It is speculative but reasonable to presume that each population of FSMs evolves initial sequences of symbols that form patterns that can be recognized by other FSMs. This allows for the identification of machines that will tend to respond to cooperation with cooperation. The specifics of such sequences will vary by trial and may be as simple as merely cooperating on the first move. But the specifics are generally unimportant. When

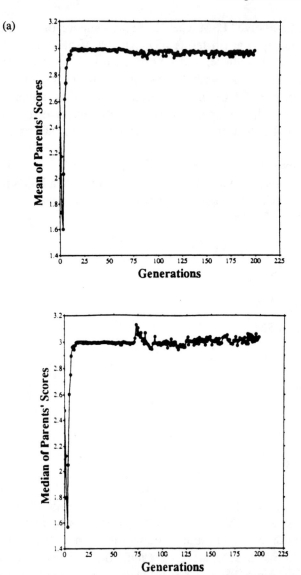

**Figure 5-13**  Evolution of the mean and median of all 50 parents' scores in the iterated prisoner's dilemma using the payoff function indicated in Table 5-4. (a) Trial 3. (b) Trial 6. The results were similar across all 20 trials.

**Figure 5-13** *continued*

**Figure 5-14** The mean (a) and median (b) of all parents' scores at each generation for populations of 50, 100, 250, 500, and 1,000 parents. The curves for populations of 50 and 100 parents represent the mean of 30 trials. The curve for the population of 250 parents represents the mean of five trials. The curves for populations of 500 and 1,000 are the results of single trials.

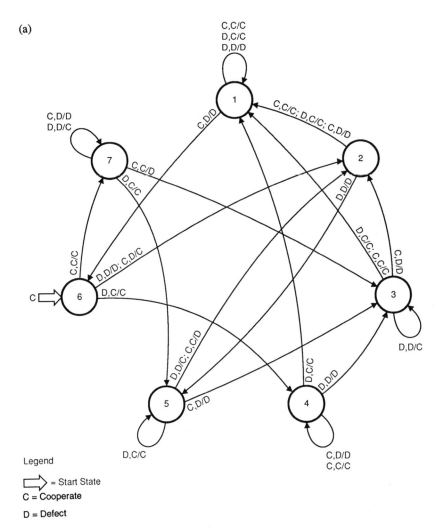

**Figure 5-15**    The best-evolved finite state machine after 25 generations for a given population size. Depicted machines for trials with 50, 100, and 250 parents are typical in terms of their behavior. (a) 50 parents. (b) 100 parents. (c) 250 parents. (d) 500 parents. (e) 1,000 parents. Angeline (pers. comm.) noted an error in Fogel (1993) relating to the output of the machine depicted in (a). The error resulted from an omitted next-state transition. The corrected machine appears above, and the corrected results appear in Table 5-5.

two FSMs from separate trials are played against each other, the resulting behavior may vary widely because no pattern of initial symbols is recognized by either player. Metaphorically, they are speaking different lan-

(b)

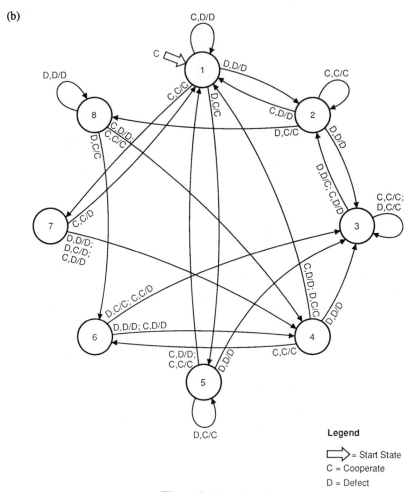

**Figure 5-15** *continued*

guages. Mutual defection or alternating cooperation and defection may be observed even though both FSMs would exhibit mutual cooperation with other FSMs from their respective populations.

A third set of experiments was conducted to examine the effects of varying the reward for defecting in the face of cooperation. When $\gamma_3$ becomes sufficiently large, it is expected that mutual cooperation will not evolve (see Eq. 5-14). Two sets of trials were conducted. A series of trials was conducted over 200 generations using 100 parents in which $\gamma_3$ ranged

(c)

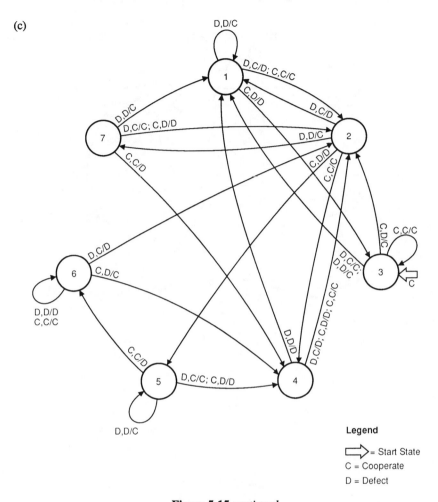

**Figure 5-15** *continued*

over the values 5.25, 5.5, 5.75, and 6.0. Note that when $\gamma_3 = 6.0$, the constraint in Eq. 5-14 is strictly violated. To garner a statistical sense for the variability of evolved behaviors, 10 additional trials were conducted with $\gamma_3 = 6.0$ and executed over 50 generations.

Figure 5-16 indicates the mean of the parents' scores at each generation in each trial with $\gamma_3$ ranging over the selected values. All trials exhibit initial mutual defection and, therefore, decreasing payoffs, followed by an increase in performance. Even when $\gamma_3 = 6.0$, the mean of the parents' scores

(d)

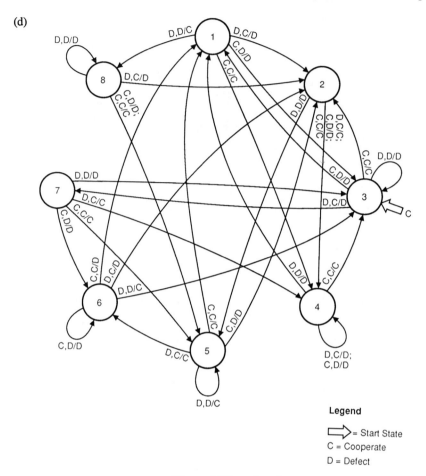

**Figure 5-15** *continued*

tends toward 3.0 at 200 generations. Figure 5-17 shows the mean of all parents' scores (average of all surviving parents' scores) at each generation when $\gamma_3 = 6.0$ in each of 10 trials. All the depicted curves exhibit similar characteristics, although the parents in trial 3 did not achieve a mean score that would be considered close to 3.0 in light of the tight clustering around this value indicated in the other nine trials.

Although it may be tempting to view these data as further evidence of "the evolution of cooperation," this interpretation would not be correct. A careful examination of the best-evolved FSMs after the comple-

(e)

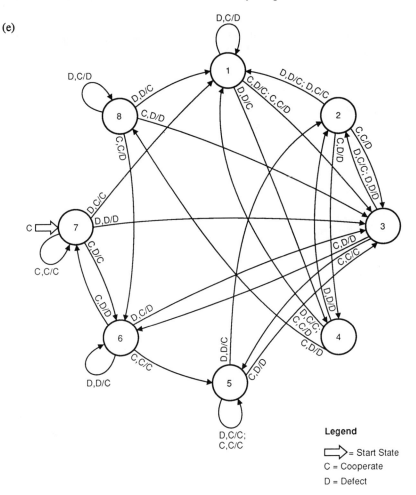

**Figure 5-15** *continued*

tion of 50 generations reveals that many of these machines were not cooperative.

Figure 5-18 depicts the highest-scoring FSM at the completion of trial 4 (denoted $FSM_4$). Across all eight states, only two (states 5 and 7) respond to (C, C) with (C), and each of these transitions respond to other states. There is no tendency for endless mutual cooperation with this FSM. But it received a score of 3.003, greater than could be achieved through mutual cooperation alone.

(a)

```
        6 7 3 3 2 1 6 4 4 1 6 4
FSM₅₀   C C D C D C D C D C D C                              C D
                                        → ALTERNATING
FSM₁₀₀  C C D D C D C D C D C D                              D C
        1 7 1 2 8 4 1 1 5 1 5 1
```

```
        1 7 1 5 1 7 1 5 1 2 8 4 1 1 5 1
FSM₁₀₀  C C D C C C D C D D C D C D C D                            C D
                                              → ALTERNATING
FSM₂₅₀  C C C C C C C D D C D C D C D C                            D C
        3 3 3 2 4 2 4 2 1 1 3 1 3 1 3 1
```

```
        3 3 3 3
FSM₂₅₀  C C C C
                        → MUTUAL COOPERATION
FSM₅₀₀  C C C C
        3 2 4 3
```

```
        3 2 4 3
FSM₅₀₀  C C C C
                        → MUTUAL COOPERATION
FSM₁,₀₀₀ C C C C
        7 7 7 7
```

Legend

---

C = Cooperate
D = Defect
The numbers above and
below the move indicate
the current state for the
respective FSM.

**Table 5-5** The results of playing the iterated prisoner's dilemma (a) with independently evolved machines in which each machine plays against a machine that was created in a separate trial with a different number of parents in the population and (b) when each independently evolved best machine plays against itself. The population size varies over 50, 100, 250, 500, and 1,000 parents. Mutual cooperation, observed when the machines play themselves, is not always the result of encounters between separately evolved machines.

(b)

```
            6  7  3  3  1  1
FSM₅₀       C  C  D  C  C  C
                                → MUTUAL COOPERATION
FSM₅₀       C  C  D  C  C  C
            6  7  3  3  1  1


            1  7  1  2  3  2  2
FSM₁₀₀      C  C  D  D  D  C  C
                                → MUTUAL COOPERATION
FSM₁₀₀      C  C  D  D  D  C  C
            1  7  1  2  3  2  2


            3  3
FSM₂₅₀      C  C
                                → MUTUAL COOPERATION
FSM₂₅₀      C  C
            3  3


            3  2  4  3
FSM₅₀₀      C  C  C  C
                                → MUTUAL COOPERATION
FSM₅₀₀      C  C  C  C
            3  2  4  3


            7  7
FSM₁,₀₀₀    C  C
                                → MUTUAL COOPERATION
FSM₁,₀₀₀    C  C
            7  7
```

Legend

---

C = Cooperate
D = Defect
The numbers above and
below the move indicate
the current state for the
respective FSM.

**Table 5-5** *continued*

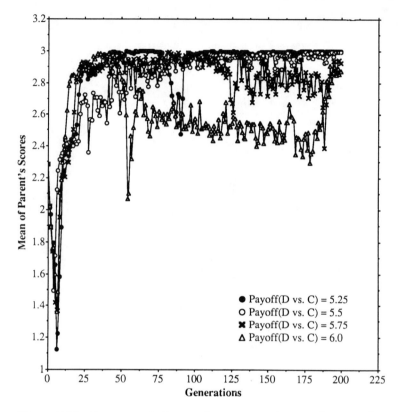

**Figure 5-16** The mean of all parents' scores at each generation as $\gamma_3$ is increased over 5.25, 5.5, 5.75, and 6.0.

Figure 5-19 indicates the structure of the highest-scoring FSM at the completion of trial 5 ($FSM_5$). The average payoff across all encounters for this machine was 3.537, again greater than could be achieved through mutual cooperation alone. The machine cooperates on the first move. If it meets another machine that cooperates on the first move, it will defect and transition to state 1. The next two possible input symbols are (D, C) or (D, D). (D, C) elicits further defection; $FSM_5$ will take advantage of the opposition as long as it continues to cooperate. $FSM_5$ would receive a higher score than Tit-for-Tat in these encounters. (D, D) elicits further defection, but not necessarily endless defection, as the machine transitions to state 5 and play then varies.

Both $FSM_4$ and $FSM_5$ are potentially vulnerable. If either were to meet a machine that defected on the first move, each would subsequently

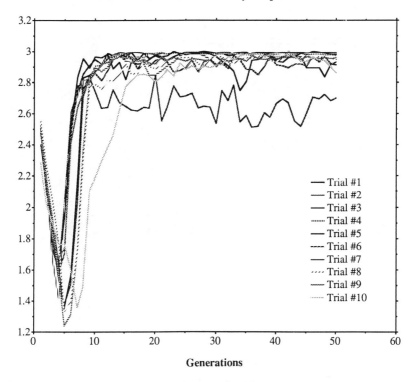

**Generations**

**Figure 5-17**  The mean of all parents' scores as a function of the number of generations in 10 trials when $\gamma_3 = 6.0$. Trial 3 appears to be a possible outlier.

cooperate and continue to cooperate as long as the opposing machine defected. The payoff for this behavior would be 0.0. There are two obvious conclusions: (1) Few if any parents in either population (trial 4 or 5) were persistent defectors, and (2) the structural complexity of parent machines was such that simply changing the initial behavior from cooperate to defect was not sufficient to exploit this apparent weakness. The first observation is logically certain; persistent defectors would have caused the mean score for $FSM_4$ or $FSM_5$ to be considerably lower. Neither would have been expected to generate the highest score in their respective population after 50 generations. The second observation can be demonstrated by playing both $FSM_4$ and $FSM_5$ against copies of themselves with only the starting symbol being varied to defection. Play proceeds as in Table 5-6. When $\gamma_3 = 6.0$, both mutual cooperation and alternating cooperation and defection receive the same reward, an average payoff of 3.0. Simply altering the

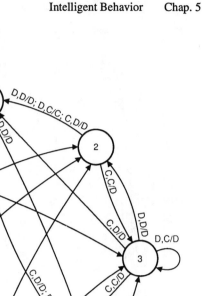

**Figure 5-18**   The highest-scoring FSM at the completion of trial 4 when $\gamma_3 = 6.0$.

initial play of cooperation to defection is not sufficient to exploit the potential vulnerability of $FSM_4$ or $FSM_5$.

The score of the best-evolved machines across nine out of all 10 trials was greater than 3.0, indicating that the increased benefit for defecting against cooperation had been exploited. Only the best machine in trial 3 (Figure 5-20) received a score of less than 3.0 (2.888). This machine cooperates on the first move and continually cooperates with other machines that reciprocate cooperation. But state 2 of $FSM_3$ is an absorbing

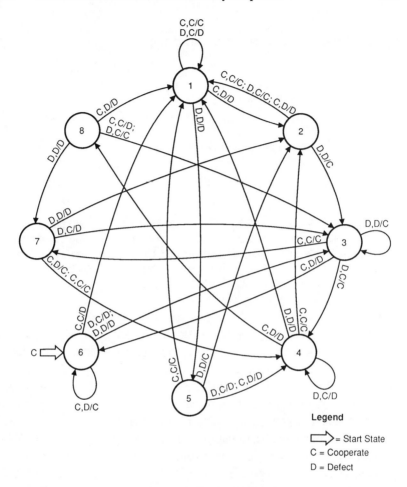

**Figure 5-19**   The highest-scoring FSM at the completion of trial 5 when $\gamma_3 = 6.0$.

defection state. If the state is entered, the machine will defect forever. Defection is common across the best-evolved machines.

Each curve depicted in Figure 5-17 indicates that the mean score for all parents in each trial was at or below 3.0. The score of the best parent in each trial, however, was typically greater than 3.0. It may be speculated that the best parent machines were not only successful in achieving mutual cooperation with other parents, and in exploiting foolish cooperators, but

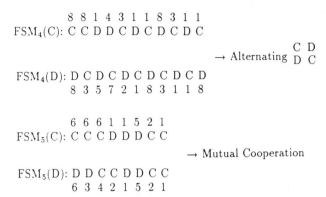

**Table 5-6** The course of play when the best FSM in trials 4 and 5 play against themselves with only the starting symbol being varied to defection. The symbol in parentheses, (C) or (D), indicates the initial play. The numbers above and below the sequence of moves indicate the current state of the machine.

they may have also evolved a propensity to generate offspring that would tend to cooperate blindly and to bolster their parents' existence further.

Evidence in support of this speculation has been obtained by recording the life span of each parent (i.e., the number of generations that each parent survived). The conditions for trial 1 were repeated and extended over 100 generations. Figure 5-21 indicates the distributions of the life span of each parent at selected generations. The histograms verify steadily increasing parental life spans; that is, in many cases, offspring were unable to displace their parents. This suggests the strong possibility that the parents were generating sacrificial offspring, FSMs that only served to increase the fitness of their parents. The evolutionary simulation apparently generated behavioral castes. Furthermore, despite selection acting solely on individuals with respect to their own success, and despite the initial evolution of purely selfish behaviors, the mean performance of the group (i.e., the reproducing population) ultimately increased to nearly 3.0.

These experiments hint at the ability of evolutionary computation to perform general problem solving. In contrast to the very specific linear models employed in the cart-pole experiments, finite state machines can in principle generate the behavior of any digital computer. Pierce (1980, p. 62) even suggested that humans may be viewed as finite state machines. Further, no specific heuristics, such as the AIC, were added to facilitate

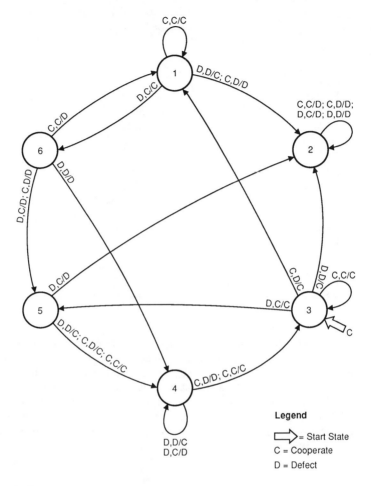

**Figure 5-20**   The highest-scoring FSM at the completion of trial 3 when $\gamma_3 = 6.0$.

modeling the environment. And the environment in question was a dynamic function of the evolution of other finite state machines. The behavior of the population tended toward that which yielded the maximum possible mean payoff, indicating that the evolutionary computation had gained an understanding of the environment in light of the varying payoffs for alternative behaviors.

(a)

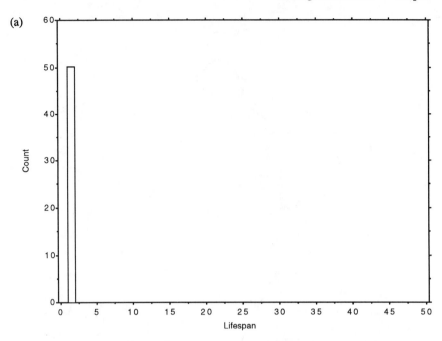

Figure 5-21  Histograms of the life spans (the number of generations that an FSM has survived in the population) of all parents in trial 1 depicted at selected generations. (a) First generation. (b) 25th generation. (c) 50th generation. (d) 75th generation. (e) 100th generation. As the generation number increases, the life span of the parents tends to increase as well. Several of the parent FSMs at the 100th generation were created before the 80th generation. The increasing life span of these parents suggests that they may have created offspring that they could subsequently exploit in competition.

## 5.4  GENERAL PROBLEM SOLVING: EXPERIMENTS WITH TIC-TAC-TOE

To provide a simple example of evolutionary general problem solving, an evolutionary program was written to discover optimal strategies in tic-tac-toe (Fogel, 1992, 1993b). The game is well known, but it will be described in detail for completeness. There are two players and a three-by-three grid (Figure 5-22). Initially, the grid is empty. Each player moves in turn by placing a marker in an open square. By convention, the first player's marker is "X" and the second player's marker is "O." The first player moves first. The object of the game is to place three markers in a row. This results

**Figure 5-21** *continued*

(d)

(e)

**Figure 5-21** *continued*

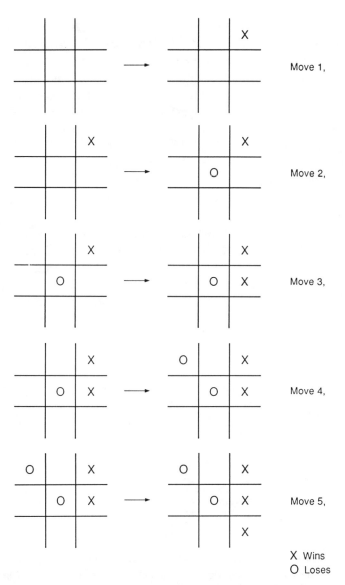

**Figure 5-22**   A possible game of tic-tac-toe. Players alternate moves in a 3 × 3 grid. The first player to place three markers in a row wins.

in a win for that player and a loss for the opponent. Failing a win, a draw may be earned by preventing the opponent from placing three markers in a row. It can be shown by enumerating the game tree that at least a draw can be forced by the second player.

Attention was devoted to evolving a strategy for the first player (an equivalent procedure could be used for the second player). A suitable coding structure had to be selected. It had to receive a board pattern as input and yield a corresponding move as output. The coding structure utilized in these experiments was a multilayered feed forward perceptron (Figure 5-23). Each hidden or output node performed a sum of the weighted input strengths, subtracted off an adaptable bias term, and passed the result through a sigmoid filter, $(1 + e^{-x})^{-1}$. Only a single hidden layer was incorporated. This architecture was selected because (1) variations are universal function approximators, (2) the response to any stimulus could be evaluated rapidly, and (3) the extension to multiple hidden layers is obvious.

There were nine input and output units. Each corresponded to a square in the grid. An "X" was denoted by the value 1.0, an "O" was denoted by the value –1.0, and an open space was denoted by the value 0.0. A move was determined by presenting the current board pattern to the network and examining the relative strengths of the nine output nodes. A marker was placed in the empty square with the maximum output strength. This pro-

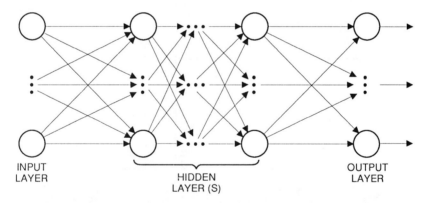

INPUT
LAYER

HIDDEN
LAYER (S)

OUTPUT
LAYER

**Figure 5-23**  A feed forward neural network. A number of input nodes pass information from the environment to nodes in a potential series of hidden layers. The final hidden layer is connected to the output layer, which yields a response of the network to any input pattern. In a multilayer perceptron, each node typically performs a dot product of the inputs to the node and their respective weights, subtracts off a bias term, and then passes the result through a nonlinear filter of the form $[1 + \exp(-x)]^{-1}$, where $x$ is the result before filtering. The networks in the current experiments used a feed forward neural network with nine input and output nodes and only a single hidden layer of a variable number of nodes.

cedure guaranteed legal moves. The output from nodes associated with squares in which a marker had already been placed was ignored. No selection pressure was applied to drive the output from such nodes to zero.

The initial population consisted of 50 parent networks. The number of nodes in the hidden layer was chosen at random in accordance with a uniform distribution over the integers $[1, \ldots, 10]$. The initial weighted connection strengths and bias terms were randomly distributed according to a uniform distribution ranging over $[-0.5, 0.5]$. A single offspring was copied from each parent and modified by two modes of mutation:

1. All weight and bias terms were perturbed by adding a Gaussian random variable with zero mean and a standard deviation of 0.05.

2. With a probability of 0.5, the number of nodes in the hidden layer was allowed to vary. If a change was indicated, there was an equal likelihood that a node would be added or deleted, subject to the constraints on the maximum and minimum number of nodes (10 and one, respectively). Nodes to be added were initialized with all weights and the bias term being set equal to 0.0.

A rule-based procedure that played nearly perfect tic-tac-toe was implemented to evaluate each contending network (see below). The execution time with this format was linear with the population size and provided the opportunity for multiple trials and statistical results. The evolving networks were allowed to move first in all games. The first move was examined by the rule base with the eight possible second moves being stored in an array. The rule base proceeded as follows:

1. From the array of all possible moves, select a move that has not yet been played.

2. For subsequent moves:

    (a) with a 10 percent chance, move randomly, else

    (b) if a win is available, place a marker in the winning square, else

    (c) if a block is available, place a marker in the blocking square, else

(d)   if two open squares are in line with an "O," randomly place
      a marker in either of the two squares, else

(e)   randomly move in any open square.

3.   Continue with step 2 until the game is completed.

4.   Continue with step 1 until games with all eight possible second
     moves have been played.

The 10 percent chance for moving randomly was incorporated to maintain
variety of play in an analogous manner to a persistence of excitation
condition (Anderson et al., 1986, p. 40; Ljung, 1987, pp. 362–363). This
feature and the restriction that the rule base only looks one move ahead
makes the rule base nearly perfect, but beatable.

Each network was evaluated over four sets of these eight games.
The payoff function varied in three sets of experiments over $\{+1, -1, 0\}$,
$\{+1, -10, 0\}$ and $\{+10, -1, 0\}$, where the entries are the payoff for winning,
losing, and playing to a draw, respectively. The maximum possible score
over any four sets of games was 32 under the first two payoff functions and
320 under the latter payoff function. But a perfect score in any generation
did not necessarily indicate a perfect algorithm because of the random
variation in play generated by step 2a, above. After competition against the
rule base was completed for all networks in the population, a second
competition was held in which each network was compared with 10 other
randomly chosen networks. If the score of the chosen network was greater
than or equal to its competitor, it received a win. Those networks with the
greatest number of wins were retained to be parents of the successive
generations. Thirty trials were conducted with each payoff function. Evolution was halted after 800 generations in each trial.

The learning rate when using $\{+1, -1, 0\}$ was generally consistent
across all trials (Figure 5-24). The 95 percent confidence limits around the
mean were close to the average performance. Figure 5-25 depicts the
improvement of the best player in the population at each generation in trial
2. The final best network in this trial possessed nine hidden nodes. The
highest score achieved in trial 2 was 31. Figure 5-26 indicates the tree of
possible games if the best-evolved network were played against the rule-
based algorithm, omitting the possibility for random moves in step 2a.
Under such conditions, the network would force a win in four of the eight
possible branches of the tree and has the possibility of losing in two of the
branches.

**Figure 5-24**   The mean score of the best neural network in the population as a function of the number of generations averaged across all 30 trials using payoffs of +1, –1, and 0 for winning, losing, and playing to a draw, respectively. The 95 percent upper and lower confidence limits (UCL and LCL) on the mean are calculated using a *t*-distribution.

The learning rate when using {+1, –10, 0} was considerably different (Figure 5-27) from that indicated in Figure 5-24. Selection in light of the increased penalty for losing resulted in an increased initial rate of improvement. Strategies that lose were quickly purged from the evolving population. After this first-order condition was satisfied, optimization continued to sort out strategies with the greatest potential for winning rather than drawing. Again, the 95 percent confidence limits around the mean were close to the average performance across all 30 trials. Figure 5-28 indicates the improvement of the best player in the population in trial 1. This network possessed 10 hidden nodes. Figure 5-29 depicts the tree of possible games if the best network from trial 1 were played against the rule-based player, omitting random moves from step 2a. It would not force a win in any branch of the tree. But it would also never lose. The payoff function was clearly reflected in the final observed behavior of the evolved network.

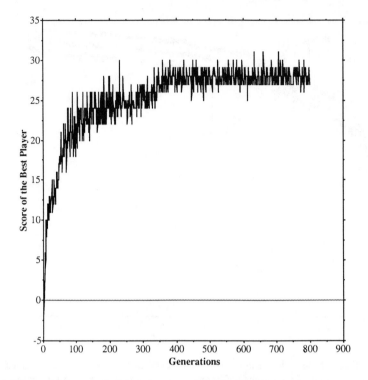

**Figure 5-25**    A typical learning curve (trial 2) depicting the improvement in the performance of the best player in the population as a function of the number of generations when the payoffs were +1, −1, and 0 for a win, loss, or draw, respectively.

The learning rate when using {+10, −1, 0} appeared similar to that obtained when using {+1, −1, 0} (Figure 5-30). The 95 percent confidence limits were wider than was observed in the previous two experiments. The variability of the score was greater because a win received 10 more points than a draw, rather than only a single point more. Strategies with a propensity to lose were purged early in the evolution. By the 800th generation, most surviving strategies lost infrequently and varied mostly by their ability to win or draw. Figure 5-31 indicates the improvement of the best score in the population in trial 1. The final best network possessed nine hidden nodes. The maximum possible score is 320 (a win in each game). This was achieved once, just before the 800th generation. The tree of possible games against the rule-based player is shown in Figure 5-32. The best-evolved network in trial 1 could not achieve a perfect score except when the

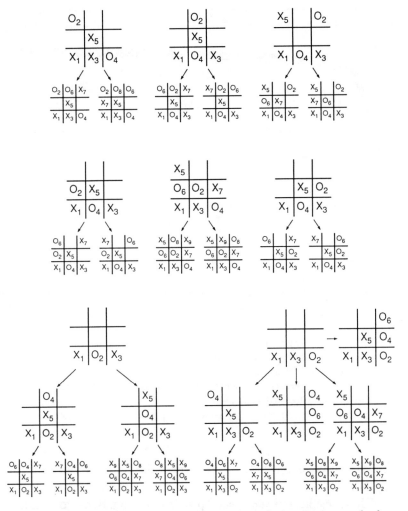

**Figure 5-26**  The tree of possible games when playing the best-evolved network from trial 2 with payoffs of +1, −1, and 0, for winning, losing, and playing to a draw, against the rule base without the 10 percent chance for making purely random moves. Each of the eight main boards corresponds to the eight possible next moves after the neural network moves first (in the lower left-hand corner). Branches indicate more than one possible move for the rule base, in which case all possibilities are depicted. The subscripts indicate the order of play.

**Figure 5-27**   The mean score of the best neural network in the population as a function of the number of generations averaged across all 30 trials using payoffs of +1, −10, and 0 for winning, losing, and playing to a draw, respectively. The 95 percent upper and lower confidence limits (UCL and LCL) on the mean are calculated using a $t$-distribution. The rate of optimization initially appears more rapid than is achieved when the penalty for losing is merely equal to the gain for winning.

rule-based procedure made errors in play through random perturbation (step 2a).

These results indicate general problem solving. Behavior was adapted to meet varying goals across a range of possible environments as determined by random chance moves on the part of the rule base. No a priori information regarding the object of the game was offered to the evolutionary program. No hints regarding appropriate moves were given, nor were there any attempts to assign values to various board patterns. The final outcome (win, lose, draw) was the only available information regarding the quality of play. Further, this information was only provided after 32 games had been played; the contribution to the overall score from any single game was not discernible. Heuristics regarding the environment were limited to the following:

**Figure 5-28**   A typical learning curve (trial 1) depicting the improvement in the performance of the best player in the population as a function of the number of generations when the payoffs were +1, −10, and 0 for a win, loss, or draw, respectively. The initial learning curve appears steeper than that observed in Figure 5-26.

1.   There were nine inputs.
2.   There were nine outputs.
3.   Markers could only be placed in empty squares.

Essentially then, the procedure was only given an appropriate set of sensors and a means for generating all possible behaviors in each setting and was restricted to act within the physics of the environment (i.e., the rules of the game).

Evolutionary programming was able to adjust both the architecture and connections of the single hidden-layer perceptron simultaneously. The final evolved neural networks operated on each in a series of observed board

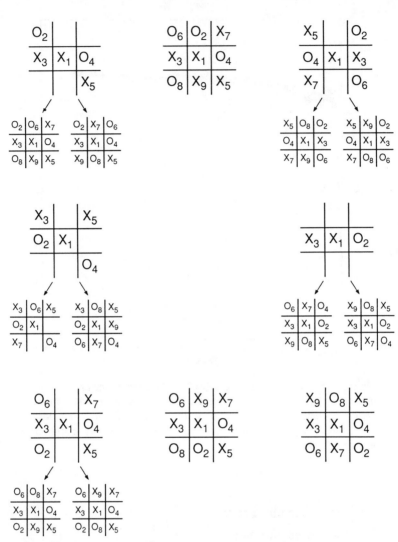

**Figure 5-29** The tree of possible games when playing the best-evolved network from trial 1 with payoffs of +1, −10, and 0, for winning, losing, and playing to a draw, against the rule base without the 10 percent chance for making purely random moves. The format follows Figure 5-26. The best-evolved network never forces a win, but also never loses. This reflects the increased penalty for losing.

**Figure 5-30**  The mean score of the best neural network in the population as a function of the number of generations averaged across all 30 trials using payoffs of +10, –1, and 0 for winning, losing, and playing to a draw, respectively. The 95 percent upper and lower confidence limits (UCL and LCL) on the mean are calculated using a *t*-distribution. The rate of optimization initially appears more similar to that which is achieved when the penalty for losing is merely equal to the gain for winning.

patterns and in turn generated a sequence of generally appropriate responses (behaviors) in light of the specified goal. The final expressed behavior was clearly dependent on the payoff function. This evolutionary procedure is robust, and no fundamental alteration of the basic algorithm is required to address problems of arbitrary complexity.

## 5.5  DISCUSSION

None of the evolutionary simulations described above is in any sense optimum. It is easy to imagine methods for improving each example by incorporating more appropriate mutation distributions or selection mechanisms or representations. But intelligence does not demand optimality.

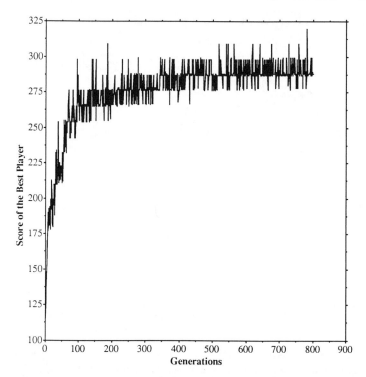

**Figure 5-31** A typical learning curve (trial 1) depicting the improvement in the performance of the best player in the population as a function of the number of generations when the payoffs were +10, −1, and 0 for a win, loss, or draw, respectively. The learning curve appears similar to that observed in Figure 5-26, with an increased variance reflecting the larger gain for winning.

Evolving species and individuals are in competition with themselves, not with any presumed "right answer." There are no absolute measures of intelligence, nor can there be under the definition offered in Chapter 1. Only a comparative evaluation of intelligent behavior can be meaningful. The more successful a system is at evolving behaviors across a wider range of environments with respect to more diverse goals, the more intelligent it is. Intelligence is a property of a system, not a solution.

Although a comparative assessment of intelligence requires a subjective judgment, the methods involved in generating intelligent behavior through evolution can be identified with complete objectivity. The evolutionary algorithms used in all three examples have four fundamental similarities. Each incorporates (1) a stochastic exploration of the state space

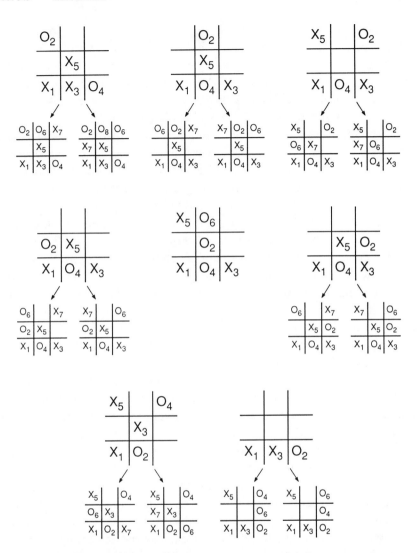

**Figure 5-32** The tree of possible games when playing the best-evolved network from trial 1 with payoffs of +10, −1, and 0, for winning, losing, and playing to a draw, against the rule base without the 10 percent chance for making purely random moves. The format follows Figure 5-26. The game tree has many of the same characteristics observed in Figure 5-26, indicating little difference in resulting behavior when increasing the reward for winning as opposed to increasing the penalty for losing.

of possible solutions, (2) a stochastic selection mechanism for purging solutions unworthy of further attention, (3) a mechanism for observing and affecting the environment, and (4) an explicit or implicit mechanism for predicting the future behavior of the environment based on alternative actions. These are the features that ensure versatility, the "essential in-gredient of intelligent behavior" (Fogel et al., 1966, p. 3).

The more familiar description of a procedure that incorporates these features is the scientific method. The resemblance between the process of evolution and the process of scientific inquiry is striking. Individual or-ganisms serve as hypotheses concerning the fundamental physics of their environment. Their behavior is an inductive inference concerning an-ticipated futures, and survival demonstrates an understanding. Offspring carry the "heredity of reasonableness" (Fogel et al., 1966, p. 112) as well as additional information as a result of genetic transformations. Simulating the scientific method and simulating evolution lead to the same basic computational procedure, a general problem-solving technique. But the recognition of intelligence as an evolutionary learning process is hardly new (Turing, 1950; Bremermann, 1958; Booker, 1982; Conrad, 1988; and others), nor has it been only recently demonstrated (Fogel, 1964; Fogel et al., 1966; Reed et al., 1967; Atmar, 1976; and others).

In that regard, the examples offered here should only be considered a contribution to the argument if they serve to highlight the fundamental importance of prediction and control in intelligent behavior. Mere opti-mization is only of minor importance. To be sure, optimization is intimately associated with evolution (Mayr, 1988, p. 104), but if, for example, op-timization is executed simply to discover the extremum of a static topog-raphy, then adaptation is made with respect to only a single goal and in only a single environment. The intelligence of such a system is inconsequen-tial. Only when the adaptive topography to be searched is a temporal function, one that is predicted and affected by the evolutionary process itself, should an observer take interest in assessing the system's potential intelligence.

A general problem-solving technique must use representations for solutions that allow for arbitrary transformations from sensed data to elicited action. Finite state machines and neural networks provide for such universal mappings within the memory limitations of the computer. Com-puter programs may also be used for such application (Koza, 1992), although no greater generality is achieved. But in each case, care must be taken as to how much a priori information is provided to the learning procedure. It is certainly useful to include operators that are specifically tailored to the problem at hand (e.g., the introduction of trigonometric functions in a spiral classification task; Koza, 1992, pp. 445–457), but their necessity suggests limited robustness. It would seem more prudent to examine cases where system responses are elicited by arbitrary mappings operating on primitive sensory inputs, as described in the neural tic-tac-toe experiments.

As tic-tac-toe is a common and relatively simple game, the profundity of the success of the evolutionary experiments may be overlooked by a casual observer. Consider a two-player game that incorporates an array of nine elements. Each player places markers in the array. Certain patterns in the array portend wins, losses, and draws, but no a priori information about the characteristics of these patterns is offered. Feedback concerning the quality of play only comes at the end of the game, when the final result becomes known. Or, even more restrictive, feedback may come only after a series of games are played so that the contribution to overall performance from any single game is unknown. Determining an optimal strategy under these conditions appears to be a significant challenge, and these are exactly the conditions that were presented to the evolutionary algorithm. Tic-tac-toe may seem simple because the notion of *in-a-row* is common in human experience and the objective of the game is agreed upon before play begins. If the patterns that define the wins, losses, and draws are arbitrary, the problem becomes much more difficult.[1]

The three simple experiments in automatic control, coevolution, and gaming illustrate evolved intelligent behavior. In each case, starting with completely random solutions to the problem at hand, the computer was able to generate increasingly appropriate behaviors in light of diverse criteria. It adapted its behavior to meet its goals across a range of environments. If intelligent decision making is viewed as a problem of optimally allocating

---

[1]If I may briefly digress to an example, I have often started lectures over the past couple of years by playing such a game with a member of the audience. I allow the participant to move first on a $3 \times 3$ grid, but do not offer what the objective of the game might be. The objective is quite simple: A win is achieved when a player places three markers on the outer squares of the grid. That is, the player moving first can force a win simply by avoiding the middle square. After we complete two or three games, I ask if anyone in the audience has any idea what the object of the game might be. The usual response is laughter. I have carried this out over as many as 10 games, yet no one has ever offered me the correct objective, despite its obvious simplicity.

available resources in light of environmental demands and goals, then these experiments do indeed serve as a foundation for the thesis that machine intelligence can be achieved by simulating evolution.

## REFERENCES

Akaike, H. (1974). "A New Look at the Statistical Model Identification," *IEEE Trans. Auto. Control*, Vol. AC-19:6, pp. 716–723.

Anderson, B. D. O., R. R. Bitmead, C. R. Johnson, P. V. Kokotovic, R. L. Kosut, I. M .Y. Mareels, L. Praly, and B. D. Riedle (1986). *Stability of Adaptive Systems: Passivity and Averaging Analysis.* Cambridge, MA: MIT Press.

Angeline, P. J. (1994). Personal communication, Loral Federal Systems, Owego, NY.

Atmar, J. W. (1976). "Speculation on the Evolution of Intelligence and Its Possible Realization in Machine Form." Sc.D. diss., New Mexico State University, Las Cruces.

Axelrod, R. (1980a). "Effective Choice in the Prisoner's Dilemma," *J. Conflict Resolution*, Vol. 24, pp. 3–25.

Axelrod, R. (1980b). "More Effective Choice in the Prisoner's Dilemma," *J. Conflict Resolution*, Vol. 24, pp. 379–403.

Axelrod, R. (1984). *The Evolution of Cooperation.* New York: Basic Books.

Axelrod, R. (1987). "The Evolution of Strategies in the Iterated Prisoner's Dilemma." In *Genetic Algorithms and Simulated Annealing*, edited by L. Davis. London: Pitman, pp. 32–41.

Barron, A. R. (1982). "Complexity Approach to Estimating the Order of a Model." Elect. Engineering 378B Final Report, Information Systems Laboratory, Stanford, CA.

Barto, A. G., R. S. Sutton, and C. W. Anderson (1983). "Neuron-like Adaptive Elements That Can Solve Difficult Learning Control Problems," *IEEE Trans. Sys., Man and Cybern.*, Vol. SMC-13:5, pp. 834–846.

Booker, L. (1982). "Intelligent Behavior as Adaptation to the Task Environment." Ph.D. diss., University of Michigan, Ann Arbor.

Boyd, R., and J. P. Lorberbaum (1987). "No Pure Strategy is Evolutionarily Stable in the Repeated Prisoner's Dilemma," *Nature*, Vol. 327, pp. 58–59.

Bremermann, H. J. (1958). "The Evolution of Intelligence. The Nervous System as a Model of Its Environment." Technical Report No. 1, Contract

No. 477(17), Dept. of Mathematics, University of Washington, Seattle, July.

Conrad, M. (1988). "Prolegomena to Evolutionary Programming." In *Advances in Cognitive Science: Steps toward Convergence*, edited by M. Kochen and H. M. Hastings. AAAS, pp. 150–168.

Fogel, D. B. (1991). "The Evolution of Intelligent Decision Making in Gaming," *Cybernetics and Systems*, Vol. 22, pp. 223–236.

Fogel, D. B. (1992). "Evolving Artificial Intelligence." Ph.D. diss., UCSD.

Fogel, D. B. (1993a). "Evolving Behaviors in the Iterated Prisoner's Dilemma," *Evolutionary Computation*, Vol. 1:1, pp. 77–97.

Fogel, D. B. (1993b). "Using Evolutionary Programming to Create Neural Networks That Are Capable of Playing Tic-Tac-Toe." In *Proc. IEEE Intern. Conf. on Neural Networks, 1993*, Piscataway, NJ: IEEE Press, pp. 875–880.

Fogel, D. B. (1994). "Evolutionary Programming: An Introduction and Some Current Directions," *Statistics and Computing*, Vol. 4, pp. 113–129.

Fogel, D. B., L. J. Fogel, W. Atmar, and G. B. Fogel (1992). "Hierarchic Methods of Evolutionary Programming." In *Proc. of the First Ann. Conf. on Evolutionary Programming,* edited by D. B. Fogel and W. Atmar. La Jolla, CA: Evolutionary Programming Society, pp. 175–182.

Fogel, L. J. (1964). "On the Organization of Intellect." Ph.D. diss., UCLA.

Fogel, L. J., A. J. Owens, and M. J. Walsh (1966). *Artificial Intelligence through Simulated Evolution*. New York: John Wiley.

Hofstadter, D. R. (1985). *Metamagical Themas: Questing for the Essence of Mind and Pattern*. New York: Basic Books.

Koza, J. R. (1992). *Genetic Programming*. Cambridge, MA: MIT Press.

Ljung, L. (1987). *System Identification: Theory for the User*. Englewood Cliffs, NJ: Prentice Hall.

Mallows, C. L. (1973). "Some Comments on $C_p$," *Technometrics*, Vol. 15, pp. 661–675.

Maynard Smith, J. (1982). *Evolution and the Theory of Games*. Cambridge: Cambridge University Press.

Mayr, E. (1988). *Toward a New Philosophy of Biology: Observations of an Evolutionist*. Cambridge MA: Belknap Press.

Pierce, J. R. (1980). *An Introduction to Information Theory: Symbols, Signals, and Noise*, 2nd ed., New York: Dover.

Rapoport, A. (1966). "Optimal Policies for the Prisoner's Dilemma." Technical Report No. 50, Psychometric Laboratory, University of North Carolina, NIH Grant, MH-10006.

Reed, J., R. Toombs, and N. A. Barricelli (1967). "Simulation of Biological Evolution and Machine Learning," *J. Theoretical Biology*, Vol. 17, pp. 319–342.

Risannen, J. (1978). "Modeling by Shortest Data Description," *Automatica*, Vol. 14, pp. 465–471.

Schwarz, G. (1977). "Estimating the Dimension of a Model," *Ann. Statist.*, Vol. 6:2, pp. 461–464.

Scodel, A., J. S. Minas, P. Ratoosh, and M. Lipetz (1959). "Some Descriptive Aspects of Two-Person Non-Zero Sum Games, " *J. Conflict Resolution*, Vol. 3, pp. 114–119.

Turing, A. M. (1950). "Computing Machinery and Intelligence," *Mind*, Vol. 59, pp. 433–460.

Wallace, C. S., and D. M. Boulton (1968). "An Information Measure for Classification," *Computer Journal*, Vol. 11:2, pp. 185–194.

Wieland, A. P. (1991). "Evolving Controls for Unstable Systems." In *Connectionist Models: Proc. of the 1990 Summer School*, edited by D. S. Touretsky, J. L. Elman, T. J. Sejnowski, and G. E. Hinton. San Mateo, CA: Morgan Kaufmann, pp. 91–102.

# 6

# Perspective

## 6.1 EVOLUTION AS A UNIFYING PRINCIPLE OF INTELLIGENCE

The theory of evolution is the great unifying theory of biology. But the impact of the theory extends even further: Evolution serves as a unifying description of all intelligent processes. Whether learning is accomplished by a species, an individual, or a social group, every intelligent system adopts a functionally equivalent process of reproduction, mutation, competition, and selection. Each such system possesses a unit of mutability for generating new behaviors and a reservoir for storing knowledge (i.e., a memory; cf. Davis, 1991, p. 3). Learning is accomplished through some form of random search and the retention of those "ideas" that provide the learning system with the greatest understanding of its environment (Atmar, 1976). The learning system evolves, adapting its behavior to achieve its goals in a range of environments.

For example, sociogenetic learning has developed in two orders of Insecta (Hymenoptera: ants, wasps, and bees, and Isoptera: termites) (Wilson, 1971). Although the origin of Isoptera is distinctly different from Hymenoptera, both have evolved a set of communicative mechanisms and caste behaviors that are quite similar. Chemical patterns are used to transmit information regarding trail following, food marking, alarm, assembly, recruitment, recognition, and so forth. Foraging appears to occur by random exploration (Wilson, 1971). An odor trail laid down by an ant can be described as an "idea" (Atmar, 1976). Ideas are reinforced through repeated traveling and remarking. Good ideas (those that increase the probability of survival of the colony) are maintained, amplified, and become the knowledge of the colony. Poor ideas are quickly forgotten; the pheromones evaporate.

Phylogenetic learning (arising within the line of descent) is the earliest form of intelligence and has given rise to ontogenetic (arising within the individual) and sociogenetic (arising within the group) learning mechanisms that serve to increase mutability and longevity substantially (Atmar, 1976). But the specific form or mechanism of learning adopted is irrelevant. Only the functional behavior of the system is exposed to selection. Species, individuals, and social groups rely on the same underlying physics to generate adaptive behavior despite using various genetic, neuronal, or cultural mechanisms, just as birds, mammals, and fish rely on the same physics for achieving flight even though the specific mechanisms employed are vastly different. Every system that incorporates the evolutionary processes of reproduction, mutation, competition, and selection, by whatever means, inherently evokes inductive learning. Intelligence is not the end result of evolution; rather, it is woven into the process itself. Intelligence and evolution cannot be separated.

## 6.2 PREDICTION AND THE LANGUAGELIKE NATURE OF INTELLIGENCE

Behavioral error is the sole quality optimized by selection, and that behavior is judged solely on its merits of predicting the forthcoming environmental conditions correctly (Atmar, 1994). Effective prediction requires the association of remembered events that are correlated in time, instances where one or more events are harbingers for some future occurrence. For example, sailors observing swallows flying low learned that this behavior was often associated with an oncoming storm. This relationship has been "used to predict bad weather: When you see the swallows flying low, prepare for bad weather. 'Swallows flying low' often precedes 'a storm' " (Lovejoy, 1975, pp. 9–10). No causality is implied in this observation, only correlation. Low-flying swallows do not cause the storm. Intelligent behavior is based on appropriately associating observations (symbols) so that future events can be anticipated and suitable actions may be taken in light of expected circumstances.

The mechanism of repeatedly mutating, testing, and selecting predictive organisms based on their survival produces systems that recognize the associations between environmental symbols and that adapt their behavior in light of these correlations. Kutas and Hillyard (1980) demonstrated that substantial neurophysiological potentials are generated in the speech regions of the human neocortex if a string of words is terminated with a grammatically proper but nonsensical terminating word, in contrast to a logical word. It must be presumed that the brain operates in a constant state of prediction (Atmar, pers. comm.). The order of observed symbols implies the rules of the environment; that is, the environment takes on a languagelike characteristic. The appropriate prediction of future environmental symbols demonstrates an understanding of that language.

The languagelike nature of intelligence becomes more obvious when language itself is studied. Bennett (1977) indicated that it is possible to randomly generate text that appears very much like English simply by taking into account the higher-order transitions across symbols (i.e., letters, spaces, and apostrophes). In examining Act III of Shakespeare's *Hamlet*, Bennett calculated the relative frequency of all symbols (first-order) and then randomly generated a sequence of text:

AOOAAORH ONNNDGELC TEFSISO VTALIDMA POESDHEMHIES-
WON PJTOMJ ITL FIM TAOFERLMT O NORDEERH HMFIOMRETW
OVRCA OSRIE IEOBOTOGIM NUDSEEWU WHHS AWUA HIDNEVE
NL SELTS ILY L CPATSDM EOLF OSTOM. . . .

But when he assessed and utilized the transition frequencies at the fourth order, he generated

A GO THIS BABE AND JUDGMENT OF TIMEDIOUS RETCH AND
NOT LORD WHAT IF THE EASELVES AND DO AND MAKE AND
BASE GATHEM I AY BEATELLOUS WE PLAY MEANS HOLY FOOL
MOUR WORK FORM INMOST BED BE CONFOULD HAVE MANY
JUDGMENT. . . .

Hayes (1983) extended Bennett's procedure to the seventh- and eighth-order transitions and created the following:

We will forthwith dispatch, and most sovereign reason, like a gulf doth hour-ly grow out of the undiscovered countries different honesty should o'er which now goes to heavens to wash it white as snow, thought, 'tis seen what a noble and feed upon whose weal depends and countries different with strings of disprized love. How now, Ophelia? Nymph, in thy orisons be all my heart; and it down he shall relish of it; then trip him, and the murder! Pray can translate beauty be the oppressor's wrong, the insolence of his likeness; this fear it is a massy whell, fix'd on the oppressor's wrong, the undiscover'd countries different with your loneliness. We shall keep those arrant she'll tax him home; and, as I think you; I your lordship?

and

Did he receive them. No, not I; I never gave you well, well, well. Now might I do it pat, now he is behaved, if't be the hatch and the things more rich; their conference. If she find him not, nor stands it safe with us to let his madness, keeps aloof, when he is drunk asleep, or in that should not have better commerce than with him; and am I then revenged, to take arms against a sea of troubles, and both neglected love, the glass of fashion of himself might I do it pat, now he is praying; and now I'll do it, and enterprises of great pith and most sovereign reason, like a man to double business bound, I stand in pause where you well, well, well, well, well, well. Now might I do it pat, now he is fit and sweat under a weary life, but like a man to double business bound, I stand in pause when I shall relish of salvation in't; then trip him, you sweet heavens! If thou dost marry, marry a fool; for which I did the murder?

Human response to even fourth- or fifth-order approximation of English "demonstrates the peculiar human compulsion to find pattern and meaning even where there is none" (Hayes, 1983). We are so conditioned to be predictive organisms that we are compelled to invent regularities in ob-served data, even when faced with purely random gibberish.

The English language may be regarded as somewhat complex. Yet an environment as complex as English text can be reasonably well predicted using no more than seventh- or eighth-order transitions. This has implica-tions on the nature of creative genius. Bennett (1977) noted that "Mozart published a pamphlet explaining how to compose 'as many German Waltzes as one pleases' by throwing dice (see Scholes, 1950, plate 37)." Bennett (1977) speculated that artistic genius may be a "simple" matter of having the "requisite high-order correlation data," with the result being a random choice with an appropriate weighting as indicated above. "Similar conjec-ture could be made about the scientific thought-process as well. . . . Even in science the initial creative thought-process frequently arises from some sort of free-associative daydreaming, which is probably equivalent in a sense to repeatedly dragging out a bunch of correlation matrices" (Bennett, 1977).

Intelligent behaviors often appear languagelike because prediction is both the essence of intelligence and is essential to the use of language. A language is defined by its symbols and their associated regularities, the rules that define the transitions across symbols. A continuously generated sequence of symbols, in any language, conveys the least measure of information (in the Shannon sense of unexpected variation) when it is completely predictable. Under such conditions, the observed sequence generates no surprise. The physical environment, essentially, presents evolving species with a continuous sequence of symbols from a language. Species' behaviors evolve to reflect the communication from the environment. Selection operates to minimize species' behavioral surprise—that is, predictive error—as they are exposed to successive symbols. Behavioral surprise can never be brought to zero, or any absolute minimum, however, because the environment always contains some element of pure randomness and because the environment is itself affected by selection acting on the species that predict it.

Prediction was implicit in each experiment presented in Chapter 5. Models of the cart-pole system were judged in terms of how well they would have predicted the plant's behavior had they been used in the past. Each move in the iterated prisoner's dilemma elicited a sequence of actions and reactions from both players, and the surviving parents were ultimately good predictors of the behavior of their opponents. The appropriateness of any move in the games of tic-tac-toe depended on the entire anticipated sequence of moves that was to follow. Placing a marker to block an opponent's possible win was only of benefit if the opponent would in fact take advantage of the presented opportunity. In each case, the evolutionary simulation learned to predict its surroundings effectively. It learned the implicit language of its environment.

## 6.3 THE MISPLACED EMPHASIS ON EMULATING GENETIC MECHANISMS

The primary evolutionary force that shapes adaptive characteristics is natural selection (Wilson, 1992, p. 75). Selection operates not on individual genes, but rather on the entire holistic phenotype that is determined by the complete genetic complement of an organism and its interaction with its environment (Spetner, 1964; and many others). In this light, models of evolution that celebrate genetic detail or rely on an operational definition of evolution as simply a change in gene frequencies have been criticized by Mayr (1963, 1982, 1988), Hoffman (1989), Atmar (1994), and many others. Yet these reductionist approaches persist. Proponents of methods for simulating evolution that employ specific abstractions of genetic transfer mechanisms have offered a different view: "Evolution is a process that operates on chromosomes rather than on the living beings they encode. . . . The process of reproduction is the point at which evolution takes place" (Davis, 1991, p. 2).

But there is no single "point" at which evolution takes place. Evolution is a continuous process comprising four operations: reproduction, mutation, competition, and selection. To identify genetic reproduction or coding structures as the keystone to evolution is to misrepresent the process. Chromosomes, genes, codons, and nucleotides are not the beneficiaries of evolutionary optimization.

Holland (1975, p. 109) offered, "Though mutation is one of the most familiar of the genetic operators, its role in adaptation is frequently misinterpreted. In genetics, mutation is a process wherein one allele of a gene is randomly replaced by (or modified to) another to yield a new structure." Such a definition may be useful in the study of and classification of possible alterations to the genetic program. But such a definition is not very useful or meaningful in terms of mutation's "role in adaptation." A mutation is simply a change in genetic material (Hartl and Clark, 1989, p. 96) and the phenotypic effect (i.e., the role in adaptation) of a random mutation can almost never be predicted with any reasonable accuracy.

It is inappropriate to model evolution as a simple process of genetic mechanisms because these mechanisms are unimportant except for the behaviors that they portend. "It is less important for the understanding of evolution to know how genetic variation is brought about than to know how natural selection deals with it" (Mayr, 1970, p. 8). The ubiquity of convergent evolution, in which strikingly similar phenotypic traits arise independently despite completely different morphological and genetic backgrounds, provides support for this perspective. Although determining the genetic bases for these phenotypic traits is of interest, such investigation may not provide a greater understanding of any trait's role in adaptation. The term *adapt* means literally *to fit*, and fitness is a property of the behavior generated by the genetic program, not directly of the program itself. The same genetic program can generate different phenotypes under varying environments, and any measure of appropriateness can only be attributed to the phenotype. Evolution is primarily a process of adaptive behavior, rather than adaptive genetics. The behavioral relationship between successive generations of organisms should be the paramount interest of abstraction, not the genetic relationship.

Simulations of evolution can be constructed to incorporate crossing-over, inversion, sexual recombination, jumping genes, introns, and other genetic attributes. But these are simply symptoms of the process of evolution, and attention should instead be devoted to pursuing a fundamental understanding of the underlying physics. For example, flapping wings are the most overt symptom of naturally evolved flight, and they are fundamental to flight in birds, but only as a mechanism for generating airflow over an airfoil. "No practical, man-carrying ornithoper has ever been built. . . . The secret to the physics of flight does not lie in the obvious flaps of the wings but in the far less obvious shape of the airfoil" (Atmar, 1992). No single symptom of genotypic transformation (e.g., crossing-over) is solely responsible for the observed patterns of behavior in the vast majority of complex systems. The overt simulation of symptoms is generally a misplaced effort.

## 6.4 BOTTOM-UP VERSUS TOP-DOWN

In general, there are two approaches to analyzing complex information structures. Bottom-up approaches segregate and emphasize individual components and their local interactions, decomposing the total system into successively smaller subsystems that are then analyzed in a piecemeal fashion. Top-down analyses emphasize extrinsically imposed forces and their associated physics (to the extent known). Neither approach is wholly satisfactory because each is a simplification of the true system, but neither do they possess equal explanatory power (Atmar, 1992).

There are inherent pitfalls in bottom-up analyses. As a system is decomposed into smaller and smaller subsystems, the interactions between these become increasingly difficult to observe until, in the limit, they are completely lost. In subsequent analysis of each tractable subsystem, there is a great propensity to attempt to optimize each component for its supposed task without regard to how it may interact with other components. Upon reassembling the entire system, all interactions become unpredictable and must be described in terms of emergent properties, patterns of behavior that could not be forecasted from analysis of isolated components. "The necessity to resort to emergent properties is a hallmark of all explanatory hypotheses which reverse the actual flow of causation" (Atmar, 1992).

Atkinson (1977, p. 6) cautioned against analyzing systems bottom-up: "An inexperienced designer often finds it necessary to overcome a tendency toward overdesign of components. He may lavish much loving care on the design of a truly superior variable-reluctance, temperature-compensated, self-orienting widget, but this perfection of one part may detract from the utility of the device in which it is to be used." But natural selection does not optimize structures from the bottom-up. Only the entire cohesive individual is evaluated through competition in its environment, and each behavioral component affects total system performance in many ways. For example, flight in birds offers clear advantages, but perhaps many more than one might first realize: increased range for foraging, increased environment for prey (including airborne prey), more effective stalking, greater chance for escape from predators, ability to nest eggs in locations that are inaccessible to many predators, and so forth (Atkinson, 1977, p. 7). As natural selection acts on the complete polyparametric phenotype, it is impossible for any single behavioral parameter to be optimized without regard to the manner in which it interacts with the phenotype as a whole.

In contrast, genetic algorithms are often described as using the bottom-up mechanism of putting together good "building blocks and eventually combining these to get larger building blocks" (Goldberg, 1983; also Goldberg, 1989, p. 45; Davis, 1991, p. 19; Holland, 1992, p. 180; Forrest, 1993; cf. Grefenstette, 1991, 1993). In this context, building blocks are analogous to functional subunits. But the identification of "good" building blocks implies a criterion by which to measure such genetic units, a method for assigning credit to them.

The credit assignment problem has been widely studied and discussed (Minsky, 1961; Doran, 1967; Holland, 1980, 1985; Cohen and Feigenbaum, 1982; Barto et al., 1983; Booker et al., 1990; and others). Minsky (1961) commented, "In playing a complex game such as chess or checkers, or in writing a computer program, one has a definite success criterion: the game is won or lost. But in the course of play, each ultimate success (or failure) is associated with a vast number of internal decisions. If the run is successful, how can we assign credit for the success among the multitude of decisions?" Newell (in Minsky, 1961) stated: "It is extremely doubtful whether there is enough information in 'win, lose, or draw' when referred to the whole play of the game to permit any learning at all over available time scales." But, metaphorically, "win, lose, or draw" is the only information on which natural selection operates.

There are no viable credit assignment algorithms for isolated genetic structures or behavioral traits, nor can there be in any system where behavioral traits are highly integrated and the relationship between the genotype and the phenotype is characterized by pleiotropy and polygeny. Credit assignment is a nonexistent problem in evolution. It is a human construction. Different algorithms for distributing credit have been offered and may be useful in certain applications. But such methods are not required for successful optimization and will generally lead to suboptimal (but perhaps adequate) performance. In contrast, a top-down approach that only emphasizes total system performance can discover optimal behavior in complex situations. The experiments in Chapter 5 with evolutionary algorithms achieved a high level of play in both the iterated prisoner's dilemma and in tic-tac-toe without the use of credit assignment algorithms.

Bottom-up analyses are also typically fraught with after-the-fact explanations. The geocentric model of the solar system is classical in this regard. After retrograde motion was observed and found inconsistent with the model, epicycles were added to the planetary orbits. "To explain the observations, Ptolemy had to assume that each superior planet revolved in its epicycle at just the right rate so that it reached perigee at the moment of opposition on every orbit" (Lightman and Gingerich, 1992). If enough epicycles upon epicycles were added, a sufficiently good fit to the data could be obtained. But such a model assumes epicycles as a "fact-in-itself" (Frisius, 1560) rather than a fact reasoned from the model. The heliocentric explanation offered by Copernicus infers retrograde motion, but explains it rather than merely accepts it.

Similar problems are associated with evolutionary simulations that are conducted from the bottom-up. When the observed evidence of evolution is in contradiction with the simulated results, there is a tendency to want to fix or improve the results by incorporating additional operations. For example, De Jong (1975) noted that the performance of genetic algorithms could be improved by making it more difficult for particular schemata to dominate the population (see also Goldberg, 1989, p. 116). To avoid this premature convergence, De Jong (1975) incorporated a clever procedure motivated by the notion of overpopulation (De Jong, pers. comm.). New solutions were made to replace solutions that were most similar based on a bit-by-bit comparison (i.e., "crowding factors"). Even though this operation can accelerate optimization in genetic algorithms and even though it has a biological inspiration, it is not characteristic of natural evolution. Natural selection acts only on the phenotypic appropriateness of individuals, not on their genetic similarity.

The natural evidence itself indicates whether or not a system is being optimized from the bottom-up. If it is, then individual coding segments must become a collection of "perfected 'genes,' informationally disconnected from one another, each operating to maximize its own optimal survival" (Atmar, 1992). But if, on the other hand, the physics of selection operates top-down, where only total system performance is evaluated and the underlying code is never directly affected but only indirectly affected, the result will be quite different. Behavior will become highly integrated functional "organs of extreme perfection" (Darwin, 1859, ch. 6), while the genetic basement will become a mélange of interwoven, overlain, and duplicated code. Only this latter pattern is observed in nature.


## 6.5  TOWARD A NEW PHILOSOPHY OF MACHINE INTELLIGENCE

Research in AI has typically passed over investigations into the primal causative factors of intelligence to more rapidly obtain the immediate consequences of intelligence (Atmar, 1976). Yet many of these efforts have not defined the intelligence they attempt to create. Efficient theorem proving, pattern recognition, and tree searching are symptoms of intelligent behavior. But systems that can accomplish these feats are not, simply by consequence, intelligent. Without a working definition of what constitutes intelligence, the field of research has fragmented into a collection of methods and tricks for solving particular problems in restricted domains of interest.

Certainly, these methods have been successfully applied to specific problems. Knowledge-based chess-playing programs have achieved a level of play that is competitive with human masters. Fuzzy systems have been applied to image processing, industrial control, and robotics. Neural networks have been used for various signal processing, spatio-temporal pattern recognition, and automatic control applications, among others. Hybrids of these methods have been applied to a great range of problems (e.g., Gallant, 1988; Kandel, 1991; Kosko, 1992). But most of these applications require human expertise. They may be impressively applied to difficult problems, but they generally do not advance our understanding of intelligence. They solve problems, but they do not solve the problem of how to solve problems.

Evolution provides the solution to the problem of how to solve problems. Moreover, the greatest gain from evolutionary computation will come when these algorithms are used to address problems that have, to date, been resistant to solution by human expertise, for evolutionary computation is not limited to recapitulating human behavior. "Recognizing that the scientific method is an evolutionary process that can be simulated opens the possibility of automating higher levels of intellect" (Fogel et al., 1966, p. 123). Such computational efforts can usefully combine research in expert, fuzzy, and connectionist systems. But any real advancement of evolutionary computation should rely on the careful observation and abstraction of the natural process of evolution.

The majority of efforts in artificial intelligence have simulated specific facets of intelligent behavior, mainly as we observe them in ourselves. Yet intelligence cannot be restricted to humans. Indeed, the life process itself provides the most common form of intelligence (Atmar, 1976). Darwinian evolution accounts for the behavior of naturally occurring intelligent entities and can be used to guide the creation of artificial entities that are capable of intelligent behavior. But more than that, if the evolutionary approach to artificial intelligence is adopted, there will truly be nothing "artificial" about it. Evolutionary machines will simply be intelligent, and the limit of such intelligence is unknowable.

## REFERENCES

Atkinson, D. E. (1977). *Cellular Energy Metabolism and Its Regulation.* New York: Academic Press.

Atmar, J. W. (1976). "Speculation on the Evolution of Intelligence and Its Possible Realization in Machine Form." Sc.D. diss., New Mexico State University, Las Cruces.

Atmar, W. (1986). Personal communication, AICS Research, Inc., Las Cruces, NM.

Atmar, W. (1992). "The Philosophical Errors That Plague both Evolutionary Theory and Simulated Evolutionary Programming." In *Proc. of First Ann. Conf. on Evolutionary Programming*, edited by D. B. Fogel and W. Atmar. La Jolla, CA: Evolutionary Programming Society, pp. 27–32.

Atmar, W. (1994). "Notes on the Simulation of Evolution," *IEEE Trans. Neural Networks*, Vol. 5:1, pp. 130–148.

Barto, A. G., R. S. Sutton, and C. W. Anderson (1983). "Neuronlike Adaptive Elements That Can Solve Difficult Learning Control Problems," *IEEE Trans. Sys., Man, and Cybern.*, Vol. SMC-13:5, pp. 834–846.

Bennett, W. R. (1977). "How Artificial Is Intelligence?" *American Scientist*, November–December, pp. 694–702.

Booker, L. B., D. E. Goldberg, and J. H. Holland (1990). "Classifier Systems and Genetic Algorithms." In *Machine Learning: Paradigms and Methods*, edited by J. Carbonell. Cambridge, MA: MIT Press, pp. 235–282.

Cohen P. R., and E. A. Feigenbaum (1982). *The Handbook of Artificial Intelligence*, Vol. 3. Los Altos, CA: Morgan Kaufmann.

Darwin, C. (1859). *On the Origin of Species by Means of Natural Selection or the Preservations of Favored Races in the Struggle for Life.* London: John Murray.

Davis, L., ed. (1991). *Handbook of Genetic Algorithms.* New York: Van Nostrand Reinhold.

De Jong, K. A. (1975). "The Analysis of the Behavior of a Class of Genetic Adaptive Systems." Ph.D. diss., University of Michigan, Ann Arbor.

De Jong, K. A. (1994). Personal communication, George Mason University.

Doran, J. (1967). "An Approach to Automatic Problem Solving." In *Machine Learning*, Vol. 1, edited by E. L. Collins and D. Michie. Edinburgh: Oliver and Boyd, pp. 105–123.

Fogel, L. J., A. J. Owens, and M. J. Walsh (1966). *Artificial Intelligence through Simulated Evolution.* New York: John Wiley.

Forrest, S. (1993). "Genetic Algorithms: Principles of Natural Selection Applied to Computation," *Science*, Vol. 261, pp. 872–878.

Gallant, S. (1988). "Connectionist Expert Systems," *Comm. of the ACM*, Vol. 31, pp. 152–169.

Frisius Reiner Gemma (1560). In Johannes Stadius, Ephemerides Novae et Auctae, Cologne, si, b3–b3cv, translated by O. Gingerich and R. S.

Westman, *The Wittich Connection: Conflict and Priority in Late Six-teenth Century Cosmology*, Trans. Am. Philos. Soc., Vol. 78, part 7, p. 42, 1988.

Grefenstette, J. J. (1991). "Conditions for Implicit Parallelism," In *Foundations of Genetic Algorithms*, edited by G. J. E. Rawlins. San Mateo, CA: Morgan Kaufmann, pp. 252–261.

Grefenstette, J. J. (1993). "Deception Considered Harmful," In *Foundations of Genetic Algorithms 2*, edited by L. D. Whitley. San Mateo, CA: Morgan Kaufmann, pp. 75–91.

Goldberg, D. E. (1983). "Computer-Aided Gas Pipeline Operation Using Genetic Algorithms and Rule Learning," Ph.D. diss., University of Michigan, Ann Arbor.

Goldberg, D. E. (1989). *Genetic Algorithms in Search, Optimization, and Machine Learning*. Reading, MA: Addison-Wesley.

Hartl, D. L., and A. G. Clark (1989). *Principles of Population Genetics*, 2nd ed. Sunderland, MA: Sinauer.

Hayes, B. (1983). "A Progress Report on the Fine Art of Turning Literature into Drivel," *Scientific American*, Vol. 249:5, pp. 18–28.

Hoffman, A. (1989). *Arguments on Evolution: A Paleontologist's Perspective*. New York: Oxford University Press.

Holland, J. H. (1975). *Adaptation in Natural and Artificial Systems*. Ann Arbor: University of Michigan Press.

Holland, J. H. (1980). "Adaptive Algorithms for Discovering and Using General Patterns in Growing Knowledge-Bases," *Intern. J. Policy Anal. Inform. Syst.*, Vol. 4, pp. 217–240.

Holland, J. H. (1985). "Properties of the Bucket-Brigade." In *Proc. of an Intern. Conf. on Genetic Algorithms and Their Applications*, edited by J. J. Grefenstette. Pittsburgh, PA: Carnegie Mellon, pp. 1–7.

Holland, J. H. (1992). *Adaptation in Natural and Artificial Systems*, 2nd ed. Cambridge, MA: MIT Press.

Kandel, A. (1991). *Fuzzy Expert Systems*. Boca Raton, FL: CRC Press.

Kosko, B. (1992). *Neural Networks and Fuzzy Systems: A Dynamical Systems Approach to Machine Intelligence*. Englewood Cliffs, NJ: Prentice Hall.

Kutas, M., and S. A. Hillyard (1980). "Reading Senseless Sentences: Brain Potentials Reflect Semantic Incongruity," *Science*, Vol. 207, pp. 203–205.

Lightman, A., and O. Gingerich (1992). "When Do Anomalies Begin?" *Science*, Vol. 225, pp. 690–695.

Lovejoy, E. P. (1975). *Statistics for Math Haters*. New York: Harper and Row.

Mayr, E. (1963). *Animal Species and Evolution*. Cambridge, MA: Belknap Press.

Mayr, E. (1970). *Populations, Species, and Evolution*. Cambridge, MA: Belknap Press.

Mayr, E. (1982). *The Growth of Biological Thought: Diversity, Evolution, and Inheritance*. Cambridge, MA: Belknap Press.

Mayr, E. (1988). *Toward a New Philosophy of Biology: Observations of an Evolutionist*. Cambridge, MA: Belknap Press.

Minsky, M. L. (1961). "Steps toward Artificial Intelligence," *Proc. of IRE*, Vol. 49:1, pp. 8–30.

Scholes, P. A. (1950). *The Oxford Companion to Music*. New York: Oxford University Press.

Spetner, L. M. (1964). "Natural Selection: An Information-Transmission Mechanism for Evolution," *J. Theo. Biol.*, Vol. 7, pp. 412–429.

Wilson, E. O. (1971). *The Insect Societies*. Cambridge, MA: Belknap Press.

Wilson, E. O. (1992). *The Diversity of Life*. New York: W. W. Norton.

# Glossary

**Adaptation.** The process of generating a set of behaviors that more closely match or predict a specific environmental regime. An increased ecological-physiological efficiency of an individual relative to others in the population.

**Adaptive Topography.** A continuous function describing the fitness of individuals and populations.

**Agnathans.** A jawless class of vertebrates represented today by lampreys and hagfishes.

**Allele.** An alternative form of a gene that occurs at a given chromosomal site (locus).

**Altruistic Behavior.** The aiding of another individual (or entity) at one's own risk or to one's own detriment.

**Asexual Reproduction.** A form of reproduction that does not involve the use of gametes.

**Behavior.** The response of an organism to the present stimulus and its present state. It is the total sum of behaviors of an organism that define the fitness of the organism to its present environment; thus it is the operative function against which selection operates.

**Chiasmata.** The X-shaped, microscopically visible figures representing homologous chromatids that have exchanged genetic material through crossing-over during meiosis.

**Chromatids.** The two identical parts of a duplicated chromosome.

**Chromosome.** Rod-shaped bodies in the nucleus of eukaryotic cells, most visible particularly during cell division, which contain the hereditary units or genes.

**Codon.**   A sequence of three nucleotide bases contained within the structure of the DNA molecule (or mRNA) that codes for a specific amino acid or for a termination signal during protein synthesis.

**Convergent Evolution.**   The independent development of similar structures in organisms that are not directly related.

**Crossing-over.**   The exchange of corresponding segments of genetic material between chromatids of homologues at meiosis.

**Diploid.**   The 2N number of chromosomes; the complete or total number; twice the number of chromosomes found in gametes.

**DNA.**   Deoxyribonucleic acid.

**Engram.**   Supposed pathway of learned neural connections.

**Ethology.**   Patterns of animal behavior. The study of patterns of animal behavior.

**Eukaryotic Cell.**   Cell with a membrane-enclosed nucleus and organelles found in animals, fungi, plants, and protists.

**Fitness.**   A summation of the quality of environmental prediction by an organism throughout its range of regimes. The probability of or propensity for survival of an individual or population.

**Founder effect.**   A cause of genetic drift attributable to colonization by a limited number of emigrants from a parent population.

**Gamete.**   A reproductive cell that joins with another in fertilization to form a zygote, most often an egg or sperm.

**Gene.**   A unit of heredity located on a chromosome and composed of DNA. The code necessary to promote the synthesis of one polypeptide chain.

**Genetic Drift.**   Changes to the gene pool of a population by chance processes alone.

**Genome.**   The total genetic constitution of an organism.

**Genotype.**   The sum of inherited characters maintained within the entire reproducing population. Often also used to refer to the genetic constitution underlying a single trait or set of traits.

**Haploid.**   The N number of chromosomes. See *diploid.*

**Heredity.**   The transmission of characteristics from parent to offspring through the gametes.

**Heterozygous.**   Having two different alleles for a given trait.

**Homologues.**   Duplicated chromosomes that look alike and have genes affecting the same traits.

**Homozygous.**   Having identical alleles for a given trait.

**Intron.**   An intervening noncoding region of a eukaryotic gene.

**Inversion.**   A reversal in order of a segment of a chromosome.

**Linkage.**   Genes on the same chromosome are linked in the sense that they tend to move together to the same gamete. Crossing-over interferes with linkage.

**Locus.**   A particular location on a chromosome.

**Meiosis.**   Type of cell division that occurs during the production of gametes, by means of which the daughter cells receive the haploid number of chromosomes.

**Morphology.**   Form and its development. Also, the study of form and its development.

**Mutation.**   A genetic change.

**Natural Selection.**   The result of competitive exclusion as organisms fill the available finite resource space.

**Neutral Mutation.**   A mutation in the genotypic structure of a population that promotes no behavioral difference in the present environment.

**Nucleus.**   A large organelle containing the chromosomes and acting as a control center for the cell.

**Ontogenetic.**   Literally "arising within the self." As a learning process, learning arising within the individual.

**Parthenogenesis.**   The development of an egg without fertilization.

**Phenotype.**   The behavioral expression of the genotype in a specific environment. The realized expression of the genotype. The functional expression of a trait.

**Pheromones.**   Small, volatile chemical signals functioning in communication between animals and acting much like hormones to influence physiology and behavior.

**Phylogenetic.**   Literally, "arising within the line of descent." As a learning process, learning arising within the phyletic line of descent.

**Phylogeny.**   The evolutionary relationships among any group of organisms.

**Pleiotropy.**   The capacity of a gene to affect a number of different phenotypic characteristics.

**Polygeny.**   The circumstance where a single phenotypic trait is affected by multiple genes.

**Prokaryotic Cell.**   A cell lacking a membrane-enclosed nucleus and organelles.

**Saltation.**   An abrupt variation in the condition of a species; a marked modification.

**Sociogenetic.**   Literally, "arising within the group." As a learning process, learning arising within a social group.

**Species.**   A group of similarly constructed organisms that are capable of interbreeding and producing fertile offspring. A population whose members are able to interbreed freely under natural conditions.

**Synapsis.**   The attracting and pairing of homologous chromosomes during meiosis.

**Teleonomic Behavior.**   Behavior that owes its goal-directedness to the operation of a program.

**Zygote.**   Fertilized egg that is always diploid.

## LITERATURE CITED FOR GLOSSARY

Atmar, J. W. (1976). "Speculation on the Evolution of Intelligence and Its Possible Realization in Machine Form." Sc.D. diss., New Mexico State University, Las Cruces.

Campbell, N. A. (1990). *Biology*, 2nd ed. Redwood City, CA: Benjamin/Cummings.

Hartl, D. L., and A. G. Clark (1989). *Principles of Population Genetics*, 2nd ed. Sunderland, MA: Sinauer.

Mader, S. S. (1983). *Inquiry into Life*, 3rd ed. Dubuque, IA: William C. Brown.

Mayr, E. (1988). *Toward a New Philosophy of Biology: Observations of an Evolutionist.* Cambridge, MA: Belknap Press.

Raven, P. H., and G. B. Johnson (1986). *Biology.* St. Louis: Times Mirror/Moseby College.

Wilson, E. O. (1992). *The Diversity of Life.* New York: W. W. Norton.

# Index